Samuel May Williams
EARLY TEXAS ENTREPRENEUR

Samuel May Williams. The portrait hangs in the Williams house in Galveston. Courtesy, Rosenberg Library, Galveston, Texas.

Samuel May Williams

EARLY TEXAS ENTREPRENEUR

By MARGARET SWETT HENSON

Texas A&M University Press

COLLEGE STATION

Library of Congress Cataloging in Publication Data

Henson, Margaret Swett, 1924–
    Samuel May Williams, early Texas entrepreneur.

    Bibliography: p.
    Includes index.
    1. Williams, Samuel May, 1795–1858.
F390.W73H46   976.4′05′0924 [B]   75-40894
ISBN 0-89096-009-7

Manufactured in the United States of America
FIRST EDITION

To Scott

Contents

List of Illustrations

Preface

SAMUEL MAY WILLIAMS has been neglected by Texas historians for too long. No major study of his life has been made since his daughter deposited the large collection of personal and business papers with the Rosenberg Library at Galveston in 1922. A brief biographical sketch by the compiler of the calendar to the Williams collection appeared in the *Southwestern Historical Quarterly* in 1952, and two unpublished master's theses barely scratched the rich store of available material.[1]

Williams arrived in Texas in 1822 and soon became Stephen F. Austin's assistant in colonial affairs. By 1831 he had acquired title to over forty-eight thousand acres of land in return for his various services to the Mexican government. During Austin's numerous absences between 1830 and 1835, Williams assumed responsibility for directing his friend's business pursuits, and, in addition, endeavored to steer the colony away from a collision with either of the political factions struggling for control of the Mexican government. When Texas committed itself to oppose Santa Anna in 1835, Williams contributed by dispatching ships, arms, ammunition, recruits, and supplies from the United States, where he had gone on personal busi-

---

[1] Ruth G. Nichols, "Samuel May Williams," *Southwestern Historical Quarterly* 56 (October 1952): 189–210; Siddie Robson Armstrong, "Chapters in the Early Life of Samuel May Williams, 1795–1836" (M.A. thesis, University of Texas, 1929); Duane Howard, "Historical Studies in the Life of Samuel May Williams: A Builder of Texas, 1795–1858" (M.A. thesis, Texas Christian University, 1947).

ness. Once independence was established, he returned again to the North seeking money for the Republic and later arranged for the construction of the Second Texas Navy, six vessels delivered in 1839 and 1840. Between September, 1835, and June, 1839, Williams spent all but eight months away from his wife and children in Texas.

In 1839 and 1840 Williams represented Galveston in the House of Representatives during the Fourth Congress of the Republic, the first to meet in the new capital at Austin. In 1843 President Sam Houston sent Williams and George W. Hockley on a diplomatic mission to Mexico to arrange an armistice ending the frontier raids being conducted by both governments. Political maneuvers, especially Houston's negotiations for annexation, doomed the efforts of the two commissioners.

Once union with the United States was accomplished, Williams unsuccessfully sought a seat in Congress. Abandoning politics, he devoted the remainder of his life to developing Texas's economic potential. In 1834 he had joined Thomas F. McKinney in the commission business on the Brazos River, and in 1837 the firm moved to Galveston Island, where it became Texas's leading mercantile establishment. McKinney and Williams were among the founders of the Galveston City Company, and because of the contributions made by the firm during the rebellion against Mexico, Williams received permission from the Texas Congress to issue paper money in 1841 in order to ease the critical shortage of circulating currency. This small banking function grew, and in 1848 Williams opened the Commercial and Agricultural Bank in Galveston, using a charter received from Mexico in 1835. Sentiment against banks of issue forced both the state legislature and the courts to doubt the legality of Williams's bank, but for ten years he successfully defended his institution from repeated attempts to close its doors. After his death in 1858, the Texas Supreme Court ruled against the Commercial and Agricultural Bank, which forced its dismantling.

Scholars have been unaware of Williams's role in the development of Texas because many of his contemporaries disliked him and conveyed this feeling to historians. Considered arrogant, brusque, and cold-hearted while serving as secretary in charge of Austin's colonial land office, Williams earned opprobrium for participating in the 1835 Monclova legislature, which was held during the crisis between the political factions in Mexico. In order to raise money and troops to oppose the centralist dictator, Santa Anna, federalist leaders in the state government authorized the sale of a little over one million acres of vacant land in Texas. Williams participated in this transaction as both legislator and purchaser and forever after was branded with the label, "Monclova speculator." His diplomatic mission to Mexico was also unpopular and was attributed to his desire to activate his Mexican banking charter obtained at Monclova.

This study attempts to clarify Williams's role during the thirty-six years he served Texas. His actions, justifiable from his point of view, were always guided by concern for his own interests, which were entwined with those of Texas. Although he lacked the popularity of the military folk-heroes of Texas, Williams made a notable contribution to the economic development of the Lone Star State.

Acknowledgments

MY greatest debt is to Sarah P. Williams and her daughter, Mary Dorothea League, who preserved Samuel M. Williams's accumulation of correspondence. Williams was in the United States in April, 1836, but Sarah carried the papers to safety when she left Quintana as the Mexican army approached the Brazos. In Galveston during the 1840's, the bundles of letters were placed in the leather trunk that had been sent to Sarah in 1837 from Baltimore. Childish scribbling on some items indicates that the children must have discovered the cache in the storeroom, perhaps on a rainy day when they were confined to the house. The trunk and its contents survived the 1900 storm at the League residence across the street from the old homestead.

Since 1922, the Rosenberg Library has housed the Williams papers, and a number of curators have arranged, calendared, and indexed the collection for scholarly use. My special thanks go to archives staff members, past and present, Robert Dalehite, Larry Wygant, and Ruth E. Kelly. Librarian John Hyatt and the board of directors have graciously granted permission to reproduce the Williams portraits and several other items belonging to the Rosenberg Library.

Others who have assisted in the research and illustration of this book include Virginia Harshman, wife of a great-grandson of Austin May Williams, who provided family information beyond what is available in Stephen W. Williams, *History of the Williams Family*. (Much of this data has been incorporated into the text and appendix; complete information is available in the Rosenberg Library Archives.) Anne Brindley and Elisabeth R. Darst of the Galveston Historical Foundation shared their special knowledge about the Williams house with me and made access to the old home easier. Robert Nesbitt, Director of Public Relations for the Port of Galveston, generously allowed the use of the port's collection of historic drawings as illustrations.

I also want to express appreciation to Professors Stanley Siegel and Edwin A. Miles of the Department of History at the University of Houston, who made valuable suggestions for both content and style. Without the able typing and proofreading by Marilyn Rhinehart, this manuscript would never have been completed.

Finally, my family and friends deserve commendation for their patience while I talked endlessly about Sam Williams and his adventures.

Samuel May Williams
EARLY TEXAS ENTREPRENEUR

CHAPTER 1

"Gone to Texas"

THE economic distress in the southern and western states following the Panic of 1819 forced many debtors to abandon their farms and homes and to seek a new beginning beyond the reach of the law. By 1822 many of these unfortunate people learned that Mexican Texas offered an asylum from the enforcement of the harsh debtor laws. Chalking "G. T. T." (Gone to Texas) on the door or the gate, the defaulter and his family would steal away, carrying as many possessions as possible and leaving the sheriff and the creditor only the real property. Poor families walked or rode west in farm wagons with their few possessions; the wealthy, accompanied by their chattel slaves and burdened with household goods, often sought passage on river and coastal vessels. Others, too, recognized the opportunities and promise of Texas—merchants, traders, adventurers, gamblers—everyone who wanted a new start in a new land.

Samuel May Williams was one of the immigrants. He and his woman companion boarded the sloop *Good Intent* at New Orleans in May, 1822, as Mr. and Mrs. E. Eccleston. Williams, like many others, left the United States owing a large sum of money, which may explain in part his resort to an alias. Captain Timothy Wightman of the *Good Intent* had just returned from a voyage to Texas as first mate on the *Only Son*, a slightly smaller vessel that was sailing again to the Texas coast. A gulf storm separated the two ships, but Wightman was able to pilot his sloop through the treacherous shallows of Matagorda Bay, and the *Good Intent* arrived at Hawkins's

Landing near the mouth of the Colorado River on June 18, only a few days after the *Only Son*.[1]

"Texas fever" pervaded the Mississippi Valley in response to advertisements placed in newspapers by Stephen F. Austin offering family men 640 acres for 12.5 cents per acre, about one-tenth the cost of similar land in the United States. At the same time that Williams embarked for Texas, the empresario was in Mexico City seeking confirmation of the grant made to his late father by the Spanish government in 1821. The death of Moses Austin and the success of the Mexican revolutionaries left in doubt the status of the colonial contract to import farmers from the United States. Austin remained in the capital until mid-1823, when he returned to Texas with permission to settle three hundred families between the Brazos and Colorado watersheds. He charged each family eighty dollars to cover the cost of surveying and issuing titles, a fee sufficiently ample to provide a surplus earmarked for Austin's creditors.[2]

The empresario quickly recognized his need for an expert bilingual clerk to assist in the preparation of deeds and in the conduct of correspondence with the Mexican authorities. Although Austin had begun to learn Spanish the previous year and felt competent in that language, the magnitude of the task of providing documents in the official language and parallel translations for the settlers overwhelmed him. From residents on the Colorado River, he learned of E. Eccleston, a "schoolmaster, who is a good clerk, and understands

[1] William Ransom Hogan, *The Texas Republic: A Social and Economic History*, p. 5; interview with Mrs. Eberly, Mary Austin Holley, "Interviews with Prominent Texans of Early Days," Mary Austin Holley Papers, Barker History Center, University of Texas at Austin; Charles Adams Gulick *et al.* (eds.), *The Papers of Mirabeau Buonaparte Lamar*, IV, pt. 1, 255–257; Milton P. Rieder, Jr., and Norma Gaudet Rieder (eds.), *New Orleans Ship Lists*, II, 33; Joseph H. Hawkins to S. F. Austin, February 6, 1822, in Eugene C. Barker (ed.), *The Austin Papers*, I, 476. (All citations to the Austin correspondence will use this shortened reference. Volumes I and II were published in the American Historical Association's *Annual Report*, 1919 and 1922, volume III by the University of Texas.)

[2] Eugene C. Barker, *The Life of Stephen F. Austin: Founder of Texas, 1793–1836*, pp. 27, 29, 30–37.

Spanish and French." If he proved to be a man "of good confidence," the empresario wanted to employ him.[3]

Austin met Williams during the autumn, and by November, 1823, the secretary was established in San Felipe and busy with the empresario's correspondence. Williams ended his masquerade as E. Eccleston at this same time, which suggests that Austin had penetrated the disguise he had adopted when fleeing Louisiana.[4] Only a few years earlier, both men had lived and worked quite near each other in New Orleans, and it is possible that they were acquainted, although no evidence exists to prove that supposition. For the next thirteen years, Williams would be closely associated with Austin, to their mutual benefit, in the task of developing the economic potential of Texas.

Williams's education and experience had well prepared him for the role he was to play. Born October 4, 1795, in Providence, Rhode Island, he had received traditional family names that went back five generations. Samuel was the first of eight children born to Howell Williams, a ship captain, and his wife, Dorothy Wheat. After 1810 young Sam went to Baltimore, where his uncle, Nathaniel Felton Williams, maintained a commission house and shop on Bowly's Wharf. Here the boy learned the techniques of commerce from the elder Williams, who in addition to his business was active in politics and also served as a director of a bank and an insurance company. When Samuel's younger brother Nathaniel Felton arrived to begin his apprenticeship, the young merchant sailed as supercargo on a vessel bound for Rio de la Plata. Commerce at Buenos Aires had first opened to foreigners when Napoleon's brother Joseph occupied the Spanish throne in 1808, and Baltimore clippers carried surplus foodstuffs to Argentina to exchange for hides and specie. Baltimore

---

[3] S. F. Austin to J. H. Bell, August 6, 1823, *Austin Papers*, I, 681–683.

[4] The earliest specimen of Williams's handwriting among Austin's correspondence is Voluntary Subsidy, November 22, 1823, Moses and Stephen F. Austin Papers, Barker History Center, University of Texas at Austin (also *Austin Papers*, I, 708–709). Williams wrote and signed his own name to Deposition concerning the loss of horses in San Felipe, October 18, 1823, *Austin Papers*, I, 669–670.

merchants increased their trade with the rebellious Spanish colonies
after the restoration of the Bourbon king in 1814. Williams remained
for a while in the Argentine capital, where he may have found employment with one of the numerous American merchants.[5] He
learned Spanish and possibly French in the cosmopolitan metropolis
and had an opportunity to observe Latin republicanism at close
hand. His experience in Buenos Aires later proved useful in colonial
Texas.

Just when Williams returned to the United States is unknown,
but it was not in time to serve as secretary to Andrew Jackson during the Battle of New Orleans, as later asserted by the British consul in Galveston. (William Kennedy, the British consul at Galveston from 1842 to 1845, confused the story about Sam Williams and
"John Williams," the alias used by Major A. Lacariere Latour, Jackson's chief engineer, when he associated with Jean Lafitte.)[6] Late in
1818 Sam Williams was in Washington, D.C., where he boarded at
the same hotel as the notorious Lafitte. The buccaneer and his
brother had bought sails from Nathaniel F. Williams when fitting
out a privateering expedition sponsored by the rebel Argentine government. Lafitte was in the capital at this time to confer with the
Spanish minister about exchanging several important Spanish hos-
tages for his crew members imprisoned in Cuba. The following winter Williams again encountered the corsair, this time in New Or-

[5] Stephen W. Williams, *History of the Williams Family*, pp. 122–
124; Siddie Robson Armstrong, "Chapters in the Early Life of Samuel
May Williams, 1795–1836" (M.A. thesis, University of Texas, 1929),
appendix A (see the genealogical charts in the appendix); Charles W.
Hayes, *Galveston: History of the Island and the City*, pp. 823–824; advertisements in the *Baltimore American and Commercial Advertiser*, April
6, 1808; January 3, February 4, May 10, 1811; July 2, September 10,
1818; Charles C. Griffin, "Privateering from Baltimore during the Spanish American Wars of Independence," *Maryland Historical Magazine* 35
(March 1940): 3–5; Frank R. Rutter, *South American Trade of Baltimore*, pp. 9–15; William Eckel to S. M. Williams, February 11, 1832,
Samuel May Williams Papers, Rosenberg Library, Galveston (references
to the Williams Papers, unless otherwise indicated, are to this collection).

[6] Kennedy to Lord Aberdeen, June 18, 1844, in Ephraim D. Adams
(ed.), *British Diplomatic Correspondence Concerning the Republic of
Texas, 1838–1846*, p. 341; Jane Lucas de Grummond, *The Baratarians
and the Battle of New Orleans*, p. x.

leans, where Lafitte was arranging for the defense of his captains.[7] Lafitte had recently moved his base camp to Galveston Island, just outside United States jurisdiction, where he remained until 1821. The ruins of the pirate settlement were still visible when the *Good Intent*, with Williams on board, passed the island the following year.

Williams lived in New Orleans in 1819, where he served in a volunteer militia that searched the nearby swamps for returning members of James Long's unsuccessful filibustering expedition to Nacogdoches, in Spanish Texas. Because of pending diplomatic negotiations with Spain to establish the southwestern border, the United States authorities paraded the captives down Chartres Street to publicize official displeasure with such illicit ventures in the neighboring territory. Sam Williams found employment as a clerk in the office of Morgan, Dorsey and Company, a mercantile company located on the corner of Magazine Street and Gravier just above Canal Street. At this time, Stephen F. Austin worked briefly as a writer for the *Louisiana Advertiser*, whose office was near the Merchants' Exchange on Canal and Chartres, about three blocks away from Williams's employer. Both young men boarded with families who lived within one block of Magazine and Poydras streets. Austin left New Orleans in June, 1821, and about that time Williams accepted a position as an agent for Osborn and Bowers, commission merchants near the foot of Canal Street. Although he was earning one hundred dollars per month, he left the firm at the end of February after working only eight months. He owed over seven hundred dollars to his employers for advances made to him, and he left New Orleans without making arrangements to repay the sum.[8]

During this period Williams bought furniture, utensils, and clothing, which indicates that he had established his own household. Why he and the lady left for Texas using her name as an alias re-

[7] Information on Lafitte from Col. Williams [1838], *Lamar Papers*, III, 228–230, V, 351.

[8] History Notes from Samuel M. Williams, *Lamar Papers*, V, 351; Greenbury Dorsey to S. M. Williams, March 9, April 4, 1843, Williams Papers; S. F. Austin to his mother [January 20, 1821], *Austin Papers*, I, 373–374; S. M. Williams to wife, June 10, 1844; W. C. Bowers to S. M. Williams, July 13, 1831, Williams Papers.

mains unclear. According to one rumor, Williams was involved in a serious dispute with three New Orleans residents, one the brother of a well-known physician. One of Austin's correspondents believed that Williams fled to avoid capital punishment, but there is no evidence to prove such an allegation.[9] Gossips in Texas blamed his flight on illicit romance, and the mysterious lady has been variously described as an actress, the wife of a circus owner, a rich widow, and a "high born Spanish lady" from Cuba. Local residents believed that Williams later banished her in 1826 in order to marry a younger woman. At least one child, Joseph Guadalupe Victoria Williams, was born of the union, and Williams retained custody of the infant, who was born in San Felipe in 1825. In spite of the scandal accompanying the woman's departure, Williams received sympathetic understanding from James E. Brown Austin, the empresario's younger brother, who was glad to hear that "Williams 'devil'" had finally started on her journey. He added that Williams should now have "more peace of mind."[10]

Before Williams accepted the position with Austin in the autumn of 1823, he had been using his clerical and linguistic talents

[9] Statements from various merchants in 1822 listing purchases made between July, 1821, and May, 1822, Williams Papers; William Fairfax Gray, *From Virginia to Texas, 1835: Diary of Col. Wm. F. Gray*, p. 182; James Erwin to S. F. Austin, September 30, 1825, *Austin Papers*, I, 1213–1216. The clerk of the Criminal District Court, Parish of Orleans, says few records exist prior to 1835 and there is nothing pertaining to Williams (Daniel B. Haggerty to author, March 21, 1972). The New Orleans Louisiana *Courier*, June 28, 1820, carried a notice from William Clark, Governor of the Territory of Missouri, advertising for Samuel M. Williams who had been indicted for the murder of Joseph Marsh, but neither Williams nor Marsh appears in the index to C. E. Carter (comp. and ed.), *The Territorial Papers of the United States*, vol. 15: *Louisiana-Missouri, 1815–1821*.

[10] Holley, "Interviews," Holley Papers; Sterling C. Robertson to Governor [Vidaurri], May 4, 1834, Sutherland Collection, translated by Malcolm D. McLean and in his possession; "More Ballads and Songs of the Frontier Folk," in J. Frank Dobie (ed.), *Foller de Drinkin' Gou'd*, pp. 155–160; Memoir of Annie Williams Corbin, n.d., in possession of author, which says that when Williams's Cuban wife died, he brought Joseph to Texas and raised him like the children of his 1828 marriage with Sarah P. Scott; J. E. B. Austin to S. F. Austin, August 22, 1826, *Austin Papers*, I, 1430–1434.

throughout the colony. Soon after his arrival on the *Good Intent* in June, 1822, he negotiated with a band of Karankawa Indians that came to Hawkins's Landing to trade for tobacco. The colonists suspected that the Indians were not entirely as peaceful as they seemed, and Williams sternly warned the "savages" that they must respect the goods and persons of the newcomers or suffer dire consequences. Most of the passengers from the vessels continued up the Colorado River to the permanent camp erected by the advance party, but Williams (as E. Eccleston) accompanied the Louisiana horse traders to the San Antonio River where he interpreted the interchange with the Spanish-speaking residents. He may have visited the provincial capital at Bexar before returning to the Colorado settlement.[11] During his first winter in Texas, Williams did clerical work for Jared Ellison Groce, a recent immigrant from Georgia by way of Louisiana, who possessed great material wealth and also many creditors in the United States.[12] The summer of 1823 found Williams employed as tutor at the home of Robert Kuykendall, who served as interim justice of the peace on the Colorado during Austin's absence in Mexico City. When neighbors captured a French-speaking Louisiana horse thief, Williams again used his talents to aid in the interrogation. The man received immediate frontier justice—thirty-nine lashes and banishment.[13]

By the end of 1823 Williams had joined Austin at John McFarland's ferry crossing on the Brazos, where the empresario had determined to locate the capital of the colony. Named San Felipe de Austin by Luciano García, governor of Texas, in honor of his patron

[11] Holley, "Interviews," Holley Papers; *Lamar Papers*, IV, pt. 1, 255–256; John Henry Brown, *History of Texas from 1685–1892*, I, 94–95; J. H. Kuykendall (ed.), "Reminiscences of Early Texans," *The Quarterly of the Texas State Historical Association* 6 (January 1903): 237–247; deposition concerning loss of horses, October 18, 1823; Hanna and Hawkins to Thomas C. Banks, April 25, 1823 (witnessed by E. Eccleston in the hand of S. M. Williams); Littlebury Hawkins to S. F. Austin, October 2, 1824, *Austin Papers*, I, 669–670, 632, 917–922.

[12] Andrew Erwin to S. F. Austin, August 29, 1825; James Erwin to S. F. Austin, September 30, 1825, *Austin Papers*, I, 1185–1187, 1213–1216.

[13] Kuykendall, "Reminiscences of Early Texans," *The Quarterly of the Texas State Historical Association* 7 (July 1903): 33.

saint and the empresario, the tiny settlement began with a handful of log cabins. Austin and Williams complemented each other in many ways. In addition to his facility in Spanish and his fine Spencerian penmanship, Williams understood commerce and banking and had valuable mercantile contacts with the eastern seaboard and the Gulf coast. Besides his experience in South America, he was familiar with Mexican culture and manners through his acquaintance with several of the leading revolutionary exiles in New Orleans. Austin, for his part, was a graduate of Transylvania University at Lexington, Kentucky, knew personally many of the important figures living in the Mississippi Valley, and proved adept in attracting settlers from that portion of the United States. He had served in the Missouri territorial legislature, thus gaining practical experience in government at its formative stage.[14]

Physically and mentally the pair resembled each other to some degree. Both were short in stature and slight in build, although Williams later added weight. Whereas the empresario had dark wavy hair, large hazel eyes, and skin that tanned evenly when exposed to the sun, his assistant was a reddish blond with a tendency to freckle and had piercing blue eyes.[15] Each man was introspective and tended to be moody, and neither possessed the magic charisma to attract a large popular following. Neither man accepted the democratic frontier spirit, agreeing with each other and a few select friends that the "sovereigns" should accept the leadership of their betters.[16] Austin often vacillated, trying to please everyone, an impossible goal that led to inner tension and physical illness at each crisis in his career.[17] Williams compromised as little as possible, and his brusque, businesslike, matter-of-fact manner alienated many of the settlers, who

[14] Juan Nepomuceno Almonte to S. M. Williams, October 10, 1834; S. F. Austin to S. M. Williams, July 1, 1832, Williams Papers; Barker, *Life of Austin*, pp. 17, 19, 21–22.

[15] The description of Austin is by his nephew, Moses Austin Bryan, in "Recollections of S. F. Austin," M. A. Bryan to son, September 25, 1889, Moses A. Bryan Papers, Barker History Center, University of Texas at Austin. Williams's description is pieced together from family sources.

[16] David G. Burnet to S. F. Austin, July 18, 1829; S. F. Austin to W. H. Wharton, April 24, 1829, *Austin Papers*, II, 228–229, 207–212.

[17] His changing position on slavery is classic; see Barker, *Life of Austin*, pp. 223–224.

resented his air of superiority. The sincere efforts of the empresario and his lieutenant to guide the colony toward success were often interpreted by others as self-seeking ambition.[18]

Although Austin's contract had been granted by the national government during the brief rule of Emperor Agustín de Iturbide in 1823 and approved by the succeeding constituent congress, the empresario had to wait for the arrival of a land commissioner appointed by the state government before titles could be issued. In spite of objections from influential native Texans, the Mexican congress had united sparsely populated Texas with Coahuila, its ranching and mining neighbor to the southwest, and placed the state capital at Saltillo, seven hundred miles away from the Brazos. This unnatural union of disparate interests and cultures encompassed an extremely large geographic area, and both the distance and the dissimilarities of the population were to pose problems during the next decade. Moreover, the state government was slow in forming, and the commissioner, the Baron de Bastrop, did not arrive at San Felipe until July, 1824, and then remained in the colony only a few months. Subsequent contracts to settle additional American immigrants were made with the state of Coahuila-Texas within the broad guidelines of the national colonization law that invited law-abiding, industrious Roman Catholics to settle the frontier.

Williams was extremely busy after Bastrop finally arrived. Besides writing each settler's application for land in Spanish and keeping track of the surveys, he wrote the original deed, usually two or three sheets, on the specially stamped government paper and in-included a Spanish translation of the surveyor's plot plan and field notes. The loose sheets of the original remained in the land office, and Williams provided a certified copy for the owner when all the fees had been paid. Austin had originally intended that the eighty dollars he charged for one section (640 acres at 12.5 cents) would cover all costs, but the Mexican government authorized each family to receive a headright of one league (4,428 acres) of grazing land and one *labor* (177 acres) of farm land, which increased the cost of surveying. The government allowed surveyors, clerks, and the land commissioner to receive small fees but expected the empre-

[18] S. F. Austin to W. H. Wharton, April 24, 1829, *Austin Papers*, II, 207–212.

sario to be content with generous premiums in land for settling a stated number of colonists. When the settlers learned that Austin would receive over sixty-five thousand acres, they refused to pay the fee stipulated in the original agreement. This action was a severe blow to his plans to recoup his family's fortune.[19]

Williams received two leagues and three *labores* in 1824; the additional forty-seven acres beyond the usual headright represented recompense for the privations he had undergone during the first two years in Texas and recognition of his value as assistant to the empresario. He located both leagues bordering the lower San Bernard River and chose a *labor* in three separate farming tracts laid off above, below, and opposite the capital, San Felipe de Austin. Williams sold the lower half of one league for one hundred dollars in 1825, less than five cents an acre, but a little later the fertile and convenient *labor* north of the village brought fourteen cents per acre.[20]

The Baron de Bastrop stayed with Williams while he was in San Felipe, which suggests that the two found a common bond. Described as a loquacious storyteller, the baron allegedly had been a Spanish spy who had lost large grants of land in Louisiana when it was sold to the United States. In reality, Philip Hendrick Nering Bogel had assumed his bogus title when he fled his wife and creditors in Holland about 1793. He later received an empresario contract to import Dutch and American wheat farmers into present-day northeastern Louisiana, a project that failed miserably. He subsequently immigrated in the early 1800's to San Antonio, where he became a respected citizen. The baron served Moses Austin as interpreter, and the Missourian offered him an interest in his colonial venture.[21]

[19] Lester G. Bugbee, "The Old Three Hundred," *The Quarterly of the Texas State Historical Association* 1 (October 1897): 108–109; Virginia H. Taylor, *The Spanish Archives of the General Land Office of Texas*, p. 17–18; Barker, *Life of Austin*, pp. 97–105, 232.

[20] Deed Record Book 2, 386, Spanish Archives, General Land Office, Austin; Brazoria County Deed Records, Spanish Records, 18; Austin County Deed Records, photostats of Colonial Records, W, 56.

[21] Kuykendall, "Reminiscences of Early Texans," *The Quarterly of the Texas Historical Association* 7 (January 1903): 248; Charles A. Bacarisse, "The Baron de Bastrop: The Life and Times of Philip Hendrick

As Austin's secretary, Williams was promised a salary of $1,000 a year, an amount that seemed adequate at first but proved to be meager compensation for the prodigious amount of work involved. Austin lacked the funds to pay even this modest sum, however, and in an effort to find public money to provide for Williams's salary, he suggested to the authorities the creation of the office of public recorder, similar to that of a county clerk in the United States. Mexican officials refused, however, because recording deeds was a function of the *ayuntamiento* (town council), and they expected to install such a body in the future at San Felipe to serve the entire colony. They did approve the position of colonial secretary which set a precedent for a bilingual clerk in the other Anglo-American colonies, but they left the problem of compensation in the hands of each empresario.[22] Williams introduced another innovation in record keeping in Texas when he received permission to transfer the titles from the loose sheets into a bound record book. Although the deeds were more secure from loss and pilfering in the leather-covered volume, the task increased Williams's clerical duties because each page had to be checked against the original and certified by the commissioner, the empresario, and two other officials.[23]

As colonial secretary Williams also recorded judicial proceedings from the alcalde's court and the appellate cases decided by Austin. These proceedings then had to be translated into Spanish for transmission to the authorities in San Antonio. He answered inquiries about land from prospective immigrants and often provided them copies of the surveyor's maps.[24] Because his work was so vital

Nering Bogel, 1759–1827" (Ph.D. dissertation, University of Texas, 1955), pp. 7, 8, 11, 68–69, 193, 200, 235–236, 266, 305.

[22] S. F. Austin to José Antonio Saucedo, August 26, 1824, August 11, 1825, *Austin Papers*, I, 881, 1166–1168.

[23] J. A. Padilla to Gaspar Flores, May 31, 1827, *ibid.*, pp. 1649–1650. The ledger arrived by ship in Galveston Bay, April 11, 1825, but Williams did not record titles in it until 1827 (Robert Lewis to S. F. Austin, April 11, 1825, *ibid.*, p. 1074). The Registro, measuring approximately eighteen by thirteen inches, four inches thick, and 612 pages long, is held in the Spanish Archives, General Land Office.

[24] Court costs for *Imla Keep* v. *Jared E. Groce* [May 8, 1826]; J. A. E. Phelps to S. F. Austin, January 16, 1825, *Austin Papers*, I, 1329, 1020–1021.

to the continued operation of the colony, Williams received an exemption from militia duty and remained in the capital when Austin was called away as commander of the volunteer army.[25] Until 1826, the empresario's absences from the colony were of short duration, but later, when business demanded his presence elsewhere for longer periods, he left routine colonial affairs under Williams's supervision.

Sam Williams became the major bureaucrat in Anglo-American Texas. One of the major sources of income for the state was from the sale of stamped paper for all legal documents, and Williams became the official dispenser for the entire colony.[26] He was also appointed postmaster for San Felipe in 1826, a patronage plum that he held until 1835, and when the government levied tonnage duty on foreign shipping, Williams was made collector on the Brazos.[27] In keeping with Spanish tradition, he kept a percentage of money collected as his fee for making the detailed reports required by his superiors. The secretary aided in framing petitions to both the state and national governments asking for laws to aid in developing the colony. Among the changes desired by the settlers were an official port on Galveston Bay, mail connections to Natchitoches, freedom of religion, and a judicial system more in keeping with Anglo-American practice. Few of the requests were granted immediately, but by persistence most of the proposals eventually became law. Of prime importance for the continued growth of the colony were requests to protect slave property brought into Mexico in spite of the known antipathy toward Negro slavery and to provide a debtor relief law to prevent creditors in the United States from harassing settlers through agents resident in the colony.[28] The latter affected many immigrants, including both Austin and Williams, and though the empresario and his assistant made arrangements for the gradual re-

[25] Minutes of a militia meeting, [April 28, 1826?], *ibid.*, pp. 1309–1310.

[26] Surety Bond, May 7, 1827; S. F. Austin to Saucedo, June 1, 1827; *ibid.*, pp. 1637, 1652.

[27] Erasmo Seguin to Postmaster, May 18, 1826; Francisco Campo Redondo to Collector, June 16, 1827; Treasury Department printed circular from José Ignacio Pavón, January 2, 1828, Williams Papers.

[28] Memorial to the Legislature, December 23, 1824, *Austin Papers*, I, 996–1002.

payment of their debts, they remained vitally interested in securing legal protection to prevent the seizure of their property.

The creation of the *ayuntamiento* in San Felipe in 1828 relieved Austin from the perplexities of administering and adjudicating for the settlers, although he would continue to locate families under the provisions of his contracts made with the state. Williams ceased to function as colonial secretary in 1827, but he continued to serve as Austin's assistant. The popularly elected council traditionally governed the four contiguous leagues granted each town by Mexican law, but the *ayuntamiento* at San Felipe had jurisdiction over the entire area encompassed in Austin's contract, from the San Jacinto to Lavaca rivers and from the coast to the San Antonio Road. Later, as the population increased, the legislature authorized additional councils at several towns. The administrative-judicial body combined the duties of modern city and county governments to preserve law and order and to guard the health and welfare of the residents.

Austin, assisted by Williams, installed the officers of the *ayuntamiento* on the second Sunday in February, 1828. In the meeting that immediately followed, the new officials asked Williams to accept the appointive office of secretary, but he refused, explaining that his business with the empresario absorbed all his time. Both men felt that the time had come for the residents of the growing colony to assume more responsibility for governing themselves. Up to this time, Williams had done the translating and clerical work that now belonged to the *ayuntamiento,* and if he should become its secretary, the council would continue to depend on him and the empresario. But under pressure from those who insisted that he was the only person who understood Spanish well enough, and through his sense of duty, Williams finally agreed to serve temporarily until the body could engage a qualified person. He made it clear, however, that they must establish a separate office for him, and when the officers agreed, he ordered a desk and work table to furnish the log house that they leased. The *ayuntamiento* met only two other times during 1828, although by law it was supposed to hold monthly sessions. Not all the officials lived near San Felipe, so illness and adverse weather often prevented assembling a quorum. Williams was unable to attend the March meeting because of the arrival of

the land commissioner, and the alcalde substituted for him, recording the minutes in English.[29]

The frontier capital of San Felipe changed slowly from a pioneer settlement of sheds and cabins, and by 1828 the village had at
least one frame building among the estimated thirty dwellings and
stores. Tree stumps still remained in the streets and visitors mistook
the scattered buildings as haphazard squatting, but most had been
carefully located in accordance with the survey made in 1824. Until
1827, both Austin and Williams maintained log houses north of the
commercial plaza on Calle Comercio, the major north-south street
paralleling the river. Directly across from Williams was the tavern
of Jonathan Peyton, who, with his wife, had arrived on the same
ship as Williams in 1822.[30]

The popular saloon was the scene of a drumhead court in September, 1827, before the creation of the *ayuntamiento* and while
Austin was away attending the state legislature at Saltillo. The sensational event capped a series of denunciations and rude jests directed against the empresario and his assistant by Dr. Louis Dayton,
a visitor from the Red River settlements, which were outside any
governmental jurisdiction. Dayton disliked the stringent require-
ments for obtaining land on the Brazos, and, hearing the old gossip
concerning Williams's arrival in Texas, he determined to cause
mischief and undermine the authority of the two men. He hired a
strolling minstrel to sing "Mrs. Williams's Lament," a defamatory
barroom ballad that mocked the leaders of the community. The following is a composite of surviving verses that pertain to Williams:

> The first of those villains who came to this State
> Was runaway Stephen F. Austin the great;
> He applied to the Mexicans as I understand
> And from them got permission to settle this land.

[29] Eugene C. Barker, "The Government of Austin's Colony, 1821–
1831," *Southwestern Historical Quarterly* 21 (January 1918): 246; *idem*
(ed.), "Minutes of the Ayuntamiento of San Felipe de Austin, 1828–
1832," *ibid.*, pp. 306, 307–308; statement from M. M. Battle, October,
1828, *Austin Papers*, II, 121.

[30] Noah Smithwick, *The Evolution of a State: Or Recollections of
Old Texas Days*, p. 55; plot plan of Villa de Austin, July 1, 1824, Re-
gistro, p. 18 (see map of San Felipe); Ganey W. Bradfield, "A List of
Property Owners within the Limits of the Model [of San Felipe, ca.

Chorus:

> The United States, as we understand,
> Took sick and did vomit the dregs of the land.
> Her murderers, bankrupts, and rogues you may see
> All congregated in San Felipe.
>
> The next was my husband, for you will now see
> How Austin coaxed him to San Felipe,
> To this great Sanhedrin, and not very mild,
> That I should be banished, then robbed of my child.[31]

When Williams challenged Dayton, the doctor threatened to burn the land office. Supporters of the absent empresario apprehended the troublemaker and took him to Peyton's tavern, where they tried the culprit and then tarred and feathered him before escorting him from town. The extralegal body included Sam Williams and Austin's brother, Brown.[32]

Soon after this episode, both Austin and Williams moved away from the noisy plaza to the garden lots north of town. These plots were larger, usually about twelve acres, and the best ones bordered Agua Dulce Creek. The empresario began a house of milled lumber, but Williams delayed building his suburban home for a year, living temporarily in a log cabin that he moved to the site. Austin converted his former log house into a two-story hotel that he leased to James Whitesides.[33]

By 1828, less than six years after his arrival in Texas, Sam Wil-

---

[31] Smithwick, *Evolution of a State*, pp. 80–81; Kuykendall, "Reminiscences of Early Texans," *The Quarterly of the Texas State Historical Association* 7 (July 1903): 49–50; Dobie (ed.), *Foller de Drinkin' Gou'd,* pp. 155–160.

[32] Hosea H. League to S. F. Austin, September 10, 1827, *Austin Papers*, I, 1679–1680; information from Mrs. Eberly, *Lamar Papers*, IV, pt. 1, 254–255.

[33] Statements from M. M. Battle and John Cumings, April 19, June 21, 1828, Williams Papers; Samuel Hirams to S. F. Austin, September 8, October 23, 1826; agreement between M. M. Battle and S. F. Austin, September 12, 1827, *Austin Papers*, I, 1451–1452, 1480, 1682–1683.

1830]" (unpublished manuscript, Josey Museum, San Felipe). Bradfield did extensive research in land titles before constructing the village model on exhibit at the museum.

liams was a man of importance and substance. In addition to his headright of more than nine thousand acres that he had received in 1824, he petitioned the governor for another four leagues of land as recompense for his work as colonial secretary. Upon receiving approval, he selected two leagues between the forks of Mill Creek northwest of San Felipe, another league on the east bank of the Brazos below the outpost in the big bend, and the remaining league on the south bank of Buffalo Bayou just west of Harrisburg.[34] The Mexican government did not tax land, an arrangement that pleased Williams and other Texas land barons, who intended to hold their estates for the future. The only restriction imposed by the government limited each individual to eleven leagues, or almost forty-nine thousand acres. At this time Williams possessed a little more than one-half that amount, but he laid plans to acquire the maximum as soon as possible.

[34] Deed Record Book 2, 120, Spanish Archives, General Land Office, Austin. The Brazos league is east of Richmond on Oyster Creek and included present-day Sugarland. The Buffalo Bayou tract was between the leagues belonging to John R. Harris and John Austin, at present between the East-Tex Freeway and the turning basin in downtown Houston.

CHAPTER 2

Rising Expectations
1828-1830

SAMUEL MAY WILLIAMS could review the events of 1828 with satisfaction. Most important to his personal happiness was his marriage to Sarah Patterson Scott in March; a priest from Bexar, Padre Galindo, performed the ceremony in San Felipe. The twenty-year-old bride was the eldest daughter of William Scott, a former Kentuckian who had arrived in Texas in 1822 and settled on the San Jacinto estuary where he constructed a boat yard and operated a coasting vessel.[1] Within a year Sarah gave birth to a daughter, who was named Sophia Caroline after Williams's sister; the new baby and Williams's son, Vic, now four, stimulated his determination to expand his business activities as soon as possible into other fields.

For the present, however, Williams was inundated with land business. Since the Baron de Bastrop had left in 1824, Williams had remained busy recording the 272 titles authorized by the land commissioner. After Bastrop's death in 1827, Governor José María Viesca appointed Gaspar Flores of Bexar to complete Stephen F. Austin's original contract and also to issue titles for the five hundred families permitted by his second grant. Flores arrived in San Felipe with his kinsman, Padre Galindo, and the newly-wed Williams welcomed him into his home during the commissioner's three-month visit. A close relationship developed between Flores and Williams

---

[1] Charles W. Hayes, *Galveston: History of the Island and the City,* p. 825; Harris County Deed Records, M, 283. William Scott's two leagues and one *labor* encompassed modern Baytown and the Exxon refinery.

that would endure until Flores's death in 1836. The residents of Bexar elected Flores alcalde in 1829, and because by law he was required to remain in the municipality during his term, he was unable to issue deeds at San Felipe. Williams managed to complete some of the paperwork by sending it to Flores with the mail carrier, but the arrangement irritated Austin, who unsuccessfully endeavored to have Williams appointed commissioner.[2]

Although the *ayuntamiento* was intended by law to keep the deed records, Austin and Williams hesitated to turn over the colonial archives until a fireproof vault could be constructed. In addition, only Williams could read the Spanish documents, and while he served as secretary to the council, the authorities could be placated with the assurance that the records were in the proper hands.[3] In order to offer credit to those who could not pay the fees in full (a minimum of eighty-seven dollars plus the surveying charge per linear measure), Williams offered to "go halves," a practice common in Mexico. The colonist executed a promissory note for the charges, and if at the end of the year the man was still unable to clear the debt, Williams offered to settle the account in order that the settler might receive his deed. To secure this loan, the debtor made over one-half of his headright (2,214 acres) to the secretary, and when the note fell due, Williams accepted the land if the money was not available. Austin, his brother, and several of the surveyors also acquired half-leagues in this manner, but the practice aroused resentment.[4] Much of Williams's unpopularity stemmed from this ar-

2 Gaspar Flores to S. M. Williams, June 12, 1828, March 5, 1829, Samuel May Williams Papers, Rosenberg Library, Galveston; S. F. Austin to Ramón Músquiz, January 12, 1829; Austin to Governor Viesca, May 31, 1830, in Eugene C. Barker (ed.), *The Austin Papers*, II, 158, 399–401.

3 Stephen F. Austin, *Translation of the Laws, Orders, and Contracts on Colonization.*

4 *Samuel May Williams v. F. W. Chandler and others*, Rosenberg Library, Galveston; John M. Hensley to S. M. Williams, November 11, 1834, Williams Papers. For Austin's activities, see Charles Adams Gulick et al. (eds.), *The Papers of Mirabeau Buonaparte Lamar*, IV, pt. 1, 224–229. Williams received a ten-dollar fee plus two dollars for the stamped paper. The commissioner got fifteen dollars and, until 1830, Austin received sixty dollars, but thereafter only fifty. See Eugene C. Barker, *The Life of Stephen F. Austin: Founder of Texas, 1783–1836*, pp. 132–133.

bitrary solution; nevertheless, the increasing number of debtors agreeing to this arrangement caused the secretary to order a printed form.[5]

Williams assumed that his duties with the impotent first *ayuntamiento* had ended on New Year's Day when the officers for 1829 were installed. But the new council asked that he continue as secretary and offered to pay him $1,000 to "sacrifice" his private interests for the community for one more year. He agreed to serve temporarily, insisting that they find a competent person to replace him because he intended to devote his efforts to support his "small but growing family." Nevertheless, Williams continued to act as secretary until 1830, when the council employed Dr. Thomas J. Gazley.[6]

Williams planned to enter commerce as a merchant, utilizing his family connections in New Orleans, Mobile, and Baltimore. His sister Sophie had married Samuel St. John, Jr., who was connected with the New York commission merchants and brokers known at different times as Beers and St. John, St. John & Son, and various other combinations. This family business reached the Gulf coast by the 1830's, and Samuel St. John moved his operation to Mobile and then New Orleans. In addition, Sam Williams's uncle, Nathaniel F. Williams, still conducted an extensive commission business in Baltimore, and his namesake, Sam's younger brother Nat, left his place there and joined a family friend in opening a commission house in 1827 at Mobile, Dobson and Williams. Austin envied his assistant's business acumen and regretted that his own education had ill prepared him for the mercantile world. He urged his sister to apprentice her sons to merchants in Missouri in order that the boys might learn a "gentleman's" profession, and he suggested that his nephews master French and Spanish like Williams. Realizing that the profits from selling his premium land lay far in the future, Austin and his brother ventured into a variety of profitable

[5] Promissory note, November 4, 1831, Rosenberg Library, Galveston.

[6] Eugene C. Barker (ed.), "Minutes of the Ayuntamiento of San Felipe de Austin, 1828–1832," *Southwestern Historical Quarterly* 21 (January 1918): 326, 395; Hosea H. League to S. M. Williams, January 12, 1829; S. M. Williams to the Ayuntamiento, January 15, 1829, Williams Papers; Barker, "Minutes of the Ayuntamiento," *Southwestern Historical Quarterly* 21 (April 1918): 417–423; 22 (July 1918): 78.

schemes. In 1828 James E. Brown Austin and his cousin, John Austin, bought the schooner *Eclipse*, which they intended to use as a coastal trading vessel. The pair invited Williams to join their enterprise, but he declined.[7]

He did accompany the two Austins to New Orleans on board the *Eclipse* in May, 1829. It had been seven years since he had left Louisiana, and no doubt he enjoyed renewing former friendships. He had arranged to begin repaying the indebtedness to his creditors in the city and thus could move freely about without the danger of arrest. After ordering merchandise sent to the Brazos, he continued on to Mobile to visit his younger brother Nathaniel F. Williams, who was the junior partner in Dobson and Williams, commission merchants. Sam Williams returned to New Orleans in August and rejoined the Austins, who were preparing to return to Texas. They were joined by John R. Harris, the developer of Harrisburg on Buffalo Bayou, who had recently come from Texas on his schooner.[8]

But before the men returned home, yellow fever took its toll. Brown Austin succumbed to the disease on August 17 at the home of their host, merchant John W. Collins, after three days, and Harris died a week later. Williams helped to make the necessary funeral arrangements and sent word of the tragedy to the families. The loss of his brother sent Austin to his sickbed suffering with acute melancholia in addition to his annual bout with fever. Williams, upon his return to San Felipe, moved his friend into more comfortable quarters at his own home, where Sarah could supervise the empresario's recovery.[9]

[7] S. F. Austin to Emily M. Perry, October 25, 1825; J. E. B. Austin to same, October 28, November 10, 1825, *Austin Papers*, I, 1228–1229, 1229–1230, 1232–1233; petition for a charter, September 12, 1828; J. E. B. Austin to S. F. Austin, September 16, 1828, *ibid.*, II, 107–109.

[8] Hyde and Merritt to S. M. Williams, April 15, 1827, Williams Papers; S. M. Williams to S. F. Austin, June 9, 1829; J. E. B. Austin to Emily M. Perry, May 26, August 6, 1829, *Austin Papers*, II, 221–223, 217–218, 244–245; various receipts to Williams dated June 29 to July 2 and August 6 to August 11, 1829, Williams Papers.

[9] H. D. Thompson to S. F. Austin, August 19, 1829, *Austin Papers*, II, 247–248; "Journal of Lewis Birdsall Harris, 1836–1842," *Southwestern Historical Quarterly* 25 (January 1922): 187; *Texas Gazette*, October 3, 1829; S. F. Austin to José Antonio Navarro, October 19, December 24,

As Austin grew stronger, Williams encouraged him to prepare for publication an English translation of the constitution and laws of Coahuila-Texas. Williams completed the translations while the empresario composed a history and apologia of his actions since 1822 as an introduction to the volume. The manuscript went to the printer in November, and the editor, Godwin B. Cotten, suspended publication of the *Texas Gazette* until the end of January in order to complete the book.[10] The former publisher of both the Mobile and the New Orleans *Gazette,* Cotten may have been acquainted with Austin and Williams before coming to San Felipe in 1829. He leased Williams's old residence across the street from Peyton's tavern for his printing office, which became the informal gathering place for the empresario's supporters. The convivial group centered around Luke Lessassier and Robert M. Williamson, two of the colony's most competent lawyers, and Williamson, in addition, wrote many of the editorials for the *Texas Gazette,* the four-page weekly that served Austin well by publicizing his support of government policies. Surveyor Frank W. Johnson and Dr. Robert Peebles completed the circle of friends, a junta that generally would support the empresario in subsequent political struggles. Williams occasionally joined the merrymakers, but Austin never could relax and enjoy the rowdy company.[11]

Early in 1830 Williams entered into a law partnership with Luke Lessassier, who had arrived recently from Louisiana. In order to prepare for his licensing examination at Saltillo, Williams borrowed copies of Spanish law books from Hosea H. League, a member of the *ayuntamiento.*[12] It seems doubtful that he had an op-

---

1829; John Austin to S. F. Austin, December 27, 1829, *Austin Papers,* II, 271–273, 302–303, 304–306.

[10] S. F. Austin to José Antonio Navarro, October 19, 1829, *Austin Papers,* II, 271–273; Charles A. Bacarisse, "The Texas Gazette, 1829–1831," *Southwestern Historical Quarterly* 56 (October 1952): 246. See Austin, *Translation of the Laws,* also in Gammel (comp.), *Laws of Texas,* I, 3–58.

[11] Bacarisse, "Texas Gazette," pp. 239–241; Noah Smithwick, *The Evolution of a State: Or Recollections of Old Texas Days,* pp. 71–72.

[12] *Texas Gazette,* April 10, 1830, January 15, 1831; memorandum to G. B. McKinstry, March, 1830; Thomas Jefferson Chambers to S. M. Wil-

portunity to go to the capital before 1835, and no certification to practice law exists among his papers; yet he did represent various local merchants and assisted the empresario in drafting a will. Lessassier and Williams ended their association about 1832, principally because by then Williams was devoting all his energy to commerce.

Capitalizing on his family connections and having re-established credit in New Orleans during his visit in 1829, Williams expected to open a commission house on the Brazos. He would buy the residents' cotton and pelts to be exchanged in New Orleans for merchandise suitable for both the Anglo-American market on the Brazos and Colorado rivers and for the Mexican market at San Antonio and the interior. The latter was illegal, but Williams and others were well acquainted with traditional Spanish practices designed to circumvent legal difficulties. Four of Williams's family had come to San Felipe during 1830 in connection with the commercial ventures. His youngest brother, Matthew, had arrived in the spring with a consignment of goods for trade and some personal items requested by Sarah, including a large family Bible. As a bachelor resident, Matthew was eligible for only one-quarter of a league of land, but because of his "good habits" and "special qualifications" (not further clarified), the legislature granted him an entire league, which he located on the lower Colorado River. He never resided there, and in 1836 he sold the tract for one dollar per acre to a speculator. Matthew assisted his brother in the land office and directed their mercantile efforts on the upper Brazos in Coles's Settlement in present-day Washington County. Sam Williams's oldest brother, Henry Howell, ended his service as a ship captain in the Colombian navy and paid the fees for a headright in the colony, but instead of remaining in Texas to legalize his claim, he returned to Baltimore and entered the commission business with their uncle. Their remaining brother, Nathaniel Felton, came to Texas from Mobile to investigate commercial opportunities and brought their widowed sister, Eliza Williams Sweet, for an extended visit. She remained when Nat returned to Alabama at the end of the summer.[13]

---

liams, October 15, 1830; H. H. League to S. M. Williams, February 9, 1831, Williams Papers.

[13] John Austin to S. M. Williams, February 3, 1830; Cone and Ormsbee, Ltd., to Williams, March 12, 1830; Morgan and Company to Wil-

These visitors and the birth of Austin May Williams on June 16, 1830, encouraged Williams to enlarge his house. Within the year, the white frame story-and-a-half home was completed on the bluff overlooking Agua Dulce Creek. Williams imported window sashes, glass and paint from New Orleans, but local craftsmen supplied brick for the kitchen floor, well, and fireplaces, cypress shingles for the roof, and milled lumber for framing and siding.[14]

Williams's rising expectations received a temporary setback when the central government enacted on April 6, 1830, a law to discourage immigration from the United States. The authorities, uneasy about the ever-increasing number of Anglo-Americans in Texas, had sent a party in 1828 toward the Sabine River, ostensibly to determine the eastern boundary but also to ascertain the number and location of the non-native population. When the expedition reached San Felipe, Austin and Williams offered lavish hospitality to Manuel Mier y Terán, the commander, in hopes of winning his support for their enterprise. Their efforts were not altogether successful. In addition to being an engineer, natural scientist, and artillery officer, Terán was a potent political figure whose negative report on Texas inspired the restrictive law of April 6, 1830. Intended to Mexicanize the Anglo settlements, the plan permitted only native Mexicans and Europeans to immigrate to Texas and ended the subterfuge of importing Negroes as indentured servants to circumvent the laws against admitting slaves. Garrisons were to be erected at all ports of entry along the coast and also on the overland routes into Austin's

---

liams, April 15, 1831, Williams Papers (the Bible was destroyed by fire in the early 1900's); Deed Record Book 7, p. 63, Spanish Archives, General Land Office, Austin; Matagorda County Deed Records, D, 17, 19, 21; George Dobson to S. M. Williams, April 11, 1830; promissory note from Henry H. Williams, November 13, 1830; N. F. Williams to brothers and sisters, August 7, 1830, Williams Papers.

[14] Statements to Williams from John Cummings, May, 1830; from C. C. Givens, June 16, 1830; from W. K. Wilson, July 26, 1830; from George Robinson, August 10, 1830; William P. Harris to Williams, September 27, 1830; statements from Brown and Bennet, January 11, 1831; from John S. Evans, September 13, 1834; Edmund Andrews to S. M. Williams, April 14, 1831; statement from Thomas Slaughter, July 4, 1832, Williams Papers. A rambling house remains on the site, but the present owner believes it to be only about sixty years old.

colony; the soldiers were to intimidate the residents and also to enforce the collection of duties scheduled to commence later in the year. The colonists had enjoyed a temporary exemption from the tariff on goods intended for their own use. Although the Mexican congress lifted the ban against foreign vessels participating in the coasting trade, the Anglo-Americans regarded the law as an anathema, and the empresario worked to soothe suspicions on both sides.[15]

Austin and Williams privately feared that the law, which threatened to end the stream of potential landowners, might destroy everything for which they had worked. In a careful reading of the law, they discovered two vaguely worded passages that could be used to their advantage if they could convince the government that the law did not apply to Austin's colony. Their case relied on the word *established* as applied to colonies, and they insisted that the prohibition against further Anglo-American immigration restricted only incomplete empresario contracts, not those of Austin, who had already been awarded premium land for filling his contractual obligations. Terán, who had been appointed federal commissioner in addition to commandant general for Texas-Coahuila and portions of Nuevo León and Tamaulipas, allowed Austin's interpretation to stand, and as a result immigrants continued to enter under his remaining contracts.[16]

Entry into Austin's colonies was readily solved by the use of passports issued to the potential immigrant by the empresario or his agent. The collection of the tariff, however, continued to cause trouble. The treasury authorized opening of a customs house for the colony six months before the exemption granted to the settlers expired. The federal government sent George Fisher, a naturalized Mexican citizen of Serbian ancestry, to open the *aduana* (customs house) at the mouth of the Brazos in May, 1830, about the same

[15] José María Sánchez, "A Trip to Texas in 1828," Carlos E. Castañeda (trans.), *Southwestern Historical Quarterly* 29 (April 1926): 270–272; S. F. Austin to Terán, May 24, June 30, 1828, *Austin Papers*, II, 43–45, 56–66; Alleine Howren, "The Causes and Origin of the Decree of April 6, 1830," *The Quarterly of the Texas State Historical Association* 16 (April 1913): 378–422.

[16] Barker, *Life of Austin*, pp. 255–274; Virginia H. Taylor, *The Spanish Archives of the General Land Office of Texas*, p. 155.

time that confirmation of the law of April 6 arrived. Fisher was a controversial political opportunist who had fled his native land in 1815, arriving in Mississippi where he became a naturalized United States citizen. He married a local girl and tried to become a planter, but in 1825 adventure attracted him to Mexico, where he was associated with Joel Poinsett, the United States chargé d'affaires. Abandoning his family in Mississippi, Fisher organized York rite Masonic lodges at Poinsett's request, a step that the conservative, monarchist Scottish rite Masons interpreted as a political device to encourage even more republicanism. With the influence of powerful York Masons, Fisher obtained the post of collector at Galveston and returned to the United States with Poinsett in 1829. He remained in New Orleans until May, 1830, when he arrived in Texas, ostensibly representing the more conservative government that was imposing itself on the Mexican republic. Fisher's political alliances were unclear, and Austin and Williams, wishing to offend neither of the developing factions, handled the inspector with caution.[17]

Fisher confiscated two hundred bales of tobacco from an American schooner in June, and other vessels, hearing about the difficulty at the *aduana,* either avoided a confrontation or dumped their cargo. Supposedly imported only for the colonists' own use, the tobacco was actually intended for trade with the Indians and Mexicans farther inland. Fisher requested that Williams provide him with a copy of the exemptions granted to the colony, but Williams delayed, explaining that in view of the new instructions, he was unsure of the procedure himself.[18] Unable to enforce the law until the arrival of the troops, Fisher received permission to suspend his activities.

[17] George Fisher to S. F. Austin, May 18, 1830, *Austin Papers*, II, 391–392; Bessie Lucille Letts, "George Fisher" (M.A. thesis, University of Texas, 1929), pp. 5–12, 19, 25.
[18] George Fisher to S. M. Williams, July 6, 1830, Williams Papers; Ramón Músquiz to Governor, February 14, 1830, *Austin Papers*, II, 332; Smithwick, *Evolution of a State*, pp. 52–53; [Ashael Langworthy], *A Visit to Texas: Being the Journal of a Traveller through Those Parts Most Interesting to American Settlers . . .*, pp. 196–198; list of goods for Bejar, [1830]; copies of letter to G. Fisher, July 27, 1830; George McKinstry to S. M. Williams, May 27, 1830; George Fisher to S. M. Williams, May 27, 1830, Williams Papers.

At this juncture, John G. Holtham, the second man to serve as secretary to the *ayuntamiento* since January, resigned. The council pressed Williams into service on July 5, and because Fisher was available, Williams suggested that the members employ him until such time as the customs house might reopen. The versatile adventurer accepted the position with alacrity, possibly hoping to discover Anglo-American secrets to transmit to Terán. The council appointed Fisher, Williams, and Austin to prepare a suitable September 16 celebration to commemorate the twentieth anniversary of the beginning of Mexican independence.[19]

A series of sensational events—three murders and one jail break —interrupted the planned fiesta and left the townspeople stunned. One of the crimes, the murder of Holtham, former secretary to the *ayuntamiento*, involved alderman Hosea H. League and Seth Ingram, the leading surveyor, who were accused of the deed.[20] A few weeks later, the council discovered that Fisher had been making copies of the records, and the members assumed that he was acting as a spy for the conservative party that had recently assumed power in the capital. The *ayuntamiento* dismissed Fisher, but he refused to relinquish certain letters and documents given to him by Williams in connection with the secretarial duties. The members felt that some of the correspondence might be misinterpreted by the authorities, and they asked Williams and the sheriff to accompany them to Fisher's room to recover the papers. The sheriff uncovered a bundle of the records hidden in a trunk; Williams identified them as belonging to the council. Fisher left the colony for Matamoros, where Terán maintained his headquarters, and in order to defend himself, he commenced a series of articles denouncing the Anglo-Americans in the *Advertiser of the Port of Matamoros*, a newspaper that he edited for the next year.[21]

[19] Barker, "Minutes of the Ayuntamiento," *Southwestern Historical Quarterly* 22 (1918–1919): 86–88, 90–95, 181–182, 272–273.

[20] *Ibid.*, 23 (July 1919): 73–77; Smithwick, *Evolution of a State*, pp. 84–88; S. F. Austin to J. F. Perry, September 22, 1830; S. F. Austin to Ramón Músquiz, November 30, 1830, *Austin Papers*, II, 493–497, 547–548.

[21] Barker, "Minutes of the Ayuntamiento," *Southwestern Historical Quarterly* 22 (January 1919): 274–278; S. F. Austin to Alamán, October 18, 1830, *Austin Papers*, II, 512–515; S. F. Austin to S. M. Williams, Jan-

Williams resumed the secretaryship of the beleaguered council in October and served the remainder of the year. He accepted the responsibility for 1831 and may have continued to serve until he turned the records over to William B. Travis, who became secretary in February, 1834. The three surviving minute books end with the entry of January 3, 1832, but Williams composed some of the subsequent correspondence with the authorities. He retained his position as special collector of tonnage on foreign shipping, and he sent his reports through Fisher, who remained on the Rio Grande until Terán again sent him to Texas in November, 1831.[22]

As 1830 drew to a close, Williams helped the empresario get his business affairs in order so that Austin might attend the state legislature to which he had been elected. Williams had served as an elector representing San Felipe at the departmental canvass held in Bexar during the first week in September. Texas was allowed two deputies, and Austin felt flattered that he was selected; yet he dreaded the upcoming session, which promised to be stormy because of the political struggle between the centralist and federalist factions. By law, candidates could not campaign for office, and once elected they were required to attend all sessions during the two-year term or face a fine. The empresario made his will and named Williams one of the executors before leaving on the seven-hundred-mile journey to Saltillo. He also urged his brother-in-law, James F. Perry, to hasten his proposed move to Texas from Missouri in order to take charge of Austin's "money matters," which had been long neglected.[23]

uary 9, March 12, 1831, Williams Papers; George Fisher to Governor, February 19, 1831, *Austin Papers*, II, 598–599; Letts, "George Fisher," pp. 65–70.

[22] Robert E. Davis (ed.), *The Diary of William Barret Travis, August 30, 1833–June 26, 1834*, p. 129; petition to Supreme Government, February 18, 1832, *Austin Papers*, II, 749–752; *Texas Gazette*, November 21, 1830; S. M. Williams to Governor, June 30, 1831, Williams Papers.

[23] Election return in Williams's hand, September 5, 1830, in private collection of Frell Albright, Houston, Texas; Francisco Ruiz to S. M. Williams, September 18, 1830, Williams Papers; S. F. Austin to J. F. Perry, September 22, December 14, 19, 1830, *Austin Papers*, II, 493–497, 555–556, 564–565.

Austin left colonial matters in Williams's hands, and even before his election to the legislature, he had arranged for his lieutenant to assume the responsibility for settling the one hundred families in the "little colony" on the upper Colorado River, the fourth contract negotiated by the empresario in 1827. In return for his work, Williams was to receive one-half the premium land due to Austin as empresario. If the settlement was completed by 1833, the secretary would be entitled to 9,000 acres. The pair had every reason to believe that the Colorado tract could be filled on time; the 1830 census showed over four thousand persons already in Austin's grant, and immigration continued despite the attempt to restrict it by the law of April 6, 1830. So far, the empresario had received title to over 148,000 acres as his bonus for locating families, and he expected to earn additional premium lands during the remaining four years of his contracts.[24]

Williams received permission from the state to increase his land holdings by seven leagues as compensation for his services to the *ayuntamiento* and other colonial duties for which he had received no pay because of the lack of circulating currency. He chose one league opposite San Felipe above the *labor* plots, one in present-day Washington County on the La Bahia Road, another in Burleson County west of the Brazos on the Bexar Road, two wooded leagues on Buckner's Creek in Fayette County, one league east of the Colorado above the village of Bastrop, and the last league southwest of that village.[25]

On his journey to the state capital, Austin wrote to his associate from Bexar, warning that the coming year threatened to bring many changes and disturbances and that they should both exercise caution when dealing with the authorities.[26] The empresario had no way of knowing how extensive those changes would be when he made the gloomy prediction. Austin referred to such external events

[24] Memorandum, April 4, 1830, Williams Papers; Barker, *Life of Austin*, pp. 131, 272, 275; Taylor, *Spanish Archives*, p. 155.

[25] Erasmo Seguin to Williams, May 13, 1830, Williams Papers; Deed Record Book 36, p. 117, Spanish Archives, General Land Office; Taylor, *Spanish Archives*, p. 255.

[26] S. F. Austin to S. M. Williams, December 29, 1830, Williams Papers.

as the unstable political climate that would affect the development of his colony, but internal developments would result in an even greater change. Austin's efforts at land speculating beyond his colonial grants was a major cause of the ensuing changes. His purchase of three eleven-league tracts for himself and his instructions to Williams to facilitate the location of other such grants for political friends brought about misunderstandings between the two associates. In spite of Williams's insistence that his private affairs must take precedence over those of the empresario, Austin continued to rely on Williams to supervise the new speculations and complete the old contracts. Thus 1831 would be a watershed: no longer would Williams submerge his own ambition in order to further the colonial enterprises of his friend. Beginning in 1831, Williams's own activities took precedence and Austin's business was relegated to second place.

CHAPTER 3

Playing the Double Game
1831-1833

WHEN Stephen F. Austin arrived in Bexar on his way to Saltillo in late 1830, he learned about the politically unstable situation that was intensifying throughout Mexico in response to the centralist party's assumption of power. Fighting appeared imminent between the centralist and federalist factions, and Austin wanted to avoid antagonizing men of influence on either side. He warned Williams to use "silence, prudence, and vigilance."

> There can scarcely be a more difficult thing than to play a *double game*, it is dangerous, and it is at times, a nice a point to draw the distinction between such a game and dishonor—we are so situated that we must keep a good understanding with Teran and Alaman, —but at the same time all our best friends at Saltillo and in Mexico are very hostile to both. . . .[1]

Throughout the winter and spring the empresario urged his lieutenant to "say little or nothing, *and nothing deffinite* [*sic*], as many smooth words without meaning as you please."[2] Samuel May Williams heeded this advice and acted in a circumspect manner when the occasion requiring diplomatic finesse arose.

Idealistic federalists, admiring the success of the republican United States, had joined self-serving pragmatists to create a decentralized federal republic when they adopted the Mexican constitu-

---

[1] S. F. Austin to S. M. Williams, December 28, 1830, Samuel May Williams Papers, Rosenberg Library, Galveston.

[2] S. F. Austin to S. M. Williams, January 13, February 5, 19, March 5, 12, April 2, 16, 1831, *ibid*.

tion in 1824. Many of its features were alien to traditional Spanish government, and elitists among the military, clergy, and aristocracy united in an effort to return to a more centralized and familiar form of control that would lessen the independence and powers of the individual states. Frauds in the second presidential election in 1828 served as an excuse for unconstitutional usurpation of the executive office by both factions, but the centralists succeeded in retaining control in 1830. Lucas Alamán, the leader of the aristocratic party, headed the cabinet of President Anastasio Bustamante, and General Manuel Mier y Terán carried out the administration's policy in the northeastern states that included Coahuila-Texas. The struggle between the two factions dominated politics for the next decade and set the stage for the Texas Revolution in 1835–1836. Texas and its neighbors rejected centralism, and northeastern Mexico provided the leadership for federalist opposition.[3] Most of the influential men at Bexar and Monclova were federalists, while Saltillo provided what little support the centralists could muster in the area. Austin and Williams could scarcely expect to avoid conflict in such a potentially incendiary situation.

Williams's first challenge appeared at Anahuac, the new garrison erected near the mouth of the Trinity River on upper Galveston Bay. In November, 1830, Terán dispatched John Davis Bradburn, a renegade Kentuckian who had earned Mexican citizenship through service in the revolutionary army, with troops to construct the fort in anticipation of reopening the customs house. Outside any empresario grant, the site was strategic for controlling smuggling activities in the area but extremely inconvenient for ships delivering goods to the Brazos. To overcome the difficulty Bradburn appointed a deputy at Brazoria, the normal head of navigation, which lay less than twenty miles above the mouth of the Brazos. One American captain, however, refused either to pay the duties or to recognize the deputy's authority; other insults and threats followed, which resulted in the officer's resignation in early 1831. Williams, acting as

[3] Emilio Rabasa, *La constitucion y la dictadura: Estudio sobre la organización política de México*, p. 14; Henry George Ward, *Mexico*, I, 216–217, 211–223. David Martel Vigness, "The Republic of the Rio Grande: An Example of Separatism in Northern Mexico" (Ph.D. dissertation, University of Texas, 1951), pp. 48, 69, 81–82, 91.

special collector for the treasury department, asked the alcalde to call out the militia to preserve order, an action that earned him the label of "tory" within a few months.[4]

In addition to the controversy over the collection of the tariff, Bradburn's arrogant attitude toward the Americans brought on a crisis. Settlers on the lower Trinity had received official permission to locate there, although it was outside the jurisdiction of an empresario or an *ayuntamiento*, but no land commissioner had been sent to issue deeds. Finally, in 1831, just after Austin left for the legislature, Commissioner Juan Francisco Madero arrived and established a town council at Liberty and began recording titles. An ardent federalist from Coahuila, Madero had received his appointment from Governor José María Viesca, also a federalist. His action appeared to violate the national decree of April 6, 1830, which restricted Anglo-American settlers. Zealously protecting his career as an officer of the centralist administration, Bradburn arrested Madero and dissolved the new *ayuntamiento*, placing the residents under martial law until clarification could come from his superiors. Williams remained aloof and refused to take sides, even though the arrest of Madero prevented the commissioner from locating large tracts of land along the Trinity that Austin had promised to federalist friends in Bexar and Saltillo. From Saltillo, the empresario complimented his associate for the correct and cautious actions he had taken.[5]

Austin returned before summer, but the situation at Anahuac smoldered dangerously and came to a climax in December, 1831. Terán visited the fort in November and reinstalled George Fisher to collect customs duties. At the end of the month, with the general's

[4] S. Rhodes Fisher to S. F. Austin, January 10, 1831; S. M. Williams to W. D. Dunlap, March 10, 1831; S. M. Williams to [John Austin], [March 20, 1831?]; S. M. Williams to F. W. Johnson, March 20, 1831, in Eugene C. Barker (ed.), *The Austin Papers*, II, 583–584, 609–610, 621–622; Bradburn to S. M. Williams, March 31, 1831, Williams Papers.

[5] Edna Rowe, "The Disturbance at Anahuac in 1832," *The Quarterly of the Texas State Historical Association* 6 (April 1903): 270–278; Victor Blanco to S. F. Austin, November 17, 1830; S. F. Austin to S. M. Williams, January 9, March 12, 1831; Francisco Madero to S. M. Williams, March 15, 1831, Williams Papers.

approval, Fisher issued an order for all vessels, including those already in port, to clear their papers with him at Anahuac. Two captains at Brazoria who had already disposed of their cargoes and were loading for the return voyage to New Orleans violently objected to both the inconvenient overland journey around Galveston Bay and the *ex post facto* aspect of the decree. Encouraged by local residents, they determined to defy the order and started downstream. Jeremiah Brown, captain of the *Sabine* and a resident of Brazoria, offered a bribe to the officials, which was refused. The schooner then ran past the garrison at the mouth of the river, exchanging cannon shots with the troops. When the boat was finally out of range, the passengers emerged from below and cheered, among them Eliza Williams Sweet, who was returning to Mobile after her long visit with her brother. A few days later the *Nelson* fired on the soldiers, killing one. Mary Austin Holley, on board a third vessel departing about the same time, experienced no difficulty in leaving Velasco even though the papers were not in order.[6]

Austin, who attended protest meetings at Brazoria late in December, denounced Fisher's orders as "utterly impractical" and impossible to enforce. Williams helped him prepare an explanation of the events for Terán that stressed the Texans' loyalty to the government but deplored the inconvenience of the customs regulations. The general, however, replied that the Americans must obey the laws, and he ordered the "pirate" ships to be confiscated should they dare to return. He also appointed a permanent officer to collect duties at Brazoria before the ships unloaded their goods. Blaming Fisher for the turmoil, Austin asked Terán to remove him. Shortly thereafter, the controversial agent resigned and returned again to Matamoros. But within five months, Austin characteristically reversed his attitude toward Fisher and begged Williams and the others to forget the past and welcome the adventurer back.[7]

[6] Bessie Lucille Letts, "George Fisher" (M.A. thesis, University of Texas, 1929), pp. 85–87; P. E. Pearson, "Reminiscences of Judge Edwin Waller," *The Quarterly of the Texas State Historical Association* 4 (July 1900): 35; S. F. Austin to Mary A. Holley, January 14, 1832, *Austin Papers*, II, 736–738.

[7] Charles D. Sayre to S. F. Austin, February 7, 1832, "Notes and Documents," *Southwestern Historical Quarterly* 63 (January 1960): 456;

Williams again assumed the responsibility for Austin's colonial activities when the empresario returned to the state capital in 1832. Pleading poor health, the reluctant deputy postponed his departure until March, and thus he did not arrive in Saltillo until April, less than one month before adjournment. From the capital Austin warned Williams to stay clear of the political struggle between the crumbling centralist regime and the followers of General Antonio López de Santa Anna, who had raised a revolt against centralist military control and had declared in favor of restoring the Constitution of 1824 and the "democratic republican federal party." Austin predicted victory for the Santana party and warned the Texans to maintain a "dead calm'" because the *santanistas* might use any turmoil as an excuse to end the colonization system. Moreover, he estimated that seventeen hundred troops were poised above Matamoros with additional soldiers at Tampico, all of whom could be landed in Texas immediately should a rebellion occur.[8]

Williams wrote his associate in April and assured him that all remained quiet in Texas, but by the time the empresario received the letter, Bradburn and the settlers near Anahuac were quarreling again. The Anglo-Americans organized a militia company to protect themselves against "Indians," a euphemism for the Mexican troops, some of whom were convicts sent to the frontier rather than to prison. Petty pilfering and insolence by the soldiers aroused American resentment and led to the formation of the volunteer company, headed by Patrick Jack as their elected leader. A recent immigrant from Georgia, Jack was one of three brothers destined to play a large role in succeeding events. Bradburn arrested Jack for organizing a military force intended for use against the administration and also incarcerated William B. Travis, who had tried to recover some runaway slaves for a Louisiana client. Bradburn had irritated local

---

S. F. Austin to Emily M. Perry, December 23, 1831; S. F. Austin to Bradburn, December 30, 1831; S. F. Austin to Terán, January 8, 1832; Terán to S. F. Austin, January 27, 1832; S. F. Austin to Terán, February 5, 1832, *Austin Papers*, II, 725, 731–732, 733–734, 743–744, 747–748; S. F. Austin to S. M. Williams, July 1, 1832; May 31, 1833, Williams Papers.

[8] S. F. Austin to S. M. Williams, April 9, 12, 28, March 21, 1832, Williams Papers.

slaveholders by using their black labor in building his fortress, and at the same time telling the blacks that slavery was illegal in Mexico. Friends and relatives demanded the release of the pair, but Bradburn refused, threatening to send the prisoners to Saltillo for trial. Volunteers on the Brazos decided to march to Anahuac and force the release of the men.[9]

As a government agent, Sam Williams could not support the plan and tried to discourage the volunteers from imprudent action. He offered Frank W. Johnson, the leader of the expedition, advice in keeping with Austin's admonitions. The Texans should demand to see copies of the commandant's orders and any other official documents that ultimately might be used as evidence to force his removal. Williams warned Johnson to remain cool when he met with the authorities and to be sure to have several witnesses present. Bradburn, however, proved adamant and refused to release his prisoners. Before commencing the siege, the attackers withdrew temporarily to Turtle Bayou to await the arrival of a cannon from Brazoria, but three small vessels, including the five-ton *Stephen F. Austin* belonging to Williams's father-in-law, blockaded Galveston Bay and prevented supplies and relief from reaching Bradburn.[10]

The band of insurgents waiting on Turtle Bayou drew up the first *santanista* declaration in Texas to explain their attack on Bradburn as the representative of the centralist regime. The Turtle Bayou Resolutions were not a callous subterfuge adopted during the immediacy of the situation; they represented instead a sincere expression of sympathy toward the federalist cause. Many of the participants in the events that occurred between 1832 and 1836 drew analogies between their actions and those of their grandfathers' generation against the British. Republican sentiment underlay the Anglo-American rhetoric against military oppression and taxation, and the Texans adopted famliar means to overcome the parent na-

[9] S. F. Austin to S. M. Williams, May 8, 1832, *Austin Papers*, II, 770–772; Rowe, "The Disturbance at Anahuac in 1832," pp. 280–282.

[10] Francisco M. Duclor to S. M. Williams, June 2, 1832, Williams Papers; S. M. Williams to Frank W. Johnson, June 3, 1832, Edward C. Hanrick Papers, Barker History Center, University of Texas at Austin; Carroll A. Lewis, Jr., "Fort Anahuac: The Birthplace of the Texas Revolution," *Texana* 1 (Spring 1969): 4, 7.

tion: petitions for redress of grievances, committees of correspondence, and volunteer troops.[11]

The residents of Brazoria also declared in favor of Santa Anna and the federalist party when John Austin returned from Galveston Bay for the cannon. This political ardor was in response to immediate events, but *santanista* agents had prepared the way when they had visited Texas earlier to publicize the movement and seek recruits. Even Father Michael Muldoon, the Roman Catholic priest sent to Texas in 1831 by the authorities in Mexico City, caught the enthusiasm and offered himself as hostage for Jack and Travis. The rebels seized the *aduana,* rolled out the cannon, and placed it on board the merchant schooner *Brazoria,* which had just arrived from New Orleans. The party started downstream on June 22, well prepared for trouble with the garrison at Velasco.[12]

Williams had written to John Austin early in June in an attempt to forestall precipitate action, but the Brazoria alcalde had already left for Anahuac and did not receive the letter until his return two weeks later. He told Williams what had occurred with Bradburn and that an attack on the fort was necessary to force the release of the prisoners.[13] Although Williams managed to prevent the San Felipe junta from endorsing the *santanista* movement, his associates, Johnson, Lessassier, and Williamson, preferred to confront the centralist authorities and accompanied William H. Jack to Anahuac. Stephen F. Austin's former supporters no longer agreed with his conciliatory policies; only Williams and newcomers Ira R. Lewis and Thomas Jefferson Chambers remained advocates for the empresario.

The insurgency of the Anglo-Americans brought Ramón Músquiz, the political chief, from Bexar on June 25. At his suggestion, the San Felipe *ayuntamiento* called a *cabildo abierto,* a seldom-used

[11] For an example of familiar phrases, see the Turtle Bayou Resolutions, in Charles Adams Gulick *et al.* (eds.), *The Papers of Mirabeau Buonaparte Lamar,* I, 142–143.

[12] Citizens' meeting [Brazoria, ca. June 20, 1832], *Lamar Papers,* I, 97–98; S. F. Austin to S. M. Williams, April 28, 1832, Williams Papers; John Austin to Francisco M. Duclor, June 21, 1832, *Lamar Papers,* I, 100–101; Rowe, "The Disturbance at Anahuac in 1832," p. 289.

[13] John Austin to S. M. Williams, June 19, 1832, Williams Papers.

procedure that opened the regular council meeting to all interested citizens. Sixty residents responded, and the alcalde appointed Williams to the committee charged with drafting a protest of the action taking place at Anahuac and requesting the participants to return home immediately. The *jefe* assured the Anglo-Americans that he would investigate their charges against Bradburn as soon as possible. Williams and the committee completed the denunciation of the rebels and affirmed their loyalty to the government on June 26. Copies were dispatched to other communities in order that they might take similar action. Brazoria residents, however, announced that they were storing arms instead. William H. Wharton vigorously denounced Sam Williams's plea for peace and accused the "tories" in San Felipe of being as weak as the Mexican leaders in Bexar who feared to resist the present oppressive administration.[14]

Williams's efforts to maintain a "dead calm" in Texas failed. The schooner and land force from Brazoria converged on the small circular fortress at the mouth of the Brazos and requested the commander to join them in declaring for Santa Anna. Captain Domingo de Ugartechea declined, and after a seven-hour battle the loyal commander surrendered.[15] When this news reached San Felipe, Williams sent out an emotional appeal calling for a consultation of the entire community in order to declare allegiance to the government and thus counteract the actions of the irresponsible few: "This once happy and prosperous country is now a perfect charnel house of anarchy and confusion . . . I call on you in the name of our father and protector, Stephen F. Austin . . . rouse up your neighborhood."[16]

The empresario learned of the developments at Anahuac in mid-June while he was visiting Terán near the mouth of the Rio

[14] Ramón Músquiz, Address to the People, June 25, 1832; minutes of citizens' meeting in San Felipe, June 25, 1832; declaration of Ayuntamiento, June 26, 1832; resolutions, June 28, 1832; W. H. Wharton to Standing Committee of Brazoria, July 4, 1832, *Lamar Papers*, I, 120–122, 123–127, 139–140.

[15] John Austin to Francisco M. Duclor, June 21, 1832; report of Ugartechea [to Terán], July 1, 1832, *Lamar Papers*, I, 100–101, 132–136; John Austin to Mexía, July 18, 1832, *Austin Papers*, II, 818–820; *Advocate of the People's Rights*, February 22, 1834.

[16] S. M. Williams to Bartlett Sims, July 1, 1832, *Lamar Papers*, I, 131.

Grande. Austin counseled his associate to refer all abuses to the political chief, a step that Williams had already taken. At Matamoros, Austin witnessed a bloodless coup when *santanista* Colonel José Antonio Mexía captured the town from the administration forces. Still playing his double game, the empresario composed a diplomatic letter to Santa Anna, although only one week before he had written a sympathetic letter to Terán. Mexía and Colonel Juan Guerra, the commander of the centralist forces that had just evacuated Matamoros, agreed to set aside their differences and sail to Texas to put down the Anglo-American rebellion. They invited Austin to accompany them, and the flotilla left on July 10.[17]

While Austin's return to Texas at first appears to be a rational response to the emergency situation on Galveston Bay, it really signified the end of his efforts to conciliate both political factions. The federalists now held the major gulf ports and controlled the customs houses, a principal source of government revenue. Most of the military leaders in the northeast had joined Santa Anna, leaving only Terán to defend the administration. In poor health since 1828, the commandant general became increasingly depressed by the political developments, and, in spite of a recent military victory over the local federalist force, his mental state deteriorated and he committed suicide July 3 by plunging on his sword. The details of his death reached Matamoros a few days later and convinced Austin that his future lay with the victorious *santanistas*. Without the moderating influence of Terán, he, too, feared the political and military excesses of the centralist regime.[18]

The five vessels bearing the two generals, the empresario, and the troops arrived at the Brazos on July 16. During the voyage Austin became convinced that Texas should publicly announce support for Santa Anna and the federalist party, and soon after landing he advised the political chief in Bexar to take such a step. But in spite of

[17] S. F. Austin to S. M. Williams, June 19, July 1, 1832, Williams Papers; S. F. Austin to Terán, June 27, 1832; S. F. Austin to Santa Anna, July 6, 1832; S. F. Austin to J. A. Mexía, July 9, 1832, *Austin Papers*, II, 800–803, 811–812, 813.

[18] Ohland Morton, *Teran and Texas: A Chapter in Texas-Mexican Relations*, pp. 172, 174–178, 181–183; S. F. Austin to S. M. Williams, July 19, 1832, Williams Papers.

continued pleas from Austin, the leaders at Bexar delayed joining the movement until the end of August.[19]

The sudden political turnabout from neutrality to *santanismo* caught Williams off guard. Austin's last letter from Matamoros, written on July 2, barely preceded the arrival of the empresario himself, who wrote to his associate immediately upon reaching Texas. Since April, Austin had advised "prudence and a dead calm" in his letters, and even as he described Mexía's bloodless coup at Matamoros, he still counseled aloofness if possible. Williams, as the defender of the status quo, was now ostracized as a tory, and in his own defense he reminded the empresario that he had been following instructions. Austin answered his associate's hostile accusations from Brazoria, admitting that he had urged neutrality, but he blamed Bradburn and his imprudent actions for the entire dilemma.[20] Cynical of human behavior yet more understanding of Austin than anyone else, Williams still felt betrayed. Although the men remained close, Williams felt justified in allowing his personal affairs to take precedence over the remaining business that he had with the empresario.

The people along the lower Brazos extended an enthusiastic welcome to Colonel Mexía. He readily accepted John Austin's explanation that the Anglo-Americans had acted only against Bradburn's personal oppression and in favor of federalism. Brazoria honored the *santanistas* with a ball on July 21, and Colonel Austin no doubt wore the ornate uniform coat tailored for him in New York and copied from Mexía's own wardrobe.[21]

No ball was held in Sam Williams's honor. Instead, Brazoria rowdies hanged him in effigy along with Chambers and Lewis. The empresario admonished his lieutenant not to be upset, because some of the most prominent men in history had experienced the

[19] Eugene C. Barker, *The Life of Stephen F. Austin: Founder of Texas, 1793–1836*, pp. 344–346.

[20] S. F. Austin to S. M. Williams, April 9, 12, 28, July 1, 2, 1832, Williams Papers; S. F. Austin to S. M. Williams, May 8, 1832, *Austin Papers*, II, 770–772; S. F. Austin to S. M. Williams, July 19, 20, 1832, Williams Papers.

[21] John Austin to J. A. Mexía, July 18, 1832; J. F. Perry to S. F. Austin, October 27, December 20, 1830, *Austin Papers*, II, 818–820, 522–524, 565–566.

same "honor." All Williams had to do, he advised, was to say that "you wished to do for the best" but "may have been mistaken as to the means." If Williams remained "quite cool," it would all pass away.[22]

The residents of San Felipe belatedly rushed to join the winning side. Frank W. Johnson converted the rebels into the "Santa Anna Volunteer Company" even before Austin arrived from Brazoria, and the *ayuntamiento* and citizens reaffirmed their loyalty to the Constitution of 1824, "rejoicing" in joining Mexía and the federalist party. Formal ceremonies with speeches and cannon salutes marked the return of the empresario, and later the same day the revelers drank innumerable toasts to each Mexican state and territory, the constitution, and Santa Anna.[23] Whether Williams attended these festivities is not recorded.

Bradburn fled to the Sabine, but his troops joined Mexía, who returned to Tampico. Ugartechea left for the south immediately after the encounter at Velasco, but the soldiers who wanted to return to Mexico had to march overland; Williams secured supplies and transportation for the baggage while the troops rested at San Felipe. Ugartechea had been lenient toward the Anglo-Americans because of family friendships, Masonic ties with Austin, and a carefully concealed sympathy for the federalist cause. His token resistance and capitulation now jeopardized his military career; had the Texans been less precipitate, the amiable officer would have replaced Bradburn in June.[24]

Sam Williams took no part in the subsequent political meetings in 1832 and 1833. San Felipe called for a convention of the residents of the entire colony, and fifty-eight delegates assembled there in October. The moderate majority selected Austin to preside and

[22] S. F. Austin to S. M. Williams, July 19, 1832, Williams Papers.

[23] S. F. Austin to Ramón Músquiz, July 28, 1832, *Austin Papers*, I, 825; Mary Austin Holley, *Texas*, pp. 142–145.

[24] S. F. Austin to S. M. Williams, July 20, 22, 1832, Williams Papers; Holley, *Texas*, p. 144; S. F. Austin to Bradburn, December 30, 1831, *Austin Papers*, II, 731–732; James David Carter, *Masonry in Texas: Background, History, and Influence to 1846*, pp. 243–244; "A True Mexican" [J. M. Carabajal] to Johnson, Baker, and Givens, July 18, 1835, Williams Papers; Terán to Ugartechea *et al.*, June 29, 1832, *Austin Papers*, II, 805–806.

adopted resolutions asking for various reforms including a reduction of the tariff, reorganization of the judiciary, moderation of the law of April 6, 1830, and separate statehood for Texas. The political chief in Bexar condemned the proceedings as unconstitutional, although he sympathized with the demands.[25] Uneasy about further action under such circumstances, the central committee authorized by the convention took no action other than calling for another meeting in April.

At the second gathering the more radical faction elected William H. Wharton president, reaffirmed the work of the previous body, and named Austin, James B. Miller, and Erasmo Seguin of Bexar to take the documents to Mexico City. The latter was chosen to encourage the participation of native Mexicans, but Miller and Seguin, who were not convention delegates, refused to go. In spite of Austin's urging, the cautious native Mexican leaders declined to endorse the documents, which unfortunately made the demands appear to be solely Anglo-American. Austin's detractors complained that he was "too soft" to press for the reforms, but none offered to make the journey in his stead. The empresario reluctantly readied himself for the long trip to the capital, thus delaying his plans to retire from public life and move to his "peach" land below Brazoria. Weary of politics, he had announced that he would refuse candidacy for office, but at the end of April, 1833, he set off on horseback for Bexar and the Rio Grande. Other than the arduous journey, the empresario anticipated little difficulty with his mission, since the federalist party had gained control of the government and installed Santa Anna as president. Austin expected to be home in four months.[26]

Williams helped his friend arrange his private business before leaving. Miguel Arciniega, the land commissioner for the "little colony," had arrived in October during the first convention, and together they worked on titles due to settlers. The empresario left

[25] Barker, *Life of Austin*, pp. 348–350. Ramón Músquiz to S. F. Austin, October 11, 1832, *Austin Papers*, II, 874–875.

[26] Barker, *Life of Austin*, pp. 360–362; S. F. Austin to J. F. Perry, April 25, 1833; S. F. Austin to Ramón Músquiz, October 10, November 15, 1832; S. F. Austin to J. F. Perry, April 20, 1832, *Austin Papers*, II, 1075–1085, 874, 888–889, 956–958.

Williams the responsibility of collecting overdue notes and also the settlement of his most pressing indebtedness, and in lieu of past and future salary, he assigned the uncollected fees due to him in the land office to his associate. Austin altered his will, leaving Williams twenty-four hundred acres, and stipulated that his elderly slave who lived with the Williams be given to Sarah. The empresario expected to be home in time to complete the third and fourth colonization contracts due to expire in November and the other six months later, but he hoped that Williams would push the land business during his absence.[27]

[27] Austin to the Public, October 9, 1832; S. F. Austin to J. F. Perry, April 19, 1833, *Austin Papers*, II, 870–871, 951–952; S. F. Austin's last will, April 19, 1833, Harris County Deed Records, F, 342.

CHAPTER 4

Businessman and Speculator
1831-1834

AFTER 1833 Samuel May Williams disappointed Stephen F. Austin by putting his own affairs ahead of remaining business with his old friend and associate. Williams left by schooner for New Orleans the same week that Austin rode off toward Bexar on his journey to Mexico City. This was the first time that both men had been absent from Texas simultaneously, but Williams expected to return within the month. Austin resented the intrusion of Williams's commercial activities, a development that he feared might delay the completion of the land business.[1] Not only was the empresario concerned about closing his contracts, but in October, 1833, time would expire for locating the three eleven-league tracts he had bought in 1831 on speculation.

In 1828 the state had authorized the sale of eleven unlocated leagues to native Mexicans, primarily to raise money and secondarily to encourage Mexican settlement within the Anglo-American colonies. The maximum price for the best land was about five cents an acre, or $250 per league, yet few native Mexicans could afford the sum and fewer still wished to move to the Texas frontier. Most who took advantage of the offer intended to subvert the intent of the law by selling their unlocated, paper grants to land-hungry Anglo-Americans at whatever price they could command. But be-

---

[1] S. F. Austin to S. M. Williams, May 9, 13, 1833, Samuel May Williams Papers, Rosenberg Library, Galveston; S. F. Austin to J. F. Perry, April 19, 20, 22, 1833, in Eugene C. Barker (ed.), *The Austin Papers*, II, 951–952, 956–958, 959–960.

cause only residents of Mexico could own land, prospective investors in the United States negotiated through a Texas agent who would hold the parcel in trust. This subterfuge was the beginning of the so-called "vast speculations" that Texans denounced for years to come.[2]

A few wealthy Mexicans, primarily members of the federalist faction in Coahuila, requested Austin to locate tracts for them, a task that devolved upon Williams, who thus became the agent for several prominent men. The matter was progressing nicely until 1831, when John Davis Bradburn removed Juan Francisco Madero, the land commissioner who had intended to issue titles for his friends. This action interrupted the completion of the venture until a more favorable political climate developed, and the problem remained unresolved when Austin left for Mexico City.[3] Williams worked to complete the business before the October deadline, and finally managed to solve the problem by working through the alcaldes who had authority to issue titles under certain conditions after 1832.[4]

Austin had bought three such tracts from three Coahuilans—José María Aguirre, Rafael Aguirre, and Santiago del Valle—when he was in Saltillo in 1831; he paid only $1,000 for the combined 145,000 acres, less than one cent per acre. Upon arriving in San Felipe, however, he discovered that he lacked some of the papers necessary to complete the titles and order the proper surveys. When he returned to the legislature the following year, he secured the documents and sent them to Williams with specific instructions for locating the grants on the upper Colorado River. The site included both

[2] Eugene C. Barker, "Land Speculation as a Cause of the Texas Revolution," *The Quarterly of the Texas State Historical Association* 10 (July 1906): 77; Virginia H. Taylor, *The Spanish Archives of the General Land Office of Texas*, p. 60.

[3] Ramón Músquiz to S. F. Austin, June 26, 1828, *Austin Papers*, II, 54–55; Victor Blanco to S. F. Austin, November 17, 1830; S. F. Austin to S. M. Williams, January 9, 1831; Juan Francisco Madero to S. M. Williams, March 15, 1831, Williams Papers.

[4] S. F. Austin to S. M. Williams, May 8, 23, 1832, *Austin Papers*, II, 770–772, 775–776; S. F. Austin to S. M. Williams, September 5, 11, 1832; Ramón Músquiz to S. M. Williams, February 28, 1833, Williams Papers; Taylor, *Spanish Archives*, p. 61.

banks of the river near the mouth of Onion Creek, encompassing a portion of the area of the present-day city of Austin; the empresario intended to create a utopian community there centered around an academy, to be financed by the sale of the remaining parcels. Following the instructions from his absent associate, Williams petitioned Alcalde Luke Lessassier, his former law partner, for the titles, using powers of attorney from Austin and the original Mexican purchasers to execute bills of sale. The land was surveyed late in 1832, but the final papers had not been filed when the empresario left for the capital.[5]

This complicated business preoccupied Austin during his mission to Mexico City. He had contracted cholera at Matamoros but by the end of May had recovered sufficiently to take passage on a miserable coasting vessel headed for Veracruz. After a difficult journey, he reached the capital in mid-July but discovered the congress recessed and most of the officials out of the city because of the spreading cholera epidemic.[6]

Disappointed and still unwell, Austin looked in vain for letters from Texas and news of Williams's progress. He finally received a brief message from John Austin in August, but the six-week-old letter failed to mention whether or not Williams had returned from New Orleans. To make matters worse, rumors in Mexico City claimed Sam Williams to be among the many cholera fatalities in Texas. Five persons had succumbed to the violent diarrhea before Austin left the colony, and before the first frost, the plague ravaged the coast and extended inland to Bexar and even to Monclova. Besides the concern felt for family and friends, Austin worried about what would happen to his investments if Williams were dead. In mid-August the empresario addressed a plaintive letter to his associate: "I know not whether I am writing to a living or a dead

[5] S. F. Austin to S. M. Williams, May 8, 1832; S. F. Austin to J. F. Perry, April 20, 1833, *Austin Papers*, II, 770–772, 956–958; S. F. Austin to S. M. Williams, August 21, 1833, Williams Papers; S. P. Brown (surveyor) to S. M. Williams, December 29, 1832, Williams Papers. The map and field notes for the José María Aguirre tract are reproduced in Walter Ewing Long, *Stephen F. Austin's Legacies*, pp. 61, 65.

[6] S. F. Austin to Ayuntamiento of Nacogdoches, May 30, 1833; S. F. Austin to Central Committee, July 24, 1833; S. F. Austin to J. F. Perry, July 30, 1833, *Austin Papers*, II, 975–977, 988–991, 991–992.

man, for I have never heard whether you have returned, or are on earth, or under it."[7]

The next mail brought a letter from Williams dated July 13 in Mobile; because of a pending sale of land to a group of Alabama investors, he had not been able to return to Texas by June as planned. Williams sent Austin two letters of credit, each for $1,000, advanced by Sam Williams's brother-in-law, Samuel St. John, and drawn on the latter's cotton factor, E. W. Gregory in New Orleans. St. John had visited the Brazos in 1832 and monopolized the cotton crop by offering eleven cents per pound; Gregory thought the price too high but deferred to the wishes of his client. St. John was connected with the eastern investment firm of Joseph D. Beers and Company and was expanding southern contacts by opening local brokerage offices in New Orleans and Mobile. Later, when Austin was unable to repay the loan, St. John accepted one of the eleven-league grants as recompense.[8]

Williams finally returned to Texas early in August and stopped at Brazoria to consult with John Austin, his partner in the sale of land to the Alabamians. The latter was recovering from the cholera at the time, but within a few weeks he suffered a relapse and died. Williams became feverish upon arriving in San Felipe and was seriously ill, perhaps with cholera, for several weeks. While her husband was away, Sarah Williams had remained at home, and on September 10, she gave birth to another son, William Howell. The two small daughters, Sophia Caroline and Eliza Ann, the latter born in October, 1831, and named for her visiting aunt, both died before the end of 1831 and were buried in the family plot near the house on Agua Dulce Creek.[9]

[7] S. F. Austin to John Austin, August 6, 1833, Williams Papers; J. F. Perry to S. F. Austin, October 26, 1833, *Austin Papers*, II, 1009–1011; Gaspar Flores to S. M. Williams, September 12, 1833; J. A. Navarro to S. M. Williams, September 11, 26, 1833; S. F. Austin to S. M. Williams, August 14, 1833, Williams Papers.

[8] S. F. Austin to S. M. Williams, August 21, 1833; E. W. Gregory to S. M. Williams, April 24, June 10, 1832, Williams Papers; S. M. Williams to J. F. Perry, July 23, 1836, quoted in James Armstrong, *Some Facts on the Eleven League Controversy*, p. 12.

[9] John Austin to S. M. Williams, August 9, 1833, Williams Papers; J. F. Perry to S. F. Austin, October 26, 1833, *Austin Papers*, II, 1009–

Austin continued to receive reports that Williams was dead, which caused him to fret about the state of his affairs. He was making little progress in Mexico City, particularly with the petition for separate statehood, a crucial matter if he expected to retain his personal influence with the settlers. Morose and depressed, Austin despaired of ever securing favorable action from the congress, and during such a mood, he wrote a letter on October 2 to the *ayuntamiento* of Bexar, suggesting that San Antonio lead other Texas municipalities in a movement to declare independence from Coahuila. Within the month, however, the federal government, again under the leadership of Santa Anna, repealed the ban on American immigration and modified the tariff, but separate statehood failed to gain the support of the dictator. Satisfied that this was all that could be gained at this time, Austin started for Texas in December.[10]

Austin's letter of October 2 caused consternation in Bexar. José Antonio Navarro censured the empresario for not following advice from San Antonio and acting instead like a rash child. To preserve its own loyalty, the *ayuntamiento* passed the damaging letter to the authorities, and when the empresario reached Saltillo in January, 1834, the commandant, on orders from the central government, arrested him for treason. In a letter written January 12 from Saltillo, Austin cautioned Williams to minimize any excitement over his arrest but urged the *ayuntamientos* to continue to work for separate statehood.[11] The administration kept the Texan in prison in the capital until Christmas Day, 1834, when he was released on parole, having to remain in the city until the following July when a blanket pardon freed all political offenders.

1011; J. F. Madero to S. M. Williams, December 29, 1831, Williams Papers; Dr. Robert Peebles Account Book, October 7, 21, 1831, Lorenzo de Zavala Papers, Barker History Center, University of Texas at Austin. The two graves are mentioned in Austin County Deed Records, C, 340.

[10] S. F. Austin to S. M. Williams, November 5, 1833, Williams Papers; J. P. Coles to Anthony Butler, July 15, 1833; S. F. Austin to Ayuntamiento of Bexar, October 2, 1833, *Austin Papers*, II, 988, 1007–1008; S. F. Austin to S. M. Williams, November 26, 1833, Williams Papers.

[11] J. A. Navarro to S. M. Williams, February 26, 1834; Thomas Mc-

Williams received the letter from Austin announcing his arrest and forced return to Mexico City at the end of January, 1834, upon his return from a business trip downriver.[12] He and Thomas F. Mc-Kinney had entered a partnership as commission merchants (probably early in 1833) and were temporarily located at Brazoria, where they bought out the interest of Walter C. White, in business there and San Felipe since 1829.[13] They intended to move the operation to land donated by Austin on the west bank of the Brazos where the river took a sharp turn eastward before emptying into the Gulf of Mexico. On this narrow spit they planned to build a warehouse, wharf, and residences, the nucleus of the new town of Quintana. Though exposed to storms and high tides, the site would provide a more convenient anchorage for coastal vessels that previously had had to make the tortuous horseshoe turns to reach Velasco and Brazoria. Each man brought his own particular talents to the merger: McKinney, who at one time had engaged in the illicit overland trade to Chihuahua, later had tried keelboating on the Neches River, and in 1830 had moved to the Brazos where he had engaged in trade, bought and transported commodities for the new firm while Williams handled the financial affairs. Austin predicted success for the new firm because of the solid reputation of the Williams family in the commercial world.[14]

During March and April, 1834, McKinney kept his partner informed about commercial and political developments at Brazoria while Williams was preoccupied in San Felipe with colonial matters. By June McKinney left the commission house in charge of an assistant and moved to Velasco, where he could supervise the construction of their buildings across the river. Williams went to New

---

Queen to S. M. Williams, February 14, 1834; S. F. Austin to S. M. Williams, January 12, 1834, Williams Papers.

   [12] Moses Austin Bryan to J. F. Perry, February 1, 1834, *Austin Papers*, II, 1045; statement from Jane Long to S. M. Williams, January 17, 1834, Williams Papers.

   [13] W. C. White to S. M. Williams, December 10, 1833, Williams Papers; *Telegraph and Texas Register*, December 30, 1837.

   [14] T. F. McKinney to S. F. Austin, November 24, 1830, *Austin Papers*, II, 138–139; Brazoria *Texas Republican*, November 8, 1834; S. F. Austin to S. M. Williams, September 7, 1834; S. F. Austin to J. F. Perry, March 28, 1835, *Austin Papers*, II, 1087–1088, III, 53.

Orleans in May primarily to purchase a shallow-draft steamboat suitable for use on the Brazos, but delivery of the *Laura* was delayed until early 1835. In the interim McKinney bought a schooner, but unfortunately it foundered on the sandbar at the mouth of the Brazos and was a total loss.[15]

In addition to the new mercantile venture, Williams was involved in a political and legal contest to retain control of an empresario grant of his own. The state had awarded a joint contract to settle eight hundred European and Mexican families in the upper Brazos watershed to Austin and Williams in 1831, but they had located only a few by 1834. The grant encompassed the area north of Austin's earlier colonies and stretched from the Navasota to the Colorado rivers, including land previously set aside for the Texas Association, a group of Tennessee speculators who had received a contract from the state in 1825. Austin at first had encouraged the Nashville investors in the hope that they would aid in developing the frontier and provide a buffer from Indian attacks, but the Tennessee company lost interest and momentum when the United States failed to acquire Texas. The area was still unsettled when the law of April 6, 1830, prohibited further Anglo-American immigration and, in effect, abrogated the agreement. That same year, one of the members, Sterling Clack Robertson, decided to send a token number of families to the site in order to salvage what he could before the expiration date of the original contract in 1831. He seemed unaware of the restrictions imposed by the April 6 statute until he arrived in Texas with the families in the fall of 1830, and then he asked Austin and Williams to assist him in overcoming the difficulties with the authorities.[16]

Austin perfunctorily agreed to present a petition from Robertson to the governor when he left for the legislature in December, but he offered the Tennessean little encouragement. The empresario

[15] T. F. McKinney to S. M. Williams, March 23, 25, 27, 29, April 5, 7, 14, 18, 19, 21, 1834; Lewis G. Sturdevant to S. M. Williams, February 13, May 4, 1834; Williams to Sturdevant, May 15, 1834, Williams Papers; *Ship Registers and Enrollments of New Orleans, Louisiana,* III, 121; S. M. Williams to S. F. Austin, April 22, 1835, *Austin Papers,* III, 66.

[16] Eugene C. Barker, *The Life of Stephen F. Austin: Founder of Texas, 1793–1836,* pp. 284–296.

had only recently secured official approval for his interpretation of the phrase that permitted Americans to continue to enter his colonies. About the same time, a French company asked the state for a grant northeast of Austin's. Aware of the probable negative response to Robertson's request, Austin believed that the Europeans would be in a strong position to acquire the upper Brazos tract. Rather than allow this valuable, contiguous territory to devolve upon foreign speculators who might not develop the land for a number of years, Austin and Williams determined to secure it for themselves.[17]

Austin and Williams may have learned about the French company when they attended the departmental election at Bexar in September. Williams prepared a petition asking for an empresario contract for himself, presumably to settle non-Anglo families along the upper Brazos River. Because this document was not in the file at Saltillo when Austin arrived at the capital at the end of January, 1831, there is no way to substantiate the date or the details of the request. Anticipating that accidents might befall the mail courier traveling between Bexar and Saltillo, Williams sent a power of attorney with Austin, dated December 17, 1830, and witnessed by the alcalde in San Felipe, "to apply in his [Williams's] name for a contract" to colonize "foreign families or others," though no number was "specified nor was any region suggested." Upon discovering that Williams's petition was not on file, Austin assured his associate on February 5 that he would submit a second request, using the power of attorney. Austin added that his friend, former governor José María Viesca, guaranteed that Williams would receive the grant.[18] Williams would have had no interest in contracting for land remote from San Felipe when the upper Brazos tract was available; thus it is clear that Williams intended to acquire the former Nashville grant area for himself.

Austin subsequently filed an application in both of their names dated February 4, 1831.[19] Why he submitted the petition in that

[17] Ibid., pp. 296–298.

[18] Ibid., 297–298; S. F. Austin to S. M. Williams, February 5, 1831, Williams Papers.

[19] Barker, Life of Austin, p. 298. Possibly this date is a clerical error, because February 14 would be in logical sequence with Austin's letters. A letter to Williams, written February 25, the day of the approval, is

form is not explained, but after the legislature approved the request on February 25, Austin wrote Williams that "the power of attorney is effected in union with myself." In a portion of the letter marked "private," he warned his associate to keep the entire arrangement secret. Austin regarded himself as "operating on a pretty large scale" for such a "taciturn and noiseless man," and he hoped that General Terán might join the enterprise by sending Mexican families to settle the area, which would ensure success for Austin and Williams.[20] Although the empresario remained in Saltillo until May 9, there is no other reference to the project in his correspondence with Williams. Nor did Williams comment on the fact that the colony would be a joint venture, which suggests that such a contingency plan had been formulated prior to Austin's departure from San Felipe.

Robertson heard rumors in San Felipe that Williams had received the grant even before Austin returned. Neither partner confirmed the report, however, until later that year when the matter became common knowledge. Robertson instituted a suit in December, 1831, to recover the colony, but there is no reference to his activities in the correspondence between Austin and Williams. Austin appointed an agent to contact potential European settlers, an idea that he had been considering for over a year, but friends feared that such a scheme would prove too costly.[21] The trouble at Anahuac and Terán's subsequent suicide prevented Austin from securing support from the influential commandant general, who might have sent Mexican colonists.

At the end of 1832 Williams sent Frank W. Johnson to survey a portion of the upper Brazos tract, including the location of eight eleven-league portions along the river to be recorded in the names

mentioned in Austin's March 5, 1831, letter to Williams, but is not extant; possibly it explained why the petition was in both names.

[20] S. F. Austin to S. M. Williams, March 5, 1831, Williams Papers.

[21] S. C. Robertson to S. F. Austin, June 7, 1831, *Austin Papers*, II, 664; testimony of William Pettus, December 15, 1831, Saltillo Archives, in John Henry Brown, *History of Texas from 1685–1892*, I, 317–318; S. F. Austin to James Hope, December 5, 1831; S. F. Austin to S. Rhodes Fisher, June 17, 1830; Francisco Ruiz to S. F. Austin, December 11, 1831, *Austin Papers*, II, 721–722, 423–429, 723.

of Austin's Coahuilan friends.[22] Seven Alabama investors had already contracted for part of this valuable acreage, and Williams, his brother Matthew, and Robert M. Williamson, attorney for the group, would hold the deeds in trust until such time as the immigrants might arrive.[23] The restriction against Anglo-American immigration ended in May, 1834, but the Alabama syndicate encountered financial difficulties that prevented completion of their arrangement. A few of the members came to Texas, but Williams still held some of their titles as late as 1840.[24]

Robertson notified Williams that he planned to present evidence to regain his colony before the San Felipe *ayuntamiento* in November, 1833. At this juncture, Williams was the sole proprietor of the contract; John Austin, who had bought out Stephen F. Austin's interest, had died in the cholera epidemic in September. Williams's attorney, William B. Travis, advised an informal conference for his client with Alcalde Luke Lessassier and Robert Williamson, *sindic procurador,* the legal officer for the town council. The four

[22] S. M. Williams to [surveyor], December 1, 1832; statement of fees from F. W. Johnson to Empresarios Williams and Austin, 1833, Williams Papers. See the General Land Office's McLennan County map for the 3, 4, 5, and 11 league grants to Mexicans. The Tomás de la Vega survey was held in trust for the Alabamans until 1840, when it was deeded to Samuel St. John as reimbursement for the $2,000 loan made to Austin while he was in Mexico. This deed was held in trust until 1849, when the U.S. district court ruled in favor of St. John in a dispute between him and Williams. The St. Johns turned disposition of the land over to agents who sold it, but squatters in the territory contested the sale that ultimately involved U.S. District Judge John C. Watrous of Texas and led to his impeachment. See speech of Hon. John H. Reagan and others on proposed impeachment of Judge Watrous, *Congressional Globe*, 35 Cong., 2 sess., 11–27, 59–65, 101–102 (December 9–15, 1858); *Spencer* v. *Lapsley,* 20 *Howard* 264 (1858).

[23] R. M. Williamson, Deed of Trust, April 13, 1833, Edward C. Hanrick Papers, Barker History Center, University of Texas at Austin; E. C. Hanrick to S. M. Williams, March 9, 1833, July 3, 1834, Williams Papers.

[24] Asa Hoxey to E. C. Hanrick, November 27, 1833; S. M. Williams to E. C. Hanrick and others, June 19, 1834; Asa Hoxey and A. P. Ufford, Deed of Trust, August 25, 1840, Hanrick Papers; E. C. Hanrick to S. M. Williams, December 8, 1833, February 4, June 24, July 3, 9, 1834; S. M. Williams to E. C. Hanrick, July 6, 1834; George Whitman to S. M. Williams, October 22, 1834, Williams Papers.

met at Williams's home but decided that a court case was the only way the matter could be settled. The council postponed the case until February, 1834, when the new alcalde, Williamson, and the council decided in favor of Robertson and recommended returning his grant. Travis, now secretary to the *ayuntamiento,* wrote the resolution to be sent to the state authorities, a document based solely on Robertson's argument and testimony from residents who had "intended" to locate in the Tennessee colony but had settled in Austin's grant instead. According to the depositions, over one hundred families had so "intended" prior to April 6, 1830, and thus the Nashville grant was also an "established colony" in accordance with Austin's interpretation of the law.[25] The court heard no evidence from either Austin or Williams; the empresario, of course, was on his way to prison in Mexico, but his associate was in San Felipe during the hearing. The fact that the alcalde and the secretary of the council were close friends of Williams appears to have had no relevance to their decision.

The victor left immediately for Monclova, recently made the state capital, to recover his contract. According to Robertson family tradition, Austin sent an assassin to remove the Tennessean and, when the attempt failed, arranged that Robertson be arrested and held without bail. Both accusations are false; Austin was en route to Mexico City and unaware of the activity in San Felipe. If Robertson was attacked, it was by Indians or bandits who regularly troubled travelers west of Bexar. Also, Robertson presented his memorials to the legislature on March 22, less than six weeks after receiving his documents from the *ayuntamiento.*[26]

[25] Barker, *Life of Austin,* p. 304; Robert E. Davis (ed.), *The Diary of William Barrett Travis, August 30, 1833–June 26, 1834,* entries for October 9, 10, 11, 1833, pp. 45–46; S. C. Robertson to S. M. Williams, October 29, 1833, quoted in Barker, *Life of Austin,* p. 305; resolution of the Ayuntamiento, February 6, 1834, in Brown, *History of Texas,* I, 319–320 (see also Barker, *Life of Austin,* p. 306).

[26] Mrs. Cone Johnson, "Incident Told to Me by Sterling C. Robertson, Grandson of Major Sterling C. Robertson," undated manuscript, Harllee Collection, in possession of Malcolm D. McLean, Fort Worth; J. W. Baker, *A History of Robertson County, Texas,* p. 22; S. C. Robertson to Legislature, April 2, 1834; petition to Governor, April 26, 1834, in Brown, *History of Texas,* I, 320–331.

Williams did not send a killer after the Tennessean either, although he did dispatch Thomas McQueen as his agent to present his case to the legislature in Monclova. McQueen, acquainted with the Mexican officials in the southwest because of his trading activities with the interior, left for Bexar shortly after Robertson. There he secured copies of documents needed to prove Williams's position, but soon after starting south on the road to Presidio, he was attacked by Indians and left for dead. Fortunately a passerby discovered the unconscious agent and returned him to San Antonio, too ill to continue the mission. No other qualified agent could reach the capital in time to defend Williams, and, on advice from his friends in Bexar, Williams hastily prepared a condensed version of the facts and sent the document to the political chief to be forwarded through official channels. In addition, Williams warned the officials that for the past ten months Robertson had been stirring up trouble and fomenting rebellion among the settlers in order to create a popular movement against Williams. Surveyor Frank W. Johnson reported that "the damnable contagious poison emitted by Robinson [sic] fever" was likely to cause civil war.[27]

Williams argued that it was "idle and irrelevant" that certain families "intended" to settle in the upper colony, because they could not do so without a land commissioner to issue titles and no such officer had ever been appointed. Nor was it Austin's fault that the families preferred to remain in the lower colony where they could secure deeds. Moreover, Robertson had presented no credentials that authenticated his claim as agent of the Tennessee company, and therefore the *ayuntamiento* had erred in recognizing his claim. In answer to Robertson's charges that Williams profiteered from the locating fees, he retorted that such an allegation was like the "Canon [sic] telling the pop gun it is noisy. . . ."[28]

[27] T. McQueen to S. M. Williams, February 14, 1834; J. A. Padilla to S. M. Williams, February 26, 1834; S. M. Williams to *jefe político* (draft), March 25, 1834 (an official copy dated March 26 appears in vol. 54, p. 301, Spanish Archives, General Land Office); S. M. Williams to S. H. Jack, March 26, 1834, Williams Papers; F. W. Johnson to R. M. Williamson, March 10, 1834, *Austin Papers*, II, 1047–1048.

[28] S. M. Williams to T. McQueen, February 4, 8, 1834, Williams Papers. The fact that Robertson lacked credentials as company agent yet won approval of the *ayuntamiento* may have been the plan discussed by

While he was preparing the defense of his charter, Williams publicly proceeded as if there were no challenge. In March, 1834, he asked the governor to appoint a land commissioner to issue titles to the persons he had located in the upper colony and sent Spencer H. Jack to open the land office at Tenoxtitlán, the settlement on the west bank of the Brazos just above the San Antonio Road. He instructed his agent to levy a fifty-dollar fee for the location of speculative leagues within the eleven-league grants and advised his young assistant to place the blame for this unpalatable arrangement squarely on his shoulders as empresario. Williams felt supremely confident of his ability to administer the colony and refused to worry that this action made him unpopular.[29]

At the end of April, the legislature approved returning the contract to the Tennessee entrepreneur and sent its recommendation to the acting governor, Senior Councilor Francisco Vidaurri y Villaseñor, who had assumed the office after the death of both elected executives. Williams's letter to the authorities arrived at this juncture, and, in order to negate its influence on the governor, Robertson circulated the old story that Williams had arrived in Texas using an assumed name. The defamatory disclosure appeared in newspapers together with a vitriolic denunciation of the methods used by Austin and Williams in securing the 1831 contract. Williams refused to take public notice of the scurrilous attack when copies arrived in Texas, but he did express his views of the affair privately to Austin by letter. The empresario apparently never received this letter, which by some means appeared in Mexico City newspapers. Thomas Jefferson Chambers, Robertson's bombastic attorney, answered Williams's disparaging remarks in a newspaper advertisement addressed to the public by reiterating the ancient gossip, with embellishments.[30]

In spite of Williams's efforts, the governor revoked the Austin-

the lawyers at Williams's house in October. This omission would have been used to ask for an official review because of a technical flaw in procedure.

[29] S. M. Williams to Spencer H. Jack, March 26, 1834, *ibid.*

[30] Congress to Governor, April 26, 1834, in Brown, *History of Texas*, I, 331; S. C. Robertson to Governor, May 4, 1834; Notice to the Public, n.d., both translated by Malcolm D. McLean and in his possession.

Williams grant on May 22, 1834, saying that it had been merely a conditional contract in 1831. Friends of Williams in the capital believed that Robertson had bribed the authorities, a charge that had substance. Williams learned of the governor's decision while he was in New Orleans, and he instructed Spencer H. Jack, his assistant, to go to the capital in order to reopen the case. This request coincided with the effort being made to effect the release of Austin, and Jack was commissioned to accompany Peter W. Grayson to Mexico City to plead the case for the empresario. In this manner Jack could combine both missions because the Texans intended to join the entourage of Colonel Juan N. Almonte, an aide to President Santa Anna, who was returning overland from an inspection tour of Texas.[31]

Under the guise of making a statistical survey, Almonte was actually investigating the purpose of the conventions held in 1832 and 1833 at San Felipe. While in eastern Texas, the colonel had heard disturbing rumors that speculators close to Austin, probably meaning Williams and his associates, planned to separate Texas from Coahuila in order to facilitate the disposition of their land. If peaceful means failed, they intended to promote a rebellion. The general tenor of existing correspondence suggests that no such sentiment was considered by Williams or his friends at this time. Almonte approached San Felipe with some trepidation, but, to his surprise, he was warmly received, though Williams was absent in the United States at the time. So far, the colonel had failed to discover any treasonable conduct in Texas.[32]

Almonte proceeded down the Brazos to Velasco, where McKinney entertained him and also showed him two subversive letters received in the colony. The first had come early in spring to Sam Williams, and, though it was signed "O. P. Q.," he attributed the mischief to Anthony Butler, the United States chargé d'affaires in Mexico City. The letter warned that Almonte came as a spy and

[31] Proclamation of the Governor, May 22, 1834, in Brown, *History of Texas*, I, 333; Oliver Jones to S. M. Williams, April 2, 1834; S. H. Jack to S. M. Williams, September 16, 1834, Williams Papers; Peter W. Grayson to J. F. Perry, July 25, August 9, 1834, *Austin Papers*, II, 1065–1066.

[32] Helen Willits Harris, "The Public Life of Juan Nepomuceno Almonte" (Ph.D. dissertation, University of Texas, 1935), pp. 14, 33–46.

suggested that the Texans seize him as surety for Austin's release. Williams sent the letter to McKinney at Velasco, where a similar letter was discovered in the post office; the second letter was addressed to Branch T. Archer, a former Virginian known to his contemporaries as a "popular agitator." This second "O. P. Q." letter labeled Almonte a "corrupt, unprincipaled poltroon" who should be hanged and suggested that the only course for the Texans was to declare independence. Convinced of Butler's complicity, Almonte notified his superiors that Butler should be recalled immediately on the grounds that he owned property in San Felipe and thus was ineligible to be a foreign representative. The controversial chargé had acquired Whitesides' Hotel from Austin as partial payment on an old indebtedness stemming from their partnership in an unsuccessful Missouri lead mine.[33] Butler, however, could not receive a title to the property because he was an alien, a complication that helps explain his interest in detaching Texas from Mexico.

Williams expressed his regret for having missed Almonte when the latter visited Texas, and reminded Santa Anna's aide of their former acquaintance in New Orleans when they both had clerked in commission houses. The colonel's cordial reply began a year of epistolary exchange that Williams hoped would aid in the recovery of his grant from Robertson.[34]

The *ayuntamiento* reversed its position favoring the return of the colony to the Tennessee speculator and by autumn, 1834, it had endorsed Williams's claim, but no explanation has been found. Williams planned to attend the next session of the legislature, in January, 1835, in order to present his case in person. When Spencer Jack came back from Mexico at the end of the year, he and Williams labored over legal briefs to be presented to the state. Relying

[33] O. P. Q. to ?, February 8, 1834, in J. M. Winterbotham, "Some Texas Correspondence," *Mississippi Valley Historical Review* 11 (June 1924) 115–118; T. F. McKinney to S. M. Williams, April 14, 1834, Williams Papers; Henry Stuart Foote, *Texas and the Texans: Or Advance of the Anglo-Americans to the Southwest,* II, 11–12; O. P. Q. to B. T. Archer, January 28, 1834, in Winterbotham, "Some Texas Correspondence," pp. 109–115; Harris, "Almonte," pp. 49–50; Barker, *Life of Austin,* pp. 248–249.

[34] Juan N. Almonte to S. M. Williams, October 10, December 20, 1834, Williams Papers.

on the doctrine of vested rights, Williams argued that his property had been taken from him without due process, and he referred to *Dartmouth College* v. *Woodward* (1819) as a precedent. He also developed an argument resting on the unconstitutionality of retroactive laws, a theme also stressed in the Jack brief, referring of course to the law of April 6, 1830. Jack maintained that the Tennessee company had not completed its contract before that date, a failure that clearly allowed Austin and Williams to proceed in 1831. The young attorney asked why the pair had not been summoned, as provided by the constitution, to answer the Robertson charges. The executive decree reassigning the contract to the Nashville promoter was "singular," to say the least, and Jack believed that the "clink of gold" had been the convincing argument.[35]

Although Williams had settled some families in the upper colony, no titles had been issued, because he lacked a commissioner. When Robertson returned to Texas, he had an authorization naming William H. Steele his land commissioner. They began issuing deeds to settlers from the office at Viesca, and, though they had been ordered by the governor to recognize the rights of families located under Williams's contract, many of the boundaries overlapped and contradicted earlier grants. At the end of 1834, James F. Perry wrote to his brother-in-law in Mexico that Robertson was "undoing" everything "previously done" in the upper colony.[36]

Williams put his affairs in order before leaving for the capital. He planned to ride with a group of Texas speculators who were going there to buy vacant land at auction. On March 26, 1834, the legislature had authorized the governor to offer parcels of farming land at a minimum price of ten dollars per *labor* (177 acres) and even less for pasturage. Dependent on the poorly collected imposts for its income, the state desperately needed a new source of reve-

[35] S. M. Williams to S. F. Austin, October 29, 1834; J. F. Perry to S. F. Austin, December 7, 1834, *Austin Papers*, III, 32–35; "Upper Colony Controversy," two manuscript briefs sewn into notebooks, no dates, one in Williams's hand and the other in Spencer H. Jack's, Rosenberg Library.

[36] Proclamation of the Governor, May 22, 1834, in Brown, *History of Texas*, I, 333 (see the General Land Office's map of McLennan County for superimposed and contradictory boundaries); J. F. Perry to S. F. Austin, December 7, 1834, *Austin Papers*, III, 32–35.

nue. The scheme to sell four hundred unlocated leagues (over 1.5 million acres) outside any empresario grant might bring one hundred thousand dollars into the empty treasury; to attract investors, the state offered credit for three years. While foreigners might buy land in any amounts up to the eleven-league limit for individuals, they had to move to the state within one year; the decree banned companies from bidding for the land.[37] This law eliminated the fiction of selling land only to native Mexicans, but only one man, John T. Mason of New York, had taken advantage of the offer in 1834. Several of Williams's acquaintances were preparing to participate in the spring auction, but it is unknown whether he intended to buy any tracts himself. Instead, he wanted permission to establish a bank of issue that would alleviate the shortage of specie and Texas' dependence on fluctuating bank paper from the United States. Such a facility would aid his and McKinney's commercial activities.

[37] Hans P. N. Gammel (comp.), *The Laws of Texas, 1822–1897*, I, 357–362, 382.

CHAPTER 5

Speculator or Patriot?
1835

WHILE Samuel May Williams made plans to regain his empresario contract from the state, he had no way of knowing that his attendance at the 1835 legislative session would permanently damage his reputation. The 1835 Monclova legislature became infamous for allowing speculators to acquire approximately eight hundred leagues (3.5 million acres) of vacant land, and for years "Monclova speculator" denoted the same sort of unprincipled scoundrel that "Yazoo man" had for an earlier generation.[1] Public reaction to the Monclova transaction was greater than that in the 1880's, when the state legislature awarded ten times that number of acres to the railroad speculators. Nonparticipating Texans deplored such activity, although similar ventures were widespread and so characteristic of the westward movement of the Anglo-Americans that one historian called it "the spirit of the age."[2]

Already unpopular with many settlers because of his control over the granting of colonial headrights, Sam Williams's participa-

[1] In 1795 the Georgia legislature sold thirty-five million acres in present-day Mississippi and Alabama to four land companies, some of whose members proved to be Georgia legislators. A subsequent legislature annulled the contracts, but in 1810 the United States Supreme Court upheld the sanctity of contract and ruled that the motives of the legislators were irrelevant (C. Peter Magrath, *Yazoo: Law and Politics in the New Republic*, pp. vii, 3–17).

[2] Elgin Williams, *The Animating Pursuits of Speculation: Land Traffic in the Annexation of Texas*, pp. 9, 23.

tion at Monclova aroused "factious demagogues" who denounced the activities of "proud coldhearted Empresario Williams." Most of his neighbors utterly rejected his subsequent explanation that President Santa Anna's renunciation of the concepts in the Mexican Constitution of 1824 posed a serious threat to their political rights and that the deputies had sold the land in order to raise funds to equip an opposition force. The Texans readily accepted the emotional denunciation of the "Mammouth Speculation" that took place at the capital, and even when Williams's prediction came true with the arrival of centralist troops, contemporaries continued to be skeptical of his intent.[3]

Williams did not leave for Monclova until February, because the opening session of the legislature had been delayed by federalist and centralist squabbling in Coahuila. The seat of the state government had moved north from Saltillo to Monclova in 1834, a victory for the federalists, who dominated that year's reform-minded legislature. Learning that Santa Anna, who in two years had become a centralist dictator, had prorogued the national congress in May, the leaders at Monclova declared against the president and called for a special session of the legislature. Saltillo, however, denounced its federalist rival and chose its own *santanista* governor, a step that, in effect, brought civil war to the state. When a quorum failed to appear in August for the special session, a coup installed a centralist governor at Monclova, too; to resolve the feud, Santa Anna ordered a new election for December, 1834, thus postponing the session from January to March.[4] The president also named his brother-in-law, Martín Perfecto de Cós, as commandant-general of the northeast, garrisoned at Saltillo to quiet the political unrest.

When reverberations from these events reached Texas, Williams endeavored to remain aloof, having vowed to eschew politics since his bitter experience in 1832. But friends in Bexar, knowing that he planned to attend the upcoming session as a petitioner, pro-

[3] Jane M. McManus to S. M. Williams, January 3, 1836, Samuel May Williams Papers, Rosenberg Library, Galveston; J. G. McNeel to J. F. Perry, June 22, 1835, in Eugene C. Barker (ed.), *The Austin Papers,* III, 77.

[4] Eugene C. Barker, *The Life of Stephen F. Austin: Founder of Texas, 1793–1836,* pp. 400–401.

posed his name as deputy to represent the Brazos district. The electors, however, preferred to return Stephen F. Austin, whom they expected to be released from prison in time to reach the capital. The Monclova-Saltillo fracas inspired federalist Juan N. Seguin, political *jefe* of Bexar, to call for a Texas convention to denounce Santa Anna and also to separate from Coahuila. This summons split the Anglo-American community, with the political chief, Henry Smith of Brazoria, and Thomas Jefferson Chambers, chief justice of the new Texas high court, endorsing the plan, while the San Felipe junta rejected it. The firebrands of 1832, William H. Jack, William B. Travis, and Frank W. Johnson, suddenly became moderates; as members of the central committee authorized by the previous conventions, they considered the scheme politically unwise. The recent civil and judicial reforms had cooled agitation for separation, immigrants were arriving in gratifying numbers, and, in addition, such precipitate action might delay the release of Austin from prison. Williams praised their stand in a letter to the empresario and predicted the end for agitators like Smith and Chambers. He informed Austin that the chief justice had "bolted and barred" the door to his cell and Chambers now "exulted" in his predicament.[5]

Sam Williams, Frank Johnson, and others formed a small armed party to travel the dangerous seven hundred miles to Monclova. They arrived early in March after a relatively uneventful trip, and Williams distributed copies of his documents relating to the upper colony. Marcial Borrego, senior member of the council and acting governor, assured him that the deputies favored returning the contract to Williams because Robertson had deceived them. He suggested that the Texan patiently await a propitious moment when the legislature might reverse the matter without undue embarrassment.[6]

Austin, who had been released on bond on Christmas Day, 1834, remained in Mexico City on parole and therefore could not

[5] Ramón Músquiz to [Ayuntamiento of San Felipe], December 26, 1834, *Austin Papers*, III, 35; Barker, *Life of Austin*, p. 402; S. M. Williams to S. F. Austin, October 29, 1834, *Austin Papers*, III, 14–15.

[6] Frank W. Johnson, *A History of Texas and Texans*, ed. Eugene C. Barker and Ernest W. Winkler, I, 168–169; S. M. Williams to S. F. Austin, March 31, 1835, *Austin Papers*, III, 56–58.

attend the session. In his absence and also that of the alternate deputy from the Brazos, Thomas F. McKinney, who had remained in Texas to attend to business matters, Williams reluctantly consented to represent the department. He also pressed the state authorities to use their influence to obtain Austin's final release.[7]

The federalist party triumphed in the special election, thus making Monclova a nucleus of opposition to Santa Anna and the centralists. Governor Agustín Viesca, a friend of the Texans, finally arrived there in April, but Vice-governor Ramón Músquiz, former *jefe* of Bexar, failed to appear.[8]

While awaiting the appearance of the executive, Williams submitted his petition for a bank charter, and once the governor was installed the request was quickly approved. The charter allowed the Banco de Comercio y Agricultura to provide banking facilities on the Brazos for twenty years. Maximum capitalization was fixed at $1 million, but operation could begin when $300,000 in stock had been subscribed and the vault contained $100,000 in specie. Most importantly for Texas commerce, Williams, as empresario, could circulate his own bank notes. Before the session ended, he had sold at least $85,000 in stock to colleagues and intended to go to the United States for the remainder.[9]

The approval of the bank charter and the promise of the eventual return of the upper colony pleased Williams, but his complacency was soon shaken by political events. Former Vice-president Valentín Gómez Farías, an ardent federalist, appeared in Monclova on his way into exile after his dismissal by the congress at Santa Anna's bidding. Fearing assassination, he remained in seclusion with friends, but he warned that the president intended to reduce all opposition by force if necessary.[10] Almost immediately, the congress

[7] S. M. Williams to S. F Austin, March 31, 1835, *Austin Papers,* III, 56–58.

[8] F. W. Johnson to Gail Borden, Jr., April 15, 1835, *ibid.,* p. 61.

[9] Charter, April 30, 1835, Williams Papers, and also in Hans P. N. Gammel (comp.), *The Laws of Texas, 1821–1897,* I, 406; James Grant's will, Harris County Probate Records, B, 277; William Fairfax Gray, *From Virginia to Texas, 1835: Diary of Col. Wm. F. Gray,* p. 96.

[10] Conversation with Col. Williams, Charles Adams Gulick *et al.* (eds.), *The Papers of Mirabeau Buonaparte Lamar,* III, 267–268; Vito Alessio Robles, *Coahuila y Texas desde la consumación de la indepen-*

ordered the reduction of local militia throughout Mexico to one soldier for each five hundred inhabitants and required that all arms and ammunition be surrendered, a measure clearly designed to weaken any civilian resistance to the centralist army. Zacatecas, Coahuila's neighbor to the south, rebelled against Santa Anna's plan to lessen state power, and rumors indicated that the president himself planned to lead the army against the federalist stronghold.[11]

From his headquarters at Saltillo, General Cós fulminated against the federalist Monclova government. The deputies from Saltillo had withdrawn from the legislature soon after the formal opening, and they refused to recognize the validity of its acts. The real reason for their leaving was the election of a federalist governor, but the *santanista* deputies publicly blamed the pending land legislation. Hoping for an excuse to return the capital to Saltillo, Cós readied his troops to march against Monclova at any overt act from Viesca and Gómez Farías, who he suspected were plotting a counter coup to recover the national government still in the hands of Santa Anna. Williams complained to Juan N. Almonte that Cós was belligerent, but the aide assured his correspondent that Santa Anna had issued strict orders to act only within the law.[12]

The Anglo-Americans present in Monclova compared this military threat with that of the British in the 1770's. Ever since the violence in 1832, the Texans had adopted the rhetoric and tactics of an earlier generation, even arranging committees of correspondence to inform the scattered communities. The remaining step was to call out the militia to oppose the centralist army they assumed to be marching northward. But even by enrolling peons, Coahuila could not furnish sufficient troops; in order to attract the Anglo-Texans to

---

dencia . . . , II, 7–9, 13; Cecil Alan Hutchinson, "Valentín Gómez Farías: A Biographical Study" (Ph.D. dissertation, University of Texas, 1948), pp. 341–348.

[11] Barker, *Life of Austin*, p. 406. By this ratio, the entire state of Texas would have forty armed men—eight at Bexar and sixteen at both Nacogdoches and on the Brazos. See Juan N. Almonte, "Statistical Report on Texas," Carlos E. Castañeda (trans.), *Southwestern Historical Quarterly* 28 (January 1925): 186, 198, 206.

[12] Barker, *Life of Austin*, pp. 403–404; Louis J. Wortham, *A History of Texas*, II, 191–198; Robles, *Coahuila y Texas*, pp. 9–13; J. N. Almonte to S. M. Williams, April 22, 1835, Williams Papers.

fight away from their homes, the state would have to offer attractive bounties.

Even before Viesca and Gómez Farías arrived, Williams and John Durst, the deputy from Nacogdoches, had introduced a bill that would allow the executive to set aside four hundred leagues (over 1.5 million acres) of vacant land to muster and equip a volunteer force during the "present emergency." The act permitted wide discretion in disposing of the land without limits on foreigners or the amount granted to single individuals. At first they had intended to utilize Decree 278, passed April 19, 1834, which set aside the same amount of land to mobilize a frontier force against Indian attack, but legalists believed that the troops would have to be limited to that purpose. The new act (Decree 293), passed on March 14, 1835, limited neither the intent nor the manner of disposing of the land, whether by sale or by bounty offers.[13] In this fashion, the deputies provided a pragmatic plan to attract troops at a time when they were uncertain as to the movement or location of government forces.

Two days after the passage of this law, Williams, Durst, and James Grant, a naturalized citizen of Scottish birth and deputy from Parras, offered to buy the four hundred leagues even before public announcement of the sale. Though no official records exist, the three apparently made a cash down payment, promising to pay the balance within a few weeks. They received four hundred certificates, good for one league each for land to be located near the sources of the Trinity, Sabine, and Sulphur rivers and skirting the Red River in northeastern Texas.[14] This area, largely uninhabited except by Indians and renegades, had been awarded to an English empresario, General Arthur G. Wavell, in 1826, but because the tract was contiguous with the United States and the exact boundary remained in dispute, no titles had been issued.[15] The fact that the new empre-

---

[13] Conversation with Col. Williams, *Lamar Papers*, III, 267–268; Gammel, *Laws of Texas*, I, 391–392, 393, 380–381.

[14] Gray, *Diary*, pp. 100, 115; S. M. Williams to the People of Texas, July 20, 1835, *Lamar Papers*, I, 216–218; testimony of John Borden, Land Commissioner, *Supplement to the Journal of the House of Representatives*, 5 Texas Cong., 1 sess., 1840–1841, p. 354.

[15] Robert Amsler, "General Arthur G. Wavell: A Soldier of Fortune

sarios were all members of the legislature angered those disappointed speculators who had come from Texas expecting to acquire land under Decree 272, the 1834 law authorizing auction sales. Thomas Jefferson Chambers and Ben Fort Smith, in particular, accused the trio of using their privy knowledge for private gain. Smith had taken an interest in developing the upper colony with Williams, but, now disgruntled, he returned to the Brazos and spread word against the speculation taking place at the capital.[16]

Exactly what profit Williams anticipated earning by this transaction is difficult to assess because the contract was later abrogated by the Republic of Texas, and the opprobrium attached to the venture caused many to suppress the certificates that they had purchased from the empresarios. Williams bought one hundred certificates at $50 each, or $5,000 in aggregate, the same amount as colonists previously had paid to empresarios for each league. This small fee irritated the other speculators, because by the terms of Decree 272, March 26, 1834, the minimum price was $250 per league, five times greater than what Durst and Williams were paying. Only General John Thomson Mason, former agent for the Galveston Bay and Texas Land Company, had had sufficient capital to take advantage of the law in 1834, buying three hundred leagues by paying one-third down and the balance within two years. Decree 272 allowed anyone, even foreigners, to purchase the certificates at auction, for a minimum of $10 per *labor* (twenty-five *labores* equal one league). Thomas Jefferson Chambers, piqued by the hasty transaction, claimed that many at Monclova in 1835 were willing to pay the higher fee. He maintained that the Durst and Williams bill had been passed without a legal quorum of two-thirds, only eight deputies being present instead of the eight and two-thirds required for "important" bills as provided in the state constitution.[17] Unable to produce the sum in full as required by the contract, Williams arranged with James Grant for at least one-half of the $5,000, giving

---

in Texas," *Southwestern Historical Quarterly* 69 (July, October 1965): 13–15, 188–196.

    [16] Gray, *Diary*, p. 115; J. F. Perry to S. F. Austin, May 5, 1835, *Austin Papers*, III, 71–72.

    [17] Gray, *Diary*, pp. 99–100, 115; Barker, *Life of Austin*, p. 119; Gammel (comp.), *Laws of Texas*, I, 357–362, 168, 437.

the Scot bank shares and a promise to deliver goods to Parras, where Grant owned an iron foundry, textile mill, and ranch. At the same time, Grant gave Williams his power of attorney and returned the certificates so that Williams might sell them while he was in the United States raising capital for his bank.[18]

Information about this exchange of land to furnish troops reached Mexico City just after the central government had issued its order to reduce departmental militias. Condemning the act as revolutionary, the national congress annulled the law as unconstitutional and then debated whether to garnishee the state's revenue to pay Coahuila's share of the national debt. Cós seized this opportunity to send his troops to Monclova to end the "squandering" of the public land by a legislature that was "pandering" to the Anglo-American speculators.[19]

When the deputies learned of the approach of the centralist troops on April 7, they authorized the acting executive to "take . . . whatever measure he may think proper for securing the public tranquility. . . ." The act (Decree 297) included one section that permitted vacant lands to be offered as security for loans, an arrangement accepted by James Grant, who apparently advanced fifteen thousand dollars in return for three hundred leagues.[20]

Within a few days, the local militia engaged a small government force; Williams and the others rushed to volunteer for service, but the Anglo-Texans were excused. No shots were exchanged and the centralist party withdrew, temporarily allowing Monclova a respite. But the disturbing news from nearby Zacatecas indicated what fate awaited those who opposed Santa Anna. There the gov-

---

[18] Harriet Smither (ed.), "Diary of Adolphus Sterne," *Southwestern Historical Quarterly* 30 (1926–1927): 149, 219–220, 307, 312, 319; James Grant's will, Harris County Probate Records, B, 277. James Ogilvy, not Sterne, wrote the first three segments of this diary published in the *Quarterly* (p. 219). Ogilvy represented Hugh Grant's efforts to recover his brother's estate in 1838.

[19] Gammel, *Laws of Texas*, I, 411–413; Eugene C. Barker, "Land Speculation as a Cause of the Texas Revolution," *The Quarterly of the Texas State Historical Association* 10 (July 1906): 82–84, 89.

[20] Gammel, *Laws of Texas*, I, 394–395. Grant's contract was dated May 2, 1835, for three hundred leagues (Spanish Archives, General Land Office, vol. 35; Smither, "Diary," pp. 148, 150).

ernor and five thousand well-trained state militia were defeated by the president and his army, and in the aftermath centralist troops raped and plundered the city. The Monclova federalists feared they were next, but fortunately Santa Anna returned to Mexico City.[21]

From the capital, Austin advised Williams to urge moderation at Monclova and not to antagonize the federal government. But by the time the letter reached Coahuila, events had made a cautious path impossible. The legislature had formally protested the reduction of the militia, and when the deputies learned that the central government had abrogated the March 14 law, they drafted a statement based on the compact theory of government. In language similar to that of the South Carolina nullifiers, the lawmakers challenged the right of the centralist party to contravene the Constitution of 1824 by diminishing the powers of the states. To do so, the general government had to amend the national charter; otherwise it was enacting unconstitutional laws.[22]

Following the advice of the Texans, Governor Viesca issued a proclamation designed to arouse Anglo-American support by warning of Santa Anna's plan to reduce the area to a military province, cancel the liberal reforms granted by the 1834 legislature, and free the slaves. He requested that each department immediately send volunteers to Coahuila. Williams, Johnson, and Robert Peebles, Williams's associate and later commissioner for the upper colony, endorsed the plea, but the call failed to attract sympathy along the Brazos; it arrived there shortly after the return of Ben Fort Smith, who denounced the demand as a ploy of the speculators to save their investments. Only twenty-five men under the command of

[21] Frank W. Johnson to Gail Borden, Jr., April 15, 1835, *Austin Papers*, III, 61; S. M. Williams to Capt. Ramsay, n.d., in Willis W. Pratt (ed.), *Galveston Island: Or a Few Months Off the Coast of Texas: The Journal of Francis C. Sheridan, 1839–1840*, p. 135; Willfrid Hardy Callcott, *Santa Anna: The Story of an Enigma Who Was Once Mexico*, p. 115; A. A. Greene (trans. and ed.), "The Battle of Zacatecas," *Texana* 4 (Fall 1969): 189–200. Authorities vary, but Santa Anna had about forty-eight hundred troops.

[22] S. F. Austin to S. M. Williams, April 29, 1835, Williams Papers; Gammel, *Laws of Texas*, I, 400–401; Wortham, *A History of Texas*, II, 195–196.

Seguin left Bexar against the orders of Colonel Domingo de Ugartechea, the newly appointed military commander of all Texas.[23]

The hardier petitioners and legislators continued to transact business even amid the increasing rumors and confusion at Monclova. On May 11, the same day that Zacatecas fell, Williams, Peebles, and Johnson, at the behest of Governor Viesca, requested a contract for four hundred leagues under the terms of Decree 278, the April 19, 1834, law that permitted the sale of land to raise a frontier force against the Indians. The trio agreed to recruit and arm one thousand men for one year's service on the frontier—intended, of course, for use against Santa Anna. The state would provide the mounts and maintenance; the first five hundred volunteers would report to the governor in July, the remainder by September. The contractors would select the officers, and those serving would be compensated from the distribution of the land. Although the empresarios expected to profit from the sale of some of the land, the three men paid nothing for this contract.[24]

In contrast with the agreement made by Williams, Durst, and Grant, this arrangement was "not generally known" in Texas until after the victory at San Jacinto. The Texas constitution written in March, 1836, specifically revoked the Williams-Durst contract because it had been annulled by the Mexican congress, but, lacking concrete information concerning the militia contract, the framers failed to proscribe it.[25] Contemporaries subsequently confused the

---

[23] Johnson, A History of Texas, I, 197; Henry Austin to J. F. Perry, May 5, 1835, Austin Papers, III, 70; Robles, Coahuila y Texas, I, 536; Cós to Ugartechea, May 11, 1835; Ugartechea to Angel Flores, May 16, 1835, Bexar Archives, Barker History Center, University of Texas at Austin.

[24] Conversation with Col. Williams, Lamar Papers, III, 267–268; John Henry Brown, History of Texas from 1685–1892, I, 282. A copy of the contract appears in Supplement to the Journal of the House, 5 Texas Cong., 1 sess., 1840–1841, pp. 329–332, and Gammel, Laws of Texas, I, 380–381.

[25] Mosely Baker to Speaker of House, October, 1836, in Edward Stiff, The Texas Emigrant: Being a Narration of the Adventures of the Author in Texas . . . down to the Year 1840, pp. 155–160; Section 10, General Provisions, Constitution, in Gammel, Laws of Texas, I, 1080–1081.

two contracts because Williams's name was attached to both, and he became known as the worst of the speculators. By July, 1835, Williams had renounced his connection with the militia grant and left the matter with his associates, who issued forty-one certificates, mostly for ten leagues each, for land to be selected northeast of Nacogdoches.[26] Four of Williams's relatives and several of his associates, including McKinney, Mosely Baker, and Spencer H. Jack, each received one of these 44,000-acre tracts, and it is conceivable that each intended to raise a volunteer unit of twenty-four men, officered by themselves and rewarded by land bounties from the grant. Ugartechea, for one, assured his superiors that Williams could easily raise one thousand men to march on Bexar. Most Texans, however, considered the scheme pure speculation, and the proposal to provide troops in exchange for land remained a political millstone for the participants for years to come.[27]

During the final days of the session Williams pressed his colleagues for the return of the upper colony. The lawmakers finally overcame the legal obstacles by tortuous rhetoric and recommended that the governor give Williams the contract, though Chambers, acting for Sterling C. Robertson, tried to prevent it and again complained that a legal quorum was not present. Viesca approved the request and appointed Robert Peebles land commissioner to issue titles for Williams, asking only that the rights of settlers already located be respected.[28]

Even before he had left San Felipe, Williams had pledged to seek revenge for himself and Austin against Thomas Jefferson Chambers. He had told the empresario that he intended to "try [his]

[26] David B. Edward, *The History of Texas*, p. 236; Barker, "Land Speculation," p. 85; S. M. Williams to Robert Potter, testimony before committee, *Supplement to the Journal of the House*, 5 Texas Cong., 1 sess., 1840–1841, p. 371.

[27] *An Abstract of the Original Title of Record in the General Land Office*, pp. 175–176; Ugartechea to Cós, May 22, 1835; Ugartechea to Manuel R. Barragan, May 25, 1835, Bexar Archives; Mosely Baker to Congress, 1836, in Stiff, *Texas Emigrant*, pp. 155–157; M. B. Lamar to A. C. Horton, J. K. Allen to A. C. Horton, A. C. Horton to M. B. Lamar, August 2, 1838, *Lamar Papers*, II, 194–196.

[28] Barker, *Life of Austin*, p. 317; Gray, *Diary*, p. 115; Gammel, *Laws of Texas*, I, 415–416.

strength" against the superior judge, and if Austin could not support this plan, he should at least not oppose it. It is clear that he expected to use physical violence, saying, "if I don't lay him flat upon his back, it shall not be fore [sic] the want of trial. . . ." Whether Williams carried out that threat remains conjecture, but the controversial Chambers was arrested and detained at Monclova, and he believed that Sam Williams had engineered the charge and had tried to have him hanged.[29]

The deputies adjourned on May 20, just ahead of the appearance of troops sent from Saltillo, and the members urged the governor to remove the archives to safety in Bexar. Cós had already ordered the nearby presidios to detain Viesca and any legislators who attempted to escape, an order that caused a great deal of indecision concerning the safest route to Texas. Some, like John Durst, had seen trouble coming and had left even before adjournment. The governor and his escort started north toward Bexar but returned when they learned about the centralist patrols; the official party tarried too long and the governor was captured on June 5. One party tried the eastern road through Lampazos and Laredo, but, upon reaching the Rio Grande, Marcial Borrego, a high-ranking federalist, reconsidered and returned to Monclova to defend his action. Borrego advised Williams to do the same, but the Texan had already crossed the river at Presidio and was retracing the route he had covered three months earlier.[30]

Williams and three others who had left soon after the session closed had been arrested when they reached the Rio Grande. Several days later the government forces captured the main body of Texans, including Juan N. Seguin and Frank Johnson. All were placed under guard at Presidio, but by that time Williams had persuaded the commandant to allow him to go with an escort to Bexar in order to talk with Ugartechea. He reached San Antonio

[29] S. M. Williams to J. F. Perry, January 14, 1835; S. M. Williams to S. F. Austin, March 31, 1835, *Austin Papers*, III, 38–39, 56–58; S. M. Williams to S. F. Austin, March 31, 1835, *ibid.*, pp. 56–58; Gray, *Diary*, p. 115.

[30] Gammel, *Laws of Texas*, I, 420, 421; Robles, *Coahuila y Texas*, II, 22; Johnson, *History of Texas*, I, 195–196; Marcial Borrego to S. M. Williams, June 2, 1835, Williams Papers.

on June 3, but the colonel refused to allow him to continue to the Brazos to "quiet the populace" and instead held him awaiting further orders.[31] Four days later, Williams's friend José Antonio Navarro visited him, and to while away the hours they began a game of monte, capturing the guard's attention. Williams arose to go to his cell for more money, and, taking advantage of the soldier's distraction, he made his escape on Navarro's horse, reputed to be the fastest mount in Texas. In a surprising move for such a romantic adventure, Navarro gave his friend a receipt for the animal dated June 8, 1835. Ugartechea failed to report the incident until June 21, when his former prisoner was safe in San Felipe. The commandant had made little effort to conceal his sympathy for the Texans and the liberal cause, but this affair almost cost his career, and he soon renounced his federalist friendships.[32]

Williams eluded pursuit by heading north and crossing the Colorado River at LaGrange before turning southeast toward San Felipe. He had time to reflect on his present predicament—a fugitive from military despotism who was accused of inciting revolution. Cós had branded the Monclova legislators rebels, but what had they done except act in the interest of most Texans? The federalist party, Williams argued, wanted to preserve the constitution that the centralist regime was destroying. Even advocating the removal of the capital to Texas seemed only sensible, not just in view of the unrestrained rivalry between Saltillo and Monclova but also because of the advance of the centralist army. Why did the national government become excited over land sales in 1835, Williams wondered, when no commotion had occurred when John T. Mason, a nonresident, had contracted a like amount the previous year?[33]

[31] Johnson, History of Texas, I, 195–197; Robles, Coahuila y Texas, II, 21–22; Ugartechea to Cós, Ugartechea to M. N. Barragan, June 3, 1835; Cós to Ugartechea, June 8, 1835, Bexar Archives.

[32] Charles W. Hayes, Galveston: History of the Island and the City, p. 826; Tura Compton Cressy, "Col. Williams, Texas Pioneer" (typescript, 1932, Barker History Center), p. 2; receipt, June 8, 1835, Williams Papers; Ugartechea to Cós, June 21, 1835, Bexar Archives; James P. Caldwell to S. M. Williams, June 18, 1835; "A True Mexican" [J. M. Carabajal] to Johnson et al., July 18, 1835, Williams Papers.

[33] S. M. Williams to the People of Texas, July 20, 1835, Lamar Papers, I, 216–218.

As to what awaited him in San Felipe, Williams knew that he was unpopular with certain elements in Texas. In 1832 it had been the more radical hotheads who had criticized him for his conservatism. More recently, dissidents believed that he favored the wealthy in the manner in which he assigned land. He had never made a secret of his contempt for public opinion and popularity, and he readily admitted that he did not mind deviating from consensus when what he considered the public interest demanded such a course. Possessing high regard for his own rights, he felt responsible for the rights of others and believed that he was always guided by "strict honesty and principle."[34]

Apart from family and friends, his reception was not especially warm. His endorsement of the governor's call for volunteers appeared to many to be like the fable: the speculators cried "wolf, wolf . . . to arms, to arms!" in order to secure their land grants. The Brazoria newspaper had printed the plea for troops as a news item only and editorialized that the March 14 law was a "death blow to this rising country."[35]

Williams returned home in time for court week, and those who foresaw the danger from centralism endeavored to use the large gathering to win converts to a plan to rescue the captive governor from San Fernando de Rosas. At the end of June, José María Carbajal, the deputy from Bexar, rode into San Felipe fleeing an order for his arrest. Former alcalde Robert M. Williamson delivered a fiery demand for preparation against centralist attack and denied that calls for action came only from speculators.[36] The sense of urgency increased when trouble over tariff collections occurred again at Anahuac. William B. Travis called for volunteers to attack the fort

[34] S. M. Williams to Spencer H. Jack, March 26, 1834, Williams Papers.

[35] Noah Smithwick, The Evolution of a State: Or Recollections of Old Texas Days, p. 59; James Kerr to T. J. Chambers, July 5, 1835, and Brazoria Texas Republican, May 9, 1835, both quoted in Barker, "Land Speculation," pp. 88, 91.

[36] Ugartechea to Cós, June 21, 1835; Manuel Sabariego to Ugartechea, June 23, 1835, Bexar Archives; Ayuntamiento of San Felipe to T. J. Chambers, June 26, 1835, quoted in Ethel May Franklin, "Joseph Baker," Southwestern Historical Quarterly 36 (July 1932): 133–134; address of R. M. Williamson, July 4, 1835, Lamar Papers, I, 207–213.

in order to release the merchants being held there by the centralist officer just as he had been imprisoned in 1832.

Sam Williams took no part in these activities; he was occupied instead with moving his family from San Felipe to Quintana before leaving for the United States to seek bank financing. He resigned his postmastership, a post he had held since 1826, and left Gail Borden, a former surveyor for Austin, in charge of Austin's records at the land office. He also designated Spencer H. Jack as agent for the upper colony to join Peebles, the land commissioner. Sterling C. Robertson's commissioner refused to acknowledge the return of the colony to Williams and continued to issue titles at Viesca, while Peebles made eighty-eight grants before the Consultation closed all land offices in November.[37]

In response to the criticism of his actions at Monclova, Williams published an explanation in the Brazoria newspaper prior to his departure for the United States. He denied any intention of offending the national government or advocacy of revolution, maintaining that instead he had been working for constitutional republicanism. Because Santa Anna had violated the Constitution of 1824, he must be opposed as a tyrant. As to the land speculation, he asked the readers how the sale of land in northeastern Texas could threaten the Brazos valley. All he asked was that they give him a "fair and impartial" hearing and added that he would gladly relinquish the grant he had just purchased for the "peace" of the county, if only he could get his money returned.[38]

Williams did not learn that Cós had ordered his arrest along with five other "revolutionaries" until almost one month later in New Orleans. The commandant general issued a warrant for Travis, Williams, Williamson, Johnson, Mosely Baker, and Lorenzo de Zavala on August 1 and later added Carbajal and other federalists. Zavala,

---

[37] *Telegraph and Texas Register*, October 10, 31, 1835; Barker, *Life of Austin*, p. 319. Peebles issued a total of 152 titles and William H. Steel, Robertson's commissioner, 279, but many were void because they were dated after November 13, 1835. See Virginia H. Taylor, *The Spanish Archives of the General Land Office of Texas*, pp. 46–47.

[38] S. M. Williams to the People of Texas, July 20, 1835, *Lamar Papers*, I, 216–218.

once a supporter of Santa Anna, had assumed the leadership of the opposition and had come to Texas in July to organize Anglo-American resistance as a diversion. The federalist exiles expected this tactic to draw the administration forces to Texas and thus ensure a successful invasion of Tampico by the insurgents. Cós's order did more to unite the Texans than all the speeches. The Anglo-American law officers allowed those on the proscribed list to go into hiding, and the *Louisiana Advertiser* noted the number of "highly respected" citizens of Texas who had taken refuge in New Orleans and remarked that more were expected daily.[39]

While Williams was still in New Orleans, Stephen F. Austin arrived there from Veracruz after his release from parole. He agreed with federalist exiles there that Texas should join with liberals in the other north Mexican states to form a strong opposition force. Some merchants along the Gulf coast who traded with Mexico favored a scheme to form a separate republic of the northeastern Mexican states and Louisiana, and it is possible that Williams was among this group.[40]

Austin expressed pleasure in the plans for the bank, and he arranged to take a large block of shares. There was no estrangement between the two at this time over the land business, nor did Williams keep secret his activities at Monclova. When Austin landed in Texas in September, 1835, he defended both the individuals and the legislature, explaining that they merely intended to raise sorely needed revenue. The following summer while campaigning for the presidency of the Republic, Austin feigned surprise and shock when a friend "explained" the Monclova speculations to him, and Williams's role caused Austin to launch an attack against his former friend in order to disassociate himself from the speculators. Thus,

[39] Ugartechea to Cós, June 29, 1835, Bexar Archives; Wily Martin to Ayuntamiento at Columbia, August 10, 1835, *Austin Papers*, III, 97; Raymond Estep, "The Life of Lorenzo de Zavala" (Ph.D. dissertation, University of Texas, 1942), p. 340; *Louisiana Advertiser*, July 25, 1835, in *Lamar Papers*, I, 219–220.

[40] S. F. Austin to J. F. Perry, July 19, 1835, *Austin Papers*, III, 90–91; Hutchinson, "Gómez Farías," pp. 368–382; George Dobson to Captain Thomas Britten, September 29, 1835, Williams Papers.

fifteen months after his reunion with Williams in New Orleans, the empresario wrote, "That cursed Monclova trip of yours has indeed been a *curse* to you and to me and to the country. . . ."[41]

Prior to their parting in New Orleans, Austin had given his associate a letter of introduction to his cousin Henry Meigs in New York. Meigs's wife was the sister of Secretary of State John Forsyth, and Austin asked that Williams be given an introduction to Forsyth.[42] Although Williams traveled north on private business, Austin evidently intended that he should have unofficial access to influential persons in the United States should Texas need an advocate.

Williams left New Orleans for Mobile, Lexington, and Baltimore at the end of August, 1835, expecting to return to Texas within a few weeks. But events in Texas moved swiftly toward a confrontation between the centralist forces and the Anglo-Americans. By mid-September, Cós had landed his troops at Copano Bay, and the Texans became convinced that war was "inevitable" whether they surrendered those on his list of revolutionaries or not. Although Williams's warning concerning the intent of Santa Anna came true on October 3, 1835, when the central government announced the end of the federal system and concentrated all authority at Mexico City, criticism of Williams's participation in the land speculations continued.[43]

Williams's interrelated interests, speculation and patriotism forced him to remain in the United States until mid-1836. Though he continued to search for capital for his bank, he devoted most of his time to raising money and supplies for the rebellion taking place in Texas.

[41] S. F. Austin to S. M. Williams, August 22, 1835, Williams Papers; S. F. Austin to D. C. Barrett, n.d., quoted in Henry Stuart Foote, *Texas and the Texans: Or Advance of the Anglo-Americans to the Southwest,* II, 155–157; S. F. Austin to Gail Borden, Jr., August [18], 1836, *Austin Papers,* III, 418–420 (this letter is strictly political propaganda and was suggested by Borden for publication in the *Telegraph,* August 23, 1836; see Barker, *Life of Austin,* pp. 438–439 for a different interpretation); S. F. Austin to S. M. Williams, November 3, 1836, Williams Papers.

[42] S. F. Austin to H. Meigs, August 22, 1835, Williams Papers.

[43] S. F. Austin to P. W. Grayson, September 19, 1835, S. F. Austin to W. D. C. Hall, September 19, 1835; S. F. Austin to Provisional Government, November 30, 1835, *Austin Papers,* III, 127–135, 269.

Chapter 6

Agent for Texas
1835-1837

SAMUEL MAY WILLIAMS left Texas in 1835 to sell stock in his proposed bank, but almost immediately he became an agent for supply-
ing the volunteer army opposing the centralist dictator, Antonio
López de Santa Anna. He was in New York City when he learned
about the October 2 skirmish at Gonzales between the Texans and
the administration's cavalry. Local residents had defeated the government's attempt to repossess a cannon previously given to the
settlers for protection against Indian attack. Reporting the event and
its unifying effect on the Anglo-American community, Thomas F.
McKinney forwarded to his partner a request from the central committee, an extra-legal body formed during the past conventions,
that their firm purchase a vessel suitable for patrolling the coast.[1]
    McKinney was particularly eager to command such a priva-
teersman and had already asked for letters of marque and reprisal.
About one month before Williams had returned from Monclova, the
Correo Mexicano, a government warship, had captured McKinney
and had taken possession of his schooner, Columbia, near the mouth
of the Brazos. Although he released all passengers and McKinney,

---

[1] S. M. Williams to wife, September 30, 1835; T. F. McKinney to
S. M. Williams, October 5, 1835, Samuel May Williams Papers, Rosenberg Library, Galveston. This was prior to the meeting of the Consultation and the forming of the provisional government; that body confirmed
the request on November 25, 1835, and authorized payment on January 8,
1836 (Hans P. N. Gammel [comp.], The Laws of Texas, 1822–1897, I,
931–932, 1031–1033).

the Mexican commander had confiscated the ship for carrying con-
traband arms and ammunition. The *Correo* continued to harass the
Texas coast until September, 1835, when the *San Felipe*, McKinney's
new schooner, arrived at the Brazos and surprised the brig in the
act of seizing a United States merchantman unloading lumber at
Quintana. Stephen F. Austin was on board the *San Felipe*, returning
to Texas from New Orleans after his long imprisonment in Mexico,
and McKinney hesitated to attack the centralist vessel for fear of
endangering the life of the empresario. After sending Austin ashore,
the Texans tried to capture the ship, but unfavorable winds prevented either side from gaining an advantage until the following
morning. Then McKinney's little river steamer, the *Laura*, came out
of the harbor and, using the lumber for fuel, towed the *San Felipe*
westward until the schooner overtook the *Correo*. The Texans took
the captive crew to New Orleans to stand trial for piracy, but the
United States District Court dismissed the case when the jury could
not reach a verdict.[2]

In response to his partner's letter, Williams dispatched the *Invincible*, a sleek 125-ton schooner, from Baltimore, using the credit
of his brother, Henry Howell Williams, who operated a commission
house on Bowly's Wharf. The ship had been built for the African
trade and, being clipper rigged, could outsail most vessels. The
Invincible arrived in Texas in January, 1836, and took its first prize
three months later near the mouth of the Rio Grande. McKinney
reluctantly declined command of this ship because Williams's continued absence forced him to devote full time to business matters.
The United States Navy seized the Texas vessel in May, 1836, for
preying on merchant vessels bound for Mexican ports, but, though
charged with piracy and brought to trial in New Orleans, the crew
was not convicted.[3]

In New York City Williams encountered other Texas speculators selling land certificates. When news of the military activities

---

[2] T. F. McKinney to R. R. Royal, October 28, 1835, Thomas F. Mc-
Kinney Papers, Barker History Center, University of Texas at Austin; Alex
Dienst, "The Navy of the Republic of Texas," *The Quarterly of the Texas
State Historical Association* 12 (January 1909): 167–171.

[3] Dienst, "The Navy of the Republic of Texas," pp. 200–206, 252–
255.

arrived, James Morgan, Charles D. Sayre, Andrew Janeway Yates, and John K. and Augustus C. Allen rallied to raise money, supplies, and recruits. Colonel Juan N. Almonte and Anthony Butler also visited the city at this time, but it is doubtful that Williams sought their company.[4] Following requests from the provisional government in Texas, Williams shipped arms and ammunition from Baltimore and also interviewed prospective officers and crewmen for the *Invincible* during November.[5] McKinney and Williams furnished at least $99,000 worth of goods and services to the Texas government during the next eight months through their New Orleans agent, Thomas Toby, and Williams's brothers in Baltimore and Mobile. The advances made by these firms contributed to their failures in 1836 and 1837, although their loans to Texas were not the only reasons for bankruptcy. The debt owed by the Republic of Texas to McKinney and Williams was not repaid during their lifetimes, though McKinney continually petitioned the state until 1872. His heirs succeeded in getting the legislature to approve the scaled-down claim of $16,942.80 in 1929, but, because of a lack of revenue, the money was not paid until 1935.[6]

Popular opinion in the United States favored the Texan cause in 1835, and the federal government failed to enforce the neutrality laws against Williams and the other agents who were openly recruiting men and arms. In New York, the Committee for the Relief of the People of Texas offered money to transport two hundred "contract families" to Texas, a euphemism for recruits. Jane McManus, a New Yorker turned Texan who wrote under the pseudonym of Cora Montgomery, offered her Matagorda property as security to raise funds. Less patriotic was the offer from Samuel

[4] John P. Austin to S. F. Austin, November 8, 1835, in Eugene C. Barker (ed.), *The Austin Papers*, III, 244–247.

[5] James Hodge to S. M. Williams, November 14, 1835; E. H. Stanley to S. M. Williams, November 14, 1835, Williams Papers.

[6] Siddie R. Armstrong, "Chapters in the Early Life of Samuel May Williams, 1795–1836" (M.A. thesis, University of Texas, 1929), pp. 146–147; report to the President of the Senate and Speaker of the House of Representatives of Texas, January 24, 1838, copy in Rosenberg Library; petition of T. F. McKinney to legislature, [1869?], McKinney Papers; Senate Bill 61 and petition of T. F. McKinney heirs, *Journal of the Senate of the State of Texas*, 44 Leg., 1 sess., October, 1935, pp. 177, 202–203.

Swartwout, collector of the Port of New York, to lend money on "good" Texas lands if the interest was sufficiently high. Swartwout also believed that he could find investors who might channel funds through Williams's bank if he could get it organized.[7] Williams, however, was unable to acquire enough capital to activate his charter at this time.

Williams continued to search for wealthy and influential men in hopes of securing the needed $100,000 to open his bank. To widen his contacts, he joined the Masonic fraternity in New York City. He had intended to become a Freemason ever since Austin had tried to establish a lodge in San Felipe for members who had emigrated from the United States. The plan had to be dropped in 1829 when the Mexican government proscribed Freemasonry because rival orders had become embroiled in politics.[8] By special dispensation, on November 21, 1835, Williams was initiated, passed, and raised into the Independence Royal Arch Lodge #2, a historic blue lodge founded in 1760. Shortly afterward, he became a Knight Templar in the Morton Commandary. The following month the new member attended the national convocation of both orders in Washington, D.C., where he received charters to establish lodges in Texas. While in the capital, he contacted an old friend, George W. Slacum, recently the United States consul in Buenos Aires and now employed in the State Department. Slacum promised to arrange a meeting for Williams with Secretary of State John Forsyth and the president, but no record of any such meeting survives.[9]

[7] S. M. Williams to Daniel Jackson, Jackson to Williams, November 16, 1835, Williams Papers; Edward Stiff, *The Texas Emigrant: Being a Narration of the Adventures of the Author in Texas . . . down to the Year 1840*, p. 261; Jane McManus to Joseph D. Beers, October 29, 1835; Committee of Citizens to S. M. Williams, January 8, 1835, Williams Papers.

[8] James David Carter, *Masonry in Texas: Background, History, and Influence to 1846*, pp. 193–206, 222–227, 233–237. Carter mentions Williams's initiation but fails to give the date, which leaves the impression that Williams was a Mason when he came to Texas (see pp. 223, 246).

[9] Membership certificate, Rosenberg Library; *Texas Grand Lodge Magazine*, January 1936; Grand Lodge of New York to author, July 30, 1971, confirming Williams's initiation; George W. Slacum to S. M. Williams, November 21, 1835, Williams Papers.

In January, 1836, Williams left for Texas by way of Philadelphia, where he ordered bank notes engraved for the Commercial and Agricultural Bank of Columbia, Department of the Brazos. He continued westward and started down the Ohio River, accidentally encountering Stephen F. Austin and Branch T. Archer at Louisville. The pair had left William H. Wharton ill at Nashville and were on their way east to raise money for Texas. The Consultation of delegates had gathered in San Felipe in November and voted two to one to adhere to the federalist cause rather than declare independence as the more radical delegates, including Wharton, advocated. The representatives had also organized a provisional state government and had chosen Wharton, Archer, and Austin as commissioners to enlist aid in the United States. The empresario left the Texas volunteers who were besieging San Antonio and reluctantly prepared to join the other two commissioners, whom he considered extremists on the question of independence. By the time the three reached New Orleans early in January, however, Austin himself was convinced that without a declaration of independence from Mexico there was little likelihood of much support in the United States for the Texas cause against Santa Anna.[10]

Williams and Austin, of course, were unaware that on March 2, the day before they met on the Ohio River, delegates to the convention at Washington-on-the-Brazos had declared Texas's independence from Mexico. Williams may have accepted Austin's new position favoring independence as expedient, but McKinney did not. In a letter that Austin received while in the United States, the impetuous McKinney denounced the empresario as an "enemy of the country" and useless as a representative of "Texas' true interest." Such a vicious attack wounded Austin, who could not understand why a close friend would be hostile to his change in course. The empresario never forgave McKinney for his outburst. While McKinney actively supported the military effort against Santa Anna and

[10] Demand note for one dollar on Commercial and Agricultural Bank, Columbia, engraved by Draper, Tappan, Lonacre and Company, Philadelphia, Rosenberg Library; S. F. Austin to J. F. Perry, March 4, 1836, *Austin Papers*, III, 317–318; Eugene C. Barker, *The Life of Stephen F. Austin: Founder of Texas, 1793–1836*, pp. 420–422, 425–426.

the centralist party, he continued to oppose independence for Texas, and as late as 1839 he said that he still had "no reason" to change his mind.[11]

Williams showed the commissioners the bank notes and gave Austin a few to exhibit as an example of Texas's progress and development. Both Austin and Williams were aware of the strong anti-banking sentiment on the Brazos, caused by a democratic suspicion of privileged monopoly, but they hoped that the benefits to commerce would overcome any opposition. The pair parted amicably, and Williams continued downriver to New Orleans, where he wrote to his wife that he could leave for Texas by land on March 21. When Austin reached Lexington he presented one of the bank notes to his cousin, Mary Austin Holley, who described the handsome engraving and the proposed financial establishment in her new book about Texas published later that year. Austin and Archer joined Wharton in Washington at the end of March, and even Wharton took pride in Williams's enterprise, displaying one of the notes at a dinner party given by Senator John C. Calhoun.[12]

Before Williams could start for Texas, however, the news of the massacre at the Alamo and the declaration of independence reached New Orleans. Confident that his associates were caring for Sarah and the children, Williams hurried to Mobile, where he helped organize meetings the first week in April to raise money and volunteers. The provisional government had recently empowered Williams and McKinney to raise up to one hundred thousand dollars on the public faith and lands of Texas.[13] This special commission may

[11] T. F. McKinney to S. F. Austin, February 22, 1836, *Austin Papers*, III, 316–317; "Recollections of Stephen F. Austin," M. A. Bryan to son, September 25, 1889, Moses Austin Bryan Papers, Barker History Center, University of Texas at Austin; T. F. McKinney to Gómez Farías, March 24, 1839, Valentín Gómez Farías Papers, Latin American Collection, University of Texas at Austin.

[12] S. F. Austin to J. F. Perry, March 4, 1836, *Austin Papers*, III, 317–318; S. M. Williams to wife, March 17, 1836, Williams Papers; Mary Austin Holley, *Texas*, pp. 184, 186–187; S. H. Wharton to S. F. Austin, April 6, 1836, *Austin Papers*, III, 325.

[13] Claude Elliott, "Alabama and the Texas Revolution," *Southwestern Historical Quarterly* 50 (January 1947): 318–320; Gammel, *Laws of Texas*, I, 1029–1031.

have been the source for their courtesy military titles, because after this time, both were commonly addressed as "Colonel." Williams collected over seven thousand dollars through subscriptions and benefit concerts and deposited it with Dobson and Williams, his brother's firm in Mobile, to be used to buy and outfit a troop transport. Williams negotiated first for a schooner, but, unable to lease it at a reasonable cost, he purchased a rundown steamer, the *Emmeline*, and ordered the necessary repairs and armor. While awaiting these alterations, the busy agent returned to New Orleans in May to attend the trial of Captain Jeremiah Brown and the officers of the *Invincible*. Williams joined other Texans in praising the defense attorneys in a letter published in the *Commercial Bulletin*.[14]

While Sam Williams labored for the cause in the United States, members of his family back in Texas took part in the mass evacuation later called the "Runaway Scrape." A portion of the volunteer army retreating on orders of Sam Houston camped near Williams's deserted house in San Felipe and used his picket fence for firewood. Austin and Lorenzo de Zavala had stayed in the empty dwelling the previous September while awaiting the opening of the proposed consultation; they reported that the chimney had fallen down, and Austin asked his brother-in-law to send someone to make repairs and to bring furnishings from the lower settlements. In April, 1836, Captain Mosely Baker set fire to the village so that it would offer nothing to the advancing Mexican army, but Williams's house northwest of town escaped the flames.[15] Although Matthew R. Williams,

[14] S. M. Williams to Government of Texas, July 14, 1836; William Bryan to David G. Burnet, April 28, 1836, in William C. Binkley (ed.), *Official Correspondence of the Texan Revolution, 1835–1836*, I, 863–864, 645–646; bill of sale, May 2, 1836; copy of letter from David Soulard, owner, certifying the inability of Williams to charter the *Mobile*, McKinney and Williams Papers, Texas State Library, Austin; Dienst, "The Navy of the Republic of Texas," pp. 252–255.

[15] Jovita Courtney, *After the Alamo: San Jacinto from the Notes of Doctor Nicholas Decomps Labadie*, p. 51; S. F. Austin to J. F. Perry, September 11, 30, 1835, *Austin Papers*, III, 112, 140–141. William Bollaert, an English naturalist, visited San Felipe in 1843 and described the deserted village, but reported that the house where Austin had lived on a bluff north of town remained in good repair (W. Eugene Hollon and Ruth Lapham Butler [eds.], *Williams Bollaert's Texas*, p. 181).

Sam's youngest brother, was enrolled in Baker's company, he apparently sent a substitute until mid-April, when he joined the group on the San Jacinto River just in time for the battle on April 21.[16] He probably had escorted his wife to William Scott's home across the river from the battlefield; the spacious home of Sarah Williams's father at Point Pleasant served as a refuge for the wives and children of many prominent Texans because of its access to the overland route to Louisiana and to ships in Galveston Bay.[17] Rumors circulated that Colonel Almonte, advancing with the Mexican army, intended to claim Scott's estate as spoils, having admired it since his visit there in 1834.[18]

Sarah Williams and the three boys fled from their exposed home at Quintana along with childless Nancy McKinney, who had sheltered two close friends—Minerva Fort Fannin, whose husband commanded the outpost at Goliad, and Laura H. Jack, the wife of William H. Jack—and their children. Jack and McKinney took the women and children by boat to Georgia, a town developed by McKinney near the mouth of the Neches. A number of refugees camped near the warehouse, but the McKinney party was sheltered in a house. Williams briefly visited his family there in April, a week after the battle on April 21 that resulted in the capture of Santa Anna, but he soon returned to Mobile to finish work on the steamer. The women and children remained on the Neches until July before returning to Quintana.[19]

[16] Sam Houston Dixon and Louis Wiltz Kemp, The Heroes of San Jacinto, p. 201; Thomas Lloyd Miller, Bounty and Donation Land Grants of Texas, 1835–1888, pp. 689, 868.

[17] S. F. Austin's sister, Emily Perry, was there, as were Mrs. David Burnet and Mrs. Lorenzo de Zavala (J. F. Perry to S. F. Austin, April 8, 1836, Austin Papers, III, 326–327; Charles Adams Gulick et al. [eds.], The Papers of Mirabeau Buonoparte Lamar, I, 520–522).

[18] Andrew Forest Muir (ed.), Texas in 1837: An Anonymous Contemporary Narrative, p. 17.

[19] Mary (Sherwood) W. Helm, Scraps of Early Texas History, pp. 12–16; James K. Greer (ed.), "Journal of Ammon Underwood, 1834–1838," Southwestern Historical Quarterly 32 (October 1928): 145; S. M. Williams to wife, April 30, 1836, Samuel May and Austin May Williams Papers, Barker History Center, University of Texas at Austin; S. F. Austin to Collingsworth and Grayson, July 9, 1836, Austin Papers, III, 392–393.

Williams returned to Texas on the refurbished steamer, re-named the *Ocean*, in company with several other vessels and a num-ber of volunteers under the command of Thomas Jefferson Green. The flotilla arrived at Velasco on June 3 just as Santa Anna and his aides were embarking on the *Invincible* to sail for Veracruz. The new arrivals, however, would have preferred to hang the dictator for his war crimes instead of using him as a tool for diplomacy. Only through the intercession of cabinet member Mirabeau B. Lamar and Sam Williams was the Mexican president saved from the mob. Williams took him across the river to his house in Quintana, but, over his objections, General Green posted a guard until Wil-liam H. Patton, Sam Houston's aide, arrived to take charge.[20]

Several weeks later Williams left on the *Yellowstone* to collect his family from the Neches. The large steamer was over one hun-dred feet long with two cabins on the deck. Built in 1831 for the use of the American Fur Company on the Missouri River, the shallow-draft vessel had been purchased by Thomas Toby in 1835 for Mc-Kinney and Williams, and it had proved invaluable during the spring on the Brazos and upper Galveston Bay, transporting men and supplies. Williams's family had scarcely returned to Quintana when he had to leave to go north on business. Toby and Brother of New Orleans, who had advanced credit for McKinney and Wil-liams, failed, and in partial recompense for Toby's outstanding serv-ice, Texas authorized him to sell land scrip; Williams agreed to help dispose of some of the scrip, feeling somewhat responsible for the agent's predicament.[21]

While Williams was in the United States, political demagogu-ery caused a rupture in his long association with Austin. The em-

[20] S. M. Williams to wife, May 9, 1836, Williams Papers; Lydia Ann McHenry to brother, July 17, 1836, in George R. Nielson, "Lydia Ann McHenry and Revolutionary Texas," *Southwestern Historical Quarterly* 74 (January 1971): 403.

[21] T. F. McKinney to George W. Smythe, June 14, 1836, McKinney Papers; S. F. Austin memorandum, July 10, 1836, *Austin Papers*, III, 393–395; *Ship Registers and Enrollments of New Orleans, Louisiana*, III, 230; S. M. Williams to wife, August 2, 1836; Sarah Williams to Williams, Au-gust 14, 1836, Williams Papers; Toby and Brother to D. G. Burnet, Au-gust 5, 1836, in Binkley, *Official Correspondence*, II, 908–909; Gammel, *Laws of Texas*, I, 1136–1137.

presario bowed to pressure and entered the presidential contest in July, 1836, although he had been in poor health since his return to Texas the previous month. The contrite McKinney stopped at Peach Point to apologize to Austin but met with such a cold reception that, in a fit of pique, he joined the Sam Houston faction that had organized to persuade the general to become a candidate.[22] The hero of San Jacinto permitted his candidacy on August 20, only eleven days before the election, at which time the former provisional governor, Henry Smith, withdrew. The main issues were the unruly and unemployed army, annexation, and opening the Republic's land office. Although neither candidate offered a clear program, Houston held the advantage as the wounded hero and personal friend of President Andrew Jackson.[23] Even before Houston formally entered the race, Austin had been accused of land speculation because of his association with Williams. His enemies also charged that the empresario had enjoyed luxurious living in the United States while others had done the fighting in Texas. The persecuted empresario distributed handbills denying the allegations and said that he had only just learned of the Monclova speculations and still did not understand them. Austin made public statements castigating the speculators, but he failed to write to Williams in New Orleans. Outraged by the reports circulating in the Crescent City, Williams wrote, ". . . although I have nothing direct from you . . . I am informed that you charge me with a want of regard for your standing and character. . . . I should like to know what beyond a morbid feeling has aroused you . . . and what it is you complain in me." Blaming William H. Jack for driving a wedge between them, he assured Austin that he still esteemed him as a friend and benefactor.[24]

[22] S. F. Austin memorandum, July 20, 1836; *Telegraph and Texas Register*, August 9, 1836, *Austin Papers*, III, 399, 411; "Recollections of Stephen F. Austin," M. A. Bryan to son, September 25, 1889, Moses Austin Bryan Papers.

[23] Stanley Siegel, *A Political History of the Texas Republic, 1836–1845*, pp. 47–52.

[24] Gail Borden to S. F. Austin, August 15, 1836; S. F. Austin to Gail Borden, August 15, 1836, *Austin Papers*, III, 417, 418–421; S. M. Williams to S. F. Austin, August 29, 1836 (draft), Williams Papers; *Austin Papers*, III, 424–426.

One week after Sam Williams wrote the letter, the Texans selected Sam Houston as their first president; Austin trailed a poor third. When offered the post of secretary of state, the disappointed empresario reluctantly accepted. He received the long-delayed letter from Williams on October 1, a month after it was written. Though ill, Austin welcomed his friend's denial of wrongdoing "with such feelings as a drowning man would seize a plank."[25] Because Williams was expected home in October, Austin did not send his reply to New Orleans. Williams, however, encountered difficulties in selling the land certificates because of the increasing number of bank failures caused by President Andrew Jackson's hard money policies. Small banks in particular had too little specie in their vaults for the amount of paper notes they circulated, and by 1836 many were forced to close. Williams finally decided that he had to go north. Austin composed a second letter on November 3, his forty-third birthday, in which he deplored his friend's Monclova trip but urged that they both forget the past. "You have greatly vexed and worried and distressed me," he said, ". . . but you are so deeply rooted in my affections that, with all your faults, you are at heart, too much like a wild and heedless brother to be entirely banished. Come home."[26] But, heartsick and exhausted, Austin succumbed to illness and died December 27, perhaps before Williams had received this last letter.

Williams left New Orleans at the end of August. For the next four months he remained "constantly on the wing," disposing of Toby land scrip in such cities as Louisville, Philadelphia, New York, Baltimore, and Richmond. As sub-agent, he received a 5 percent commission, which by January 2, 1837, amounted to $1,356.75. Each certificate was for a 640-acre section worth $320. He used twenty-four certificates to buy the brig *Flight* in Baltimore for use as a troop transport, and in New York he paid for repairs to two Texas

[25] S. F. Austin to S. M. Williams, October 12, 1836, *Austin Papers*, III, 435–436. This letter is not in the Williams Papers, which suggests that it was never sent.

[26] S. M. Williams to wife, August 4, 1836; S. F. Austin to S. M. Williams, November 3, 1836, Williams Papers. The original of the Austin letter is very dog-eared and torn.

naval vessels with the land scrip. One was the *Invincible*, which he had bought two years earlier, and he rescued the schooner from a forced sale. After the ship returned to Texas, it ran aground at Galveston in August and was lost.[27]

When the *Flight* left for Texas in January, 1837, Williams sent his family some clothes and delicacies unobtainable except in the eastern cities. Distressed at being unable to return himself, he explained to his wife it was because he refused to "abandon all hope . . . because difficulties and mortifications present themselves." Only pride kept him going. Unfortunately for Sarah, the captain of the *Flight* mistook San Luis Pass west of Galveston Island for the mouth of the Brazos, and the brig went aground, breaking apart and scattering its cargo. Expecting a baby within the month, Sarah sent a friend down the beach to salvage what washed ashore. "You Seartainly have been absent long enough," she scolded her husband, adding that Samuel should not neglect his own interests. "We have done enough, lost enough, to bring things to a close on that score. . . ."[28] But because the financial situation worsened in 1837, Williams's return home grew more distant.

Williams continued to move from city to city, carefully avoiding creditors who might seek to incarcerate him for debts incurred by McKinney and Williams in 1835–1836. While banks failed and business stagnated, one bright note for the Texans occurred when the United States recognized the newly independent country, but talk of annexation was postponed. John K. Allen and George W. Hockley, a close friend of President Houston's, joined Williams to discuss plans for selling the Republic's scrip. In May, he went to Baltimore to consult with Michel B. Menard and his associate, Dr. Levi Jones, who had come east to sell shares and the scrip of the Galveston

[27] S. M. Williams to wife, January 6, 1837; various receipted hotel statements, October 5–November 20, 1836; statement of scrip sales, January 2, 1837, Williams Papers; William H. Wharton to S. F. Austin, December 31, 1836, in George P. Garrison (ed.), *Diplomatic Correspondence of the Republic of Texas*, I, 166–168; Dienst, "The Navy of the Republic of Texas," p. 261.

[28] S. M. Williams to wife, January 6, 1837; Sarah Williams to Williams, March 15, 1837, Williams Papers.

City Company. McKinney had taken a large bloc of stock for the firm, so Williams joined the pair on their tour through Virginia promoting Galveston business. Williams was in Washington in September and the following month visited Philadelphia, where he rejoined Allen for the return to Texas by way of Virginia, South Carolina, Georgia, and Alabama.[29]

The weary traveler stopped in Mobile, and his brother Nathaniel F. Williams, Nat's partner George Dobson, and Sam's brother-in-law Samuel St. John decided to accompany him to Texas. Dobson and Williams contemplated developing a new commercial enterprise in Texas, while St. John hoped to profit from his generous donation of five thousand dollars to the Texan cause in February, 1836. Sam Williams carried a quantity of specie and paper money that was intended to activate his bank charter. The Texas congress had confirmed the Mexican charter in 1836 as a means of giving relief to the firm of McKinney and Williams. The antibanking faction, however, managed to pass a measure that forbade issuing paper bank notes intended to circulate as money. It became law just as Williams started for Texas.[30]

Williams and other entrepreneurs had an additional banking scheme in reserve in case his charter was invalidated. The First Congress granted a charter to a group of investors for the Texas Rail Road, Navigation, and Banking Company, which allowed the directors to open a bank of issue when $1 million in specie was in the vault; a bonus of $25,000, also in specie, was to be paid to the treasury of the Republic shortly thereafter. Neither Williams nor the other investors in this project could raise the specie before the deadline of June, 1838, and the president turned down their offer to make up the deficit in Texas treasury notes. Thus neither Williams's "little bank" nor the "Great Bank" of the ambitious speculators

[29] Edward Hanrick to S. M. Williams, December 29, 1836; S. M. Williams to wife, May 30, June 18, October 13, December 24, 1837; statements to Williams and others from various hotels, 1837, *ibid.*

[30] William Fairfax Gray, *From Virginia to Texas, 1835: Diary of Col. Wm. F. Gray*, p. 200; Gammel, *Laws of Texas*, I, 882; J. P. Bryan (ed.), *Mary Austin Holley, The Texas Diary, 1835–1838*, p. 53; Gammel, *Laws of Texas*, I, 1135, 1389–1390.

opened in 1838. One potential investor recorded in his diary that "the Texas Bank turned out a Bubble."[31]

The vessel carrying the Williams brothers and their brother-in-law went aground at the same place where the *Flight* had foundered the previous year. Upon learning of the disaster, McKinney sent Cary, one of his slaves, with a wagon and warm clothing to rescue the shipwrecked party from the barren peninsula about fifteen miles east of Velasco. Williams learned from Cary that his infant daughter had died only days before. The baby had been born in April, 1837, and at the behest of Sarah, he had chosen her name —Sarah McKinney Williams "for her dear mother."[32]

Besides the death of their longed-for daughter, Sarah had endured many hardships while her husband was away. She had seen Williams less than two months out of the past twenty-nine; he was away a little more than eight months before he returned after the battle of San Jacinto, and this time he had been absent for over sixteen months. After the birth of little Sarah, the new mother lost her hair and thereafter always wore a cap. While Williams was in the United States, she spent part of the time at Quintana and Velasco, but during most of the time she lived with her family on the San Jacinto and was there when the great hurricane swept the Gulf coast in October, 1837. Three days after the wind subsided, her father, William Scott, died, leaving two grown sons and an eleven-year-old daughter besides Sarah and his widow. Williams learned of the death of his father-in-law in December and wrote his wife that they had had their "full portion of such afflictions." He vowed that this would be their last separation, and he hoped that she and her mother were bearing up under the strain.[33] It is doubtful that she

[31] Gammel, *Laws of Texas*, I, 1188–1192; William R. Hogan, *The Texas Republic: A Social and Economic History*, pp. 97–99; James Morgan to Samuel Swartwout, February 3, 1838, David G. Burnet Papers, Rosenberg Library; James Ogilvy on January 3, 1839, Harriet Smither (ed.), "Diary of Adolphus Sterne," *Southwestern Historical Quarterly* 30 (October 1926): 149.

[32] T. F. McKinney to S. M. Williams, January 21, 1838; Sarah Williams to Williams, May 3, 1837; S. M. Williams to wife, May 30, 1837, Williams Papers.

[33] Sarah Williams to S. M. Williams, May 3, 1837, *ibid.*; *Telegraph and Texas Register*, October 7, 11, 18, 1837; Harris County Probate Rec-

received that letter before the death of little Sarah McKinney and Williams's almost fatal shipwreck. Little did the bereaved couple know that several more long separations awaited them in the future, one only four months away.

---

ords, E, 134; S. M. Williams to wife, December 24, 1837, Williams Papers.

CHAPTER 7

"A Man Proud in His Spirit and Proud in His Character" 1838-1841

SAMUEL MAY WILLIAMS had other entrepreneurial interests besides banking after his return to Texas in 1838, for he soon became preoccupied with the reorganization of the Galveston City Company. In 1833 Michel B. Menard, a friend of Thomas F. McKinney, had conceived the plan to acquire the eastern end of Galveston Island. He arranged for a native Mexican, Juan N. Seguin, to petition the state for the site as his reward for service against the Indians, thus overcoming the proscription against the acquisition of land in the littoral by Anglo-Americans. Then, as "agent" for Seguin, Menard ordered a survey in 1834 for the strategically located league and *labor*, totaling 4,605 acres. While Williams was in Monclova, McKinney obtained for their firm a one-half interest in the project by paying Menard $400. Subsequent events, however, postponed the immediate development of the port.[1]

McKinney and Menard organized the Galveston City Company in late 1836 while Williams was still away, and they invited Congressmen Mosely Baker and John K. Allen to become investors. The five men then petitioned the Texas congress to recognize Menard's

---

[1] Charles W. Hayes, *Galveston: History of the Island and the City,* pp. 170–175; memo of Seguin Title, January 18, 1833, Galveston City Company Papers, Rosenberg Library, Galveston; T. F. McKinney to S. M. Williams, March 23, 1834; M. B. Menard to S. M. Williams, April 5, 1835, Samuel May Williams Papers, Rosenberg Library. The chapter title is a quotation from S. M. Williams to wife, July 23, 1838.

claim so that they might begin work immediately on developing the property.[2] Although the land office remained closed, most of the legislators appeared to favor the request in spite of pressure from rival claimants. The public, however, labeled this proposed transaction a new "land steal" and demanded that the valuable site be offered for sale to the highest bidder. To quiet the clamor, the government advertised the acreage in the *Telegraph and Texas Register,* but shortly thereafter, the Texas congress awarded the title to Menard for his bid of $50,000. Critics condemned the exchange and charged Baker with improper conduct, although he denied even having voted on the matter. By this act of December 9, 1836, Menard had to pay the Republic $30,000 on February 1 and the remainder by May. The rest of the thirty-one-mile-long island was to be sold at public auction the following November.[3]

Menard encountered difficulty in raising the required sum before the deadline. In order to secure the money, he mortgaged his quit claim to David White, a Mobile merchant who had helped Texas during the revolution. Already authorized to sell Texas scrip in Alabama, White also proceeded to issue stock and scrip for the Galveston Company on his own authority, and Menard soon perceived that the Alabamian intended to defraud him.[4] At this juncture, Menard encountered Robert Triplett, a wealthy Kentuckian who had amassed a fortune speculating in military scrip in that state and who held a rival claim at Galveston.[5] Triplett and nine other citizens of the United States had subscribed to a $200,000 loan

---

[2] Agreement between M. B. Menard, T. F. McKinney, and S. M. Williams, *et al.,* December 14, 1836, Williams Papers.

[3] Quit claim, December 9, 10, 1836, in Hayes, *Galveston,* pp. 177–180; Edward Stiff, *The Texas Emigrant: Being a Narration of the Adventures of the Author in Texas . . . down to the Year 1840,* pp. 161–162; Hans P. N. Gammel (comp.), *The Laws of Texas, 1822–1897,* I, 1130–1131, 1328.

[4] Gammel, *Laws of Texas,* I, 1132; Hayes, *Galveston,* pp. 179–180, 831–832.

[5] M. B. Menard to T. F. McKinney and others, April 11, 1837, typescript in Galveston City Company Papers; Arnold Harris Hord, "Genealogy of the Triplett Family," *William and Mary Quarterly,* 1st ser., 21 (July 1912): 124–125.

for Texas in January, 1836, expecting to receive in return land scrip worth fifty cents per acre and early location rights. The investors advanced $20,000 before learning that Texas politicians refused to honor the loan arrangement negotiated by the three Texas commissioners. Triplett and William Fairfax Gray, one of the contributors, staked a claim to a section of land near the eastern tip of Galveston Island, but they lacked the political influence to receive a title. Therefore, Triplett welcomed the opportunity to assist Menard with his financial arrangements in 1837 in exchange for inclusion in the Galveston City Company.[6] Menard hurried to Baltimore to consult with Williams, and they placed warnings in eastern newspapers that Menard possessed the only legitimate claim to Galveston recognized by the Republic. White relinquished his rights in the speculation and representatives of the reorganized company began selling stock.[7]

Sam Williams was elected one of the five directors at the first meeting of the reorganized company in Galveston in April, 1838. The board offered the public one thousand shares of stock, each with a face value of $1,000, but sold at discount—perhaps $800, as suggested by Menard. These negotiable certificates passed from hand to hand until redeemed by the company or exchanged for lots; the shares declined in value to a low of $100, but by 1856 they had returned to par value.[8] At the first public sale in April, Williams bought sixteen city lots worth a total of $14,125 for friends, paying one-fifth in cash as required by the charter. Surviving records do not reveal what Williams's holdings in stock and lots were, but he owned two ten-acre suburban lots and no stock at the time of his

[6] William Fairfax Gray, *From Virginia to Texas, 1835: The Diary of Col. Wm. F. Gray*, pp. 71, 132–134, 148–150, 156, 160–162, 210–211, 216, 218; Eugene C. Barker, "The Finances of the Texas Revolution," *Political Science Quarterly* 19 (December 1904): 630–632; Willard Richardson et al. (eds.), *Galveston Directory, 1859–1860*, pp. 42–44.

[7] S. M. Williams to wife, May 30, 1837; statements to Williams and others from Powhattan House, June 9, 1837, and the Eagle Hotel, June 15, 1837, Williams Papers; M. B. Menard to T. F. McKinney, June 17, 1837, Galveston City Company Papers.

[8] Richardson, *Galveston Directory, 1859–1860*, pp. 42–43; M. B. Menard to T. F. McKinney, April 22, 1837, Galveston City Company Papers. The Rosenberg Library has 173 of these certificates. The company had cancelled 713 shares by 1856.

death. The firm owned 121 shares in 1838, but the partners released 21 shares in May to pay a portion of debt owed to David White.[9]

Williams and McKinney had left their families at Quintana in order to attend the Galveston meeting, and from the island the two boarded their steamer for a trip to Houston, where the congress was in session. The raw village of Houston had been organized by their business associates, John K. and Augustus C. Allen, during the past year, and already an estimated fifteen hundred inhabitants crowded the hastily erected buildings. The Allen brothers donated three commercial lots at the foot of Milam Street to the firm of McKinney and Williams for an office and warehouse so that a branch might be established on Buffalo Bayou. McKinney invested in Houston real estate, including a one-seventh interest in the two-story frame capitol building which he and his partners intended to convert into a hotel after the congress voted in 1839 to move the government to Austin.[10]

Williams did not share in the Houston speculation, primarily because he owned the league of land just east of the Allen brothers' tract, less than one mile from the capitol building and extending about six miles down the bayou toward Harrisburg. In order to capitalize on the building boom in Houston, Williams installed a steam sawmill to cut the area's abundant timber, but within the year he found the mill a financial burden and sought a buyer. He still owned the mill ten years later, although he had sold portions of his league as the city of Houston grew and moved eastward. Only 750 acres remained in his possession in 1858, and his heirs disposed of these. Tallow Town, a facility for rendering beef tallow, hides and bones, developed in the tract about the time of the Civil War.[11]

President Houston called Williams to the capital in May, 1838, to persuade him to undertake with Albert T. Burnley a confidential

[9] Receipts and memoranda, April 1, 13, 1838; McKinney and Williams receipt, May 28, 1838, Williams Papers.

[10] Harris County Deed Records, A, 177, C, 20, 161, 165.

[11] T. F. McKinney to S. M. Williams, August 21, November 3, 1838; copy of deed to Samuel and A. C. Allen and William Richardson, November 15, 1839; J. T. Doswell to S. M. Williams, May 18, 1849, Williams Papers; inventory of S. M. Williams's estate, Galveston County Probate Records, I, 277; Jesse A. Ziegler, *Wave of the Gulf*, pp. 24–28.

mission to the United States for the purpose of negotiating a $5 million loan originally proposed in 1836. Burnley had been appointed earlier and had spent a portion of 1837 discussing the sale of Texas bonds with Nicholas Biddle, president of the state-chartered Bank of the United States of Pennsylvania. The banker, unable to accept the proposition in the form presented, made suggestions for rewording the law authorizing the sale.[12] The Texas congress passed a second act in May, 1838, and Sam Williams reluctantly agreed to accept the commission in spite of his promises to his family that they should not be separated again for a long period. A portion of the anticipated loan was earmarked for the purchase of six naval vessels to protect the Texas coast. The ships acquired in 1835 had all met disaster, and rumors circulated that the Mexicans planned to invade Texas again. While the Texans desperately needed funds for defense, creditors were reluctant to extend a loan unless assured that the Republic could maintain itself. The United States, Great Britain, and France all favored an independent Texas, but for economic reasons financial interests in those nations hesitated to make funds available lest they offend Mexico.[13]

Accompanied by Burnley, Williams left for New Orleans in June, 1838, and then journeyed up the Mississippi and Ohio rivers and overland to Philadelphia. They spent July negotiating with Biddle and were joined by Anson Jones, the Texas minister to the United States, and General James Hamilton, former governor of South Carolina and president of the Bank of Charleston, who had become interested in Texas speculations. The commissioners placed the bonds in Biddle's vault for safekeeping, but the banker remained noncommittal about the proposed sale and they feared that they might have to travel to Europe to find buyers.[14]

[12] Gammel, Laws of Texas, I, 1092–1093; Nicholas Biddle to A. T. Burnley, November 22, 1837, Letterbook, The Papers of Nicholas Biddle (Library of Congress, 1915), on microfilm in the University of Houston Library. Hereafter cited as Biddle Papers.

[13] Gammel, Laws of Texas, I, 1355–1356, 1484–1486; Sam Houston to Senate, May 21, 1838; report from Samuel May Williams, December 5, 1839, in Ernest W. Winkler (ed.), Secret Journals of the Senate, Republic of Texas, 1836–1845, pp. 110, 115.

[14] S. M. Williams to wife, May 25, July 23, 1838; Sarah Williams to

Biddle was in the midst of a manipulation designed to force up the worldwide price of cotton by cornering the market, a scheme that succeeded momentarily but absorbed his available capital. Banks had ceased paying specie in May, 1837, after the price of cotton and other agricultural commodities dropped drastically. When Williams and Burnley arrived a year later, many banks had resumed specie payments, but the Texans found themselves competing for the available capital with commissioners from various states and individual planters, merchants, and bankers. Many people, including Senator Henry Clay, believed that the Texas request would be granted, but finally in October Biddle refused to make the loan, saying that it was "inexpedient." Williams and his associates believed that abolitionist sympathizers had exerted pressure and thus forced the banker to move cautiously.[15] Privately, Williams suspected that Biddle intended to do some speculating in Texas land, a surmise that proved correct when Biddle bought $44,000 worth of stock certificates in the Galveston City Company.[16] The banker had suggested the names of some prominent persons who might furnish American money to the Texans, thus making it unnecessary for the commissioners to go abroad. Williams and Burnley contacted these individuals, but the poor economic conditions doomed their efforts and a journey to Europe appeared inevitable.[17]

Williams, July 22, 1838; James Auchincloss to S. M. Williams, July 27, 1838, Williams Papers; S. M. Williams's receipt to N. Biddle, November 20, 1838, Biddle Papers.

[15] Bray Hammond, *Banks and Politics in America*, pp. 478–481, 487–488; Henry Clay to Nicholas Biddle, September 14, 1838; A. T. Burnley to Nicholas Biddle, August 25, 1838, Biddle Papers; S. M. Williams to wife, October 13, 1838, Williams Papers; A. T. Burnley to Anson Jones, October 11, 1838, in Anson Jones, *Memoranda and Official Correspondence Relating to the Republic of Texas*, p. 143.

[16] A. T. Burnley to Nicholas Biddle, October 26, 1836, Biddle Papers; T. F. McKinney to S. M. Williams, January 5, 1839, Williams Papers; Nicholas Biddle to James Love, October 26, 1839, quoted in Joe B. Frantz, *Gail Borden: Dairyman to a Nation*, p. 151.

[17]A. T. Burnley and S. M. Williams to Henry Smith, October 8, 1838, in Seymour V. Conner (ed.), *Texas Treasury Papers: Letters Received in the Treasury Department of the Republic of Texas, 1836–1846*, I, 133–138; A. T. Burnley to Nicholas Biddle, October 10, 1838, Biddle Papers.

Williams was spared that ordeal when President Houston named him naval commissioner in August after the original appointee, Peter W. Grayson, committed suicide. This new assignment remained a secret in Texas except among the close associates of the Sam Houston faction. McKinney wrote his partner that he hoped Williams would succeed in sending at least one good ship to Texas before the end of Houston's presidential term in December. Such an accomplishment would enhance Williams's reputation, enabling him to return and "roll about this country and make a display merely to annoy your enemies."[18]

Williams experienced difficulties at the very beginning of his new assignment. The creditors of McKinney and Williams intended to initiate suits against the firm if he went into New York City, and although he surreptitiously visited Baltimore, his friends warned him that he was also in danger there. His New York agent, James Auchincloss, persuaded one of the creditors in that city to sign a letter of license granting temporary immunity from arrest so that Williams might come to their office and make arrangements to settle the account. But as the other firms had not yet signed such letters, Williams had to remain in Philadelphia until September, when Auchincloss arranged for a three-month period of grace during which he could come and go as he pleased. Early in November some of the creditors reneged, and Williams's agent warned him to stay only at William Bunker's Mansion House, a hotel at the foot of Broadway where he had stopped during previous visits. Matters evidently improved because Williams soon moved to the new deluxe Astor House, where guests enjoyed the luxury of baths and water closets on each floor, thanks to a steam pump that raised water to all levels of the hotel.[19]

Forced to negotiate for the ships without the benefit of the loan, Williams reported to the Texas congress that he had been able

[18] T. F. McKinney to S. M. Williams, August 21, 1838, Williams Papers.

[19] James Auchincloss to S. M. Williams, August 13, 1838; Asa P. Ufford to S. M. Williams, August 14, September 24, November 10, 1838; hotel receipts, October 21, 25, November 9, 28, 1838, January 15, 1839, Williams Papers; Marshall B. Davidson, *History of Notable American Houses*, p. 204.

to buy the steam packet *Charleston* for $120,000, payable in five years at 10 percent interest. Several weeks later, a personal loan arranged through the efforts of James Hamilton enabled Texas to get immediate possession of the vessel. The South Carolina financier also urged the Texas congress to transfer Williams's commission to him when the results of the September election placed Mirabeau B. Lamar in the presidency. Hamilton expected to become the naval commissioner after the inauguration in December, and he pledged Williams to secrecy in order not to endanger the pending contracts. Williams did not immediately reply, because he was personally supervising the remodeling of the steamer in New York City. The refurbished steamer, rechristened *Zavala* for the deceased vice-president, prepared to sail for Texas at the end of 1838.[20]

While Hamilton furthered his own career, Williams met with Frederick Dawson, the noted Baltimore shipbuilder. Aided by his brother, Henry Howell, now Texas consul at Baltimore, the commissioner contracted for six new vessels to be paid for by two bonds of the Republic in the amount of $280,000 each, redeemable in five years. Samuel Williams endorsed the bonds on November 29, giving them to the Girard Bank in Philadelphia to hold until completion of the ships. This act ended his primary responsibility to the Houston administration for acquiring the navy, and he could take pride in a job well done. He remained on hand to supervise the project, although he was uncertain whether he would be the naval commissioner under the new administration.[21]

Williams spent the Christmas holidays with his brother's family

[20] Alex Dienst, "The Navy of the Republic of Texas," *The Quarterly of the Texas State Historical Association* 13 (July 1909): 7; James Hamilton to S. M. Williams, October 27, 1838, Williams Papers; James Hamilton to M. B. Lamar, November 3, 1838, in Charles Adams Gulick *et al.* (eds.), *The Papers of Mirabeau Buonaparte Lamar*, II, 274–279; James Treat to S. M. Williams, November 28, 1838, Williams Papers.

[21] Robert Irion to J. P. Henderson, November 29, 1838, in George P. Garrison (ed.), *Diplomatic Correspondence of the Republic of Texas*, II, 350–354; To James Schott, President of Girard Bank, November 29, 1838, Henry Sampson volume, "Obituary Address" (Washington, 1850), Rosenberg Library; Moses A. Bryan to J. F. Perry, February 11, 26, April 16, 1839, Moses Austin Bryan Papers, Barker History Center, University of Texas at Austin.

at their country estate north of Baltimore. In January he received a letter from McKinney stating that Lamar had personally guaranteed that Williams would continue to serve as naval commissioner. But only a week after the interview with McKinney, Lamar appointed Hamilton to succeed Williams and sent Memucan Hunt to join Burnley as loan commissioner. John G. Tod, the naval agent who also had lost his appointment, believed that Biddle and Hamilton had contrived the loan refusal so that Hamilton could get the position and gain prestige for the Lamar administration by successful negotiation. Tod predicted that Texas would soon have the money. In Texas the Houston bloc was infuriated. Senator Robert Wilson of Harris County had to be expelled from the senate chamber for damning the body for its submission in Williams's dismissal. The senators passed a resolution thanking the commissioner for his efforts, and even William H. Wharton challenged anyone to name one individual who had done more for Texas than Williams. McKinney took the blame for his partner's recall. He had worked against Lamar during the presidential canvass, and the dismissal was the new president's revenge. "Like it or not," McKinney warned his friend, he intended to secure Williams's election to the next congress. He added, "May you live to place your foot on the neck of every enemy you have on earth...."[22]

Williams remained in the east until May, when he met with Hamilton in Baltimore. The new commissioner expressed his delight in Dawson's work and generously praised the Williams brothers in a letter to Lamar; although they had supported Houston, he hoped the president would find them as admirable as he did. When the first of the new vessels, the *Viper*, was completed in May, Williams, Anson Jones, recently recalled as minister, and the latter's secretary, Moses Austin Bryan, embarked as passengers for Texas. The first of three identical schooners, the ship was sixty-six feet long and designed to be manned by thirteen officers and a crew of sixty-nine

---

[22] S. M. Williams to wife, December 7, 1838; T. F. McKinney to S. M. Williams, December 13, 17, 1838, Williams Papers; John G. Tod to S. M. Williams (draft), January 22, 1839, John G. Tod Papers, Rosenberg Library, Galveston; T. F. McKinney to S. M. Williams, January 5, 27, 1839, Williams Papers.

sailors and marines. On her maiden voyage, however, a skeleton crew of five handled the ship.[23]

The citizens of Galveston welcomed the ship and subsequently honored Jones and Williams with a public dinner in June. A talented orator, Jones spoke at length, defending his action in Washington, where he had officially withdrawn the Texan offer of annexation when it became apparent that union was politically impossible. He praised the developers of Galveston for their remarkable progress in only eighteen months and predicted a rosy future for the port. Following the eloquent address, Williams apologized for the brevity of his own remarks, due primarily, he said, to his inexperience as a public speaker but also to his emotional state in response to the honor paid him. Regretting that he had been unsuccessful in procuring the loan, he nevertheless took great pride in his role in obtaining a navy that was second to none. In response to his introduction as an associate of Stephen F. Austin, Williams said that he had "loved him with the devotion of a woman," and that he had courted hatred of himself in order that Austin might be esteemed and loved by all. This hyperbole, typical of contemporary oratory, was the opening speech of Williams's campaign to represent Galveston in the lower house of the Texas congress. Less than three years after his death, the apotheosis of the empresario had already occurred, and by mid-century his name was "more potent than in life."[24]

Galveston County had been created in the spring of 1838 and had sent Mosely Baker as its first representative to congress that same autumn; the new county was combined with Harris and Liberty counties to form a senatorial district and in 1838 was served by Senator Robert Wilson.[25] The annual congressional election of 1839

[23] S. M. Williams to R. G. Dunlap, [February, 1839], in Conner, *Texas Treasury Papers*, I, 186–187; James Hamilton to M. B. Lamar, May 19, 1839, *Lamar Papers*, II, 578; Anson Jones, *Memoranda and Official Correspondence Relating to the Republic of Texas*, pp. 29, 33; Tom Henderson Wells, *Commodore Moore and the Texas Navy*, appendix C.

[24] Jones, *Memoranda*, pp. 33, 291–295; *Telegraph and Texas Register*, July 17, 1839; James Armstrong, *Some Facts on the Eleven League Controversy*, p. 11.

[25] Gammel, *Laws of Texas*, I, 1482–1483; *Biographical Directory of the Texan Conventions and Congresses, 1832–1845*, p. 27.

engendered great interest in Galveston, not only because the new congress would be forced to come to grips with the Republic's pressing financial problem, but also because a local controversy had given rise to a hotly contested movement for a congressional review of the city charter. The city of Galveston had been organized in 1838 under a charter that permitted all white male property-owners to vote for city officials, although candidates for alderman and mayor were required to hold property valued at a minimum of five hundred dollars.[26] Subsequently the islanders selected a democratic, liberal adventurer, John M. Allen, as mayor in March, 1839, along with eight aldermen of varying political views. Allen's election offended the conservative members of the community, particularly the directors of the Galveston City Company, who heretofore had enjoyed complete control over local affairs. The new mayor forced the adoption of an inflationary, though pragmatic, solution for the community's irritating shortage of coins by issuing Galveston "change scrip" in denominations of two and four bits and one, two, and three dollars, limited in number to one and one-third the value of Texas treasury notes deposited with the city. To regain control of the city and forbid such monetary policies, the wealthier segment determined to ask the congress for a new charter, one that would limit the franchise to those who owned a substantial amount of property.[27] Their candidate, of course, was Sam Williams, who agreed entirely with the antidemocratic proposal.

The candidates and their partisans bombarded potential voters with broadsides and statements during August. While the merchants and real estate speculators backed Williams, the mayor and his democratic followers supported John L. Evans, former editor of the short-lived Galveston *Intelligencer*. Evans had served as alderman since June, appointed by his friend the mayor when Gail Borden, former customs collector for the port and a member of the Galveston City Company, resigned.[28]

The Houston *Telegraph and Texas Register*, owned by Dr. Francis Moore, Jr., who was campaigning to represent the senatorial district of Harris, Liberty, and Galveston counties, attacked

[26] Gammel, *Laws of Texas*, II, 94–99.
[27] Hayes, *Galveston*, pp. 300, 338–339.
[28] *Ibid.*, pp. 349–350; Frantz, *Gail Borden*, pp. 156, 158.

Williams for his land-speculating activities. Moore had purchased the newspaper from Gail and Thomas H. Borden in 1837 and used its editorial column to vilify the followers of Sam Houston. To help counteract such derogatory publicity, McKinney and Williams took space in other papers to announce that their firm continued to accept the depreciating treasury notes at 50 cents on the dollar for both debts and goods. Because these notes sold elsewhere for 37.5 cents or less, this statement may be regarded as a political move as well as a sincere effort to restore faith in the Redbacks, as the treasury notes were commonly called.[29]

Williams defeated Evans on September 2 by a vote of 187 to 150, and he began making arrangements to attend the November opening of the Fourth Congress, the first session to be held in the new capital at Austin. The firm of McKinney and Williams had transferred its central operation from Quintana to Galveston in 1838, and in addition to the three-story warehouse and long wharf at the foot of Twenty-fourth Street, the firm also owned an interest in a tavern, rent houses, and the Tremont Hotel, as well as Mac's race course and the adjacent stables near the gulf. During Williams's absence, McKinney agreed to supervise the construction of a comfortable story-and-a-half house for his partner and one for himself on the suburban outlots that they owned about two miles west of town. In the meantime, Sarah Williams and the children lived with her mother on the San Jacinto. She had borne another daughter in November, 1838, and named her Mary Dorothea for "your and my mother," as she told her absent husband, who was then in the northeast contracting for the naval vessels.[30]

Williams left his family at the end of September, and, after transacting some business in Houston, he started for Austin on horseback by way of San Felipe, LaGrange, and Bastrop. McKin-

[29] Broadside, August 16, 21, 27, 1839, Williams Papers; Walter P. Webb (ed.), *The Handbook of Texas*, II, 229, 721; *The Galvestonian*, August 22, 1839; Edward W. Heusinger, "The Monetary History of the Republic of Texas," *Southwestern Historical Quarterly* 57 (July 1953): 85.

[30] *Telegraph and Texas Register*, September 4, 1839; T. F. McKinney to S. M. Williams, July 16, August 21, November 6, 1838, December 10, 1839; Sarah Williams to Williams, December 13, 1838, Williams Papers.

ney's slave Cary followed later with the baggage and a wagonload of provisions, but he did not arrive in the frontier capital until mid-December. Forced to wear his riding jacket until his trunk arrived, Williams passed up two lavish parties because he lacked proper attire. Louis P. Cooke, secretary of the navy, invited Williams to live with his family in one of the log cabins built to house the officials. Even though the tiny house was crowded, it was preferable to the rude hotels. In writing to his wife, Williams described the location of Austin as picturesque and healthful, in contrast to humid Houston. The raw village lay just above land along the Colorado owned by both Williams and his partner. Prior to the relocation of the seat of government, McKinney had been selling portions for less than one cent per acre; now they confidently expected the value would rise.[31]

The Fourth Congress convened on Monday, November 11, 1839, but Williams and seven others missed the opening ceremonies and President Lamar's address the following day. The Galveston representative arrived on Friday and took his oath of office during the regular session the following morning. He discovered that his friend, José Antonio Navarro, the representative from Bexar, was ill and unable to attend the session, but Juan Seguin served that district in the senate. Altogether there were over thirty new faces who had not served in previous congresses, including former President Sam Houston, representing San Augustine County in the lower house. In spite of an earlier pledge to Lamar to support administration fiscal measures, Williams usually voted with the Houston faction against the new president's alleged extravagance. He also generally supported the hero of San Jacinto and his associates in opposition to Lamar's Indian policy.[32]

Austin's first congress met in a rustic building that capped a hill west of the main avenue leading from the river. Balancing it on the

[31] S. M. Williams to wife, December 4, 29, 1839; T. F. McKinney to S. M. Williams, November 11, December 10, 1839, January 27, 1839, Williams Papers.

[32] Harriet Smither (ed.), *Journals of the Fourth Congress of the Republic of Texas, 1839–1840*, II, 3, 24; Stanley Siegel, *A Political History of the Republic of Texas, 1836–1845*, pp. 140–143; S. M. Williams to M. B. Lamar, June 22, July 11, 1839, *Lamar Papers*, III, 28, 41.

east was the two-story frame President's House, clearly the most prestigious building in town. The temporary statehouse resembled a pioneer cabin built on blocks with a porch across the front; a wide hall divided the senate chamber on the north from that of the representatives, and the western wall of both rooms had small cubicles for committee meeting rooms. When the first cold norther struck, Williams offered a resolution requesting that a fireplace and chimney be erected immediately and that the bouncing, unstable floor be shored up with stone foundation blocks.[33] Apparently the matter was corrected because no further comment exists on the uncomfortable conditions.

Speaker David S. Kaufman appointed the Galvestonian chairman of the finance committee and a member of the committee on naval affairs. The financial crisis dominated much of the session, and Williams worked with the loan commissioners who had just returned from Europe. A joint finance committee from both chambers recommended that Texas should practice rigid economy and create a sinking fund to redeem its bonds, thus strengthening its credit both in the United States and in Europe before again dispatching loan commissioners on a new foreign mission.[34]

On January 12, 1840, Chairman Williams delivered his own report, which the Austin *Texas Sentinel* described as "lucid and able." He blamed the depreciation of the Republic's promissory notes on the lack of specie and compared the new nation's dilemma with that of a bank that suspended payment. He then proposed a funding plan reminiscent of that of Alexander Hamilton in 1790: the treasury should issue interest-bearing bonds to redeem the outstanding paper immediately, and, in order to create a demand for the notes already in circulation, no more unsecured paper should be issued. Also, to increase revenue, Williams suggested a 15 percent ad valorem duty on all imports except distilled spirits, which already carried a high rate. The government should cease accepting bonds in lieu of cash from importers, and a system of drawbacks should be

[33] Ernest William Winkler, "The Seat of Government of Texas," *The Quarterly of the Texas State Historical Association* 10 (January 1907): 185–245; Smither, *Journals of the Fourth Congress*, II, 58.

[34] Smither, *Journals of the Fourth Congress*, II, 4, 170–173; Siegel, *Political History of the Republic*, pp. 114–119.

set up to aid exporters. Finally, Williams advised that a more efficient collection of direct taxes should be adopted to alleviate the immediate problems.[35]

Although these measures prompted considerable debate, all of Williams's recommendations were eventually enacted into law. He sent Nicholas Biddle a copy of the new law and, after returning to Galveston, received a complimentary letter from the banker. But in spite of his efforts, the Redback notes continued to depreciate and, by the end of 1841, brought only 12.5 cents on the dollar. About eight hundred thousand dollars' worth of interest-bearing notes were exchanged for bonds, and almost one-half that amount was collected in revenue, which left over one million dollars outstanding in the hands of speculators.[36] Thus only a portion of Williams's funding plan succeeded, which was about all that could be expected while the economy still suffered from the effects of the Panic of 1837.

Like his colleagues, Williams introduced a number of local bills to satisfy the demands of his constituents. Besides relief bills asking for restitution for losses due to military action, he successfully sponsored measures to provide Galveston with a lighthouse and a new city charter.[37] One special interest bill supported by Williams was the petition for his freedom delivered in person by McKinney's slave Cary, who had served as an express rider during the Texas Revolution. McKinney allowed him to hunt game and sell the meat to neighbors, and over the years Cary had accumulated sufficient funds to buy himself and his family. Only Cary McKinney and one other slave, Peter Martin, were emancipated by the congress because of their service to the Republic; other blacks failed to win approval because most white Texans feared that free Negroes caused unrest among the slave population. The Fourth Congress also passed an act to remove free blacks from Texas unless they obtained special

[35] Austin *Texas Sentinel*, January 15, 1840; Smither, *Journals of the Fourth Congress*, II, 293, 274–287.

[36] Gammel, *Laws of Texas*, II, 183, 209–225, 230, 453; S. M. Williams to Nicholas Biddle, February 22, 1830, Biddle Papers; S. M. Williams to James H. Starr, March 23, 1840, in Conner, *Texas Treasury Papers*, II, 422–423; Heusinger, "Monetary History," pp. 85–86.

[37] Smither, *Journals of the Fourth Congress*, II, 126, 296, 305.

dispensation from the government. Cary posted a $1,000 bond to ensure that he would not become a public charge and returned to Galveston, where he became the operator of a livery stable.[38] His family, though not free, at least belonged to him.

Before the congress adjourned on February 5, the Freemasons held a Grand Lodge in Austin with Williams presiding as Grand Worthy Master. His success in congress and recognition by the Masons pleased McKinney, who congratulated his partner for showing "this miserable community" that they knew little about him. McKinney was gratified that his friend was getting along so well in his "own quiet way." Always restless, McKinney suggested closing all their businesses in Galveston because it "was too much for mere men." All the people on the island, he added, could "go to the Devil," just as Sam had so often said.[39]

Williams's hopes to secure passage of a banking bill were again doomed. Prejudice against private banks of issue prevailed, and the only chance for any such institution was in a national bank. Lamar favored a state-owned bank; others suggested a land bank. Disappointed but willing to sacrifice his personal ambitions temporarily in order to establish some sort of facilities in Texas, Williams offered to raise some of the necessary capital for a national bank if congress passed the bill.[40] But congress failed to act in 1840, and the continuing depressed times prevented the accumulation of sufficient capital in any event. Those interested in the national bank pinned their hopes on securing a foreign loan.

[38] *Ibid.*, pp. 235, 254, 259, 305; certificate from T. F. McKinney, November 11, 1839, Williams Papers; Gammel, *Laws of Texas*, I, 1024, II, 325; Galveston County Deed Records, C, 97; Harold Schoen, "The Free Negro in the Republic of Texas," *Southwestern Historical Quarterly* 40 (October 1936): 83, 106–108.

[39] Grand Lodge notice, Austin *Texas Sentinel*, February 5, 1840; T. F. McKinney to S. M. Williams, December 10, 1839, Williams Papers.

[40] Lamar to House of Representatives, December 23, 1839, in Smither, *Journals of the Fourth Congress*, II, 231–233; James Hamilton to M. B. Lamar, January 7, 1840, *Lamar Papers*, III, 322; Willis W. Pratt (ed.), *Galveston Island: Or a Few Months Off the Coast of Texas: The Journal of Francis C. Sheridan, 1839–1840*, pp. 110–111; James Hamilton to James Starr, January 5, 1840, in Conner, *Texas Treasury Papers*, I, 354.

Williams returned to Galveston by the end of February and met his brother Henry Howell and Samuel St. John, who had come to Texas on business because commercial affairs in the east remained at a standstill. Henry Williams had talked with James Hamilton before the latter again embarked for France seeking a loan for Texas. They agreed that one of the new naval vessels should carry a cargo of Brazos cotton to LeHavre to illustrate the potential of the new republic, and Williams offered to expedite the matter. This proposal failed to win the support of Lamar, who sent the navy instead to patrol in Mexican waters. The French government had agreed to a commercial treaty with Texas the previous autumn and had sent Alphonse DuBois de Saligny to the Republic as chargé d'affaires. From New York, Saligny sent Williams, as chairman of the house financial committee, his country's recommendations regarding tariff on French imports, and by the time he reached Galveston on January 17, 1840, he had received a reply. Williams assured the chargé that the rates had been redrawn in keeping with his suggestions, good news for which Saligny took personal credit when informing his superiors.[41]

Besides endorsing the plan to ship cotton to France, Williams actively worked to influence the British in order to hasten the pending negotiations for recognition and commercial agreements. Francis C. Sheridan, a grandson of the playwright, visited Texas to analyze the conditions for the British Foreign Office. At his suggestion, Williams wrote a lengthy memoir defending the struggle against Santa Anna and emphasizing the necessity for slave labor in cotton production. Though defensive about slavery, he explained how the British could prevent the United States from annexing Texas by recognizing the independent Republic. In addition, this action would strike a blow against southern planters, an argument designed to assuage the strong abolition sentiment in England. In order to obtain British recognition, Williams suggested that Texas might assume a portion of the Mexican debt owed to English capitalists and possibly even pay something to Mexico in exchange for freedom. Sheridan incorporated this information into his report, and be-

[41] S. M. Williams to M. B. Lamar, April 9, 1840, *Lamar Papers*, III, 365–266; Saligny to Mole, January 19, 1840, in Nancy Nichols Barker (trans. and ed.), *The French Legation in Texas*, I, 120.

fore the end of the year, Great Britain signed a commercial treaty with Texas that was quickly ratified in Austin, although official recognition was delayed until the arrival of a chargé d'affaires in 1842.[42]

Complete chaos threatened Galveston in June, 1840, after the election of officials under the new charter secured by Williams. A residency requirement of one year and a property qualification of currently paid taxes on a minimum of five hundred dollars' worth of real estate disfranchised one-half the island city's voters. The new electorate chose conservative John H. Walton as mayor and elected nine aldermen in sympathy with their views, but Mayor Allen, whose term under the old charter did not expire until 1841, ignored the change and refused to surrender the records. Finally, an armed force led by McKinney stormed Allen's home, forcing his capitulation and thus ending the "Charter War." Four years later, the city obtained permission to alter the charter and subsequently dropped the property restriction and allowed the franchise for all white male taxpayers who had resided one year in the city.[43]

Williams did not run for reelection to the congress in 1840, but the conservative faction maintained its control of political affairs by electing Michel B. Menard to represent the county in the lower house. Because Francis Moore, the editor of the Houston *Telegraph*, had won the three-year term as senator for the three-county district, Galveston exerted little influence in the upper house.

Focusing his entire attention on business, Williams petitioned congress for permission to issue small denomination paper notes through McKinney and Williams to ease the lack of circulating money. Merchants in both New Orleans and Texas accepted the depreciating Texas Redbacks only at discount, which antagonized their customers. Small notes circulating at par would thus facilitate commercial transactions. Through the influence of Congressmen Menard and Houston, the measure passed in 1841, and the firm issued $30,000 in small bills in the amounts of twenty-five and fifty

[42] Pratt, *Galveston Island*, pp. vii–ix; S. M. Williams to Captain Ramsay, n.d., *ibid.*, pp. 130–148; Siegel, *Political History of the Republic*, p. 150.

[43] Gammel, *Laws of Texas*, II, 440; Hayes, *Galveston*, 363–365, 402–409, 411; Gammel, *Laws of Texas*, II, 999–1006; Galveston *Weekly News*, February 24, 1844.

cents and one, two, and three dollars. The notes were secured by $60,000 in real property—land and slaves—belonging to Sam Williams and his brother Nat, and McKinney and his younger brother, James, who composed the reorganized McKinney, Williams and Company after 1840. The commission agents agreed to pay specie on demand, restrict interest rates, and furnish annual reports to the congress. Section 10 of the act, nevertheless, expressed the reluctance of some legislators in granting such a privilege: "Banking privileges, as a general rule, being inexpedient, the privilege granted to McKinney, Williams and Company, are . . . in consideration of their having made large advances to the government at an early period of its existence." Despite one contemporary's description of the "little bank's" issue as "trifling," this new circulation of small notes had an immediate salutary effect.[44]

McKinney and Williams continued to dominate the commission business along the coast because of their favorable connections in the east. Henry Howell Williams sent his own vessels to Galveston with building material and goods to exchange for cotton, and through his efforts a large English brig direct from Liverpool anchored off the McKinney and Williams's wharf in 1839. Their chief rival, Robert Mills of Columbia, had doubted that such a vessel would come, but when the *Ambassador* actually appeared, he relinquished his claims to Brazos cotton so that the huge ship could be loaded with Texas produce. Henry Howell Williams had to guarantee Mills's advances to the planters, but the advantage of advertising the port of Galveston and Texas cotton in Great Britain was worth the effort.[45]

The Williams brothers supported Sam Houston in the vitriolic presidential campaign in 1841. David G. Burnet, who opposed the Old Hero, revived all the old charges against Sam Williams during

---

[44] Sam Houston to S. M. Williams, July 28, 1841, Williams Papers; Gammel, *Laws of Texas*, II, 598–600; Arthur Ikin, *Texas: Its History, Topography, Agriculture, Commerce, and General Statistics*, p. 86.

[45] T. F. McKinney to S. M. Williams, July 16, November 3, 1838, January 27, February 22, 1839, Williams Papers. For a detailed account of the rivalry in cotton buying, see Abigail Curlee Holbrook, "Cotton Marketing in Antebellum Texas," *Southwestern Historical Quarterly* 73 (April 1970): 431–447.

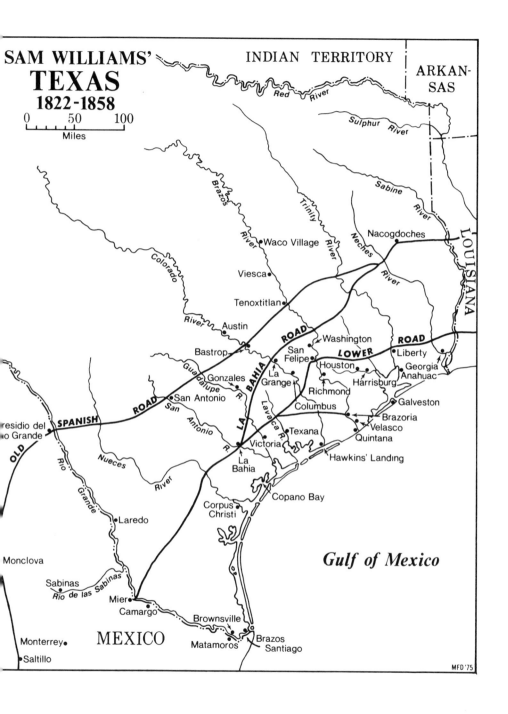

SAM WILLIAMS'
TEXAS
1822-1858

0   50   100

Miles

INDIAN TERRITORY

ARKAN-
SAS

Red River

Sulphur River

Brazos River

Sabine River

Trinity River

Neches River

●Waco Village

Nacogdoches●

LOUISIANA

Viesca●

Colorado River

Tenoxtitlan●

River   Austin

Bastrop

ROAD

Washington

ROAD

San
Felipe●

LOWER

●Liberty

Guadalupe River

●Gonzales

LA BAHIA

La
Grange

Houston●

●Georgia
Anahuac

Harrisburg●

San
Antonio

ROAD

●San Antonio

Richmond

Columbus

●Galveston

resido del
o Grande

SPANISH

Antonio R.

Lavaca R.

●Texana

Brazoria
●Velasco
Quintana

OLD

Rio Grande

Nueces River

Victoria●

La
Bahia

Hawkins' Landing

Copano Bay

●Laredo

Corpus
Christi●

Gulf of Mexico

Monclova

Sabinas
Rio de las Sabinas

Mier●

Camargo●

Brownsville

Monterrey●

●Saltillo

MEXICO

Matamoros●

Brazos
Santiago

MFD '75

Samuel May Williams in Knights Templar regalia, photograph circa 1854.
Courtesy, Rosenberg Library, Galveston, Texas.

Sarah Scott Williams. The portrait hangs in the Williams house in Galveston. Courtesy, Rosenberg Library, Galveston, Texas.

Austin May Williams, late 1860's. Courtesy, Virginia Harshman.

Thomas F. McKinney, Williams's long-time business associate. From Louis J. Wortham, *A History of Texas from Wilderness to Commonwealth.*

Plan of San Felipe de Austin, 1824. The map is in the *Registro* in the Spanish Archives. Courtesy, General Land Office, Austin, Texas.

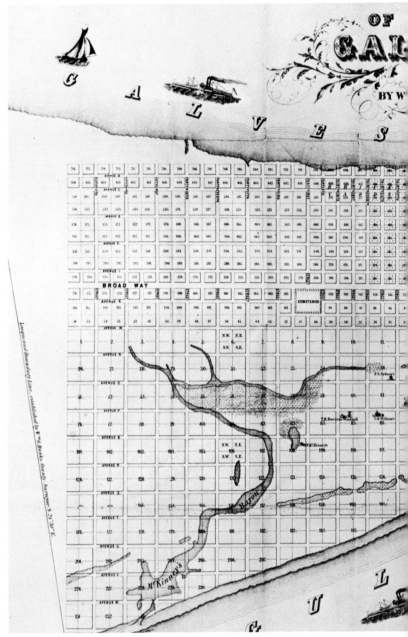

Plan of the City of Galveston, 1845. Williams's and McKinney's residences are shown on outer lots 86 and 108, respectively. Courtesy, Rosenberg Library, Galveston, Texas.

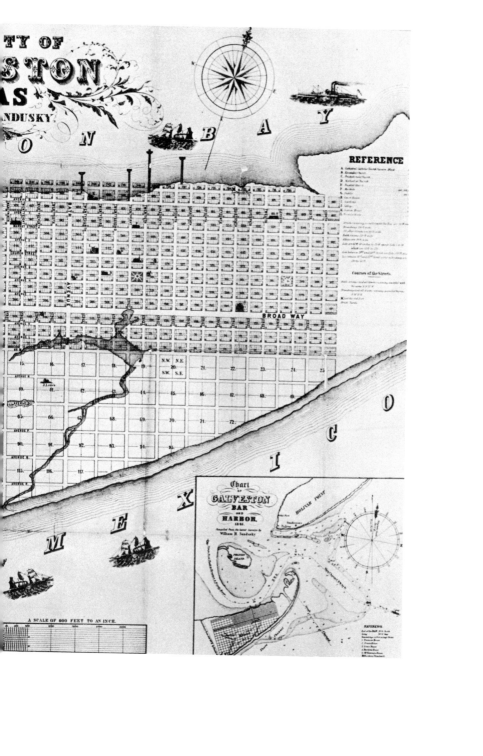

The *Invincible*, a clipper-rigged schooner purchased by Williams in Baltimore for the Republic in 1835, was seized by the U.S. Navy for piracy in 1836. Sketch by Emil Bunjes. Courtesy, Port of Galveston.

The *Zavala*. Originally called the *Charleston*, the steam packet was purchased in New York by Williams and rechristened and refurbished for service in the Texas Navy in 1838. Sketch by Emil Bunjes. Courtesy, Rosenberg Library, Galveston, Texas.

The *Austin* (*left*), flagship of the Texas Navy, and the *San Antonio,* one of three identical schooners, were among the six vessels Williams had built in Baltimore in 1839 for Texas. Sketch by F. Karppi. Courtesy, Port of Galveston.

The brig *Wharton,* built in Baltimore in 1839, sailed with the *Austin* under Texas Commodore Edwin W. Moore—against Houston's wishes— to aid rebel Yucatan in May, 1843. Sketch by Don Davis. Courtesy, Port of Galveston.

Uncirculated demand note for one dollar on the Commercial and Agricultural Bank, Columbia. William Wharton showed one of these notes to John C. Calhoun in 1836 as evidence of Texas' stability and development. Courtesy, Rosenberg Library, Galveston, Texas.

Demand note for one dollar on the Commercial and Agricultural Bank, Galveston, circulated after Williams activated his Mexican banking charter in 1848. A token fine of $2,000, for issuing just one of these notes, was finally levied against the C & A in the final antibanking suit. Courtesy, Rosenberg Library, Galveston, Texas.

Contract between Samuel May Williams, naval commissioner under Sam Houston, and Frederick Dawson, Baltimore shipbuilder, dated January 3, 1839, for six new vessels for the Texas Republic. Courtesy, Rosenberg Library, Galveston, Texas.

The Williams house in Galveston, as it looked about 1870–1880. The cupola was not rebuilt after fire damaged the upper story in the 1880's. The sketch by Don Davis is based on a photograph in the Rosenberg Library. Courtesy, Port of Galveston Magazine.

the race, not only his land-speculating activities but even the fact he had come to Texas under an assumed name. The Galveston *Civilian* and the Austin *Sentinel* defended the Galvestonian, who was rumored to be named to Houston's cabinet should he win. In their estimation, Williams had proved himself a patriot, "governed by that best of all incentives, his country's good."[46] On September 6, Williams and over seven thousand others went to the polls and cast ballots for Houston; Burnet received only half that number. Although he did not become a member of the cabinet, Williams would, nevertheless, take an active role in shaping foreign policy under the new administration.

[46] Anthony Butler to S. M. Williams, August 23, 1841; [Williams] draft to *Galvestonian*, n.d., Williams Papers; Austin *Texas Sentinel*, June 13, 1840, August 5, September 2, 1841.

CHAPTER 8

A Sam Houston Man Betrayed
1841-1844

With the reelection of Sam Houston as president, Samuel May Williams and his three brothers expected that their interests would continue to prosper. Nathaniel Felton Williams had suffered a double blow with the dissolution of Dobson and Williams at Mobile following the Panic of 1837 and the death of his wife, Elizabeth Dobson, in 1838. He moved his five children and his widowed sister, Eliza W. Sweet, to Galveston, where he had purchased a house just west of Samuel's residence. He entered the firm of McKinney and Williams in 1840 but sold his interest in 1842 when he returned to New Orleans to become a senior member in Williams, Whitman, and Company. Nat married his cousin Martha Elizabeth, the daughter of uncle Nathaniel F. Williams of Baltimore in 1841, a union that perhaps made possible the partnership in New Orleans. In addition to his commercial interests, Nat had bought the Oyster Creek league in Fort Bend County from Sam in 1838, and with the aid of Matthew R. Williams he developed a successful sugar plantation, which he sold in the 1850's at great profit.[1]

For a time, Henry Howell Williams was the most successful of the four brothers. While serving as Texas consul at Baltimore during the first Houston administration, he managed a busy commission

[1] Fort Bend County Deed Records, A, 246, 251; N. F. Williams to W. B. Ochiltree, January 25, 1845, in Seymour V. Conner (ed.), *Texas Treasury Papers: Letters Received in the Treasury Department of the Republic of Texas, 1836–1846*, III, 1075–1076; S. M. Williams to wife, May 31, 1844, Samuel May Williams Papers, Rosenberg Library, Galveston.

agency in the Maryland city and engaged in extensive commercial interests in the new republic. He invested heavily in Texas real estate, including shares in the Galveston City Company, and became president of the board in December, 1841. He bought the commission business from McKinney and Williams in 1842 and made it a branch of H. H. Williams and Company of Baltimore; eventually he relinquished his interest at Galveston to his eldest son, John.[2] Henry's wife, Rebecca Wilkins, never made Galveston her home, although she made several extended visits with Sam and Sarah in company with Henry. Rebecca preferred their country home near Green Springs, Maryland, northwest of Baltimore.

When Henry bought the commission business, Thomas F. McKinney began liquidating his interests in Galveston with the intent of moving to his ranch in Travis County across the river from Austin. McKinney had never liked banking and had always left that portion of the business to Sam. The "little bank" continued to be Sam Williams's primary interest after 1842, operating under the original title of McKinney and Williams.[3] The Texas economy was making steady recovery from the Panic of 1837 when renewed trouble with Mexico threatened in 1842, and Sam Williams would again be summoned to public service by Sam Houston.

After his inauguration in December, 1841, President Sam Houston reversed his predecessor's policy toward Mexico, but despite his efforts to return to a state of armed neutrality, problems with Mexico increased. In January, 1842, Texas learned about the capture of the Santa Fe expedition, an armed mercantile party sent by President Mirabeau B. Lamar the previous summer to enlist the support of the residents along the upper Rio Grande. The Texans were arrested and sent to prison in Mexico, where political instability had allowed Santa Anna to regain the presidency. In retaliation for the Texan incursion at Santa Fe, the Mexican leader ordered raids on San Antonio twice during 1842. Moving the government away from the frontier to Washington-on-the-Brazos, Houston reluctantly called up the militia, but only to act defensively, not to attack Mata-

[2] Galveston City Company broadside, December 20, 1841, Rosenberg Library; Galveston *Civilian*, March 9, July 27, 1842.

[3] T. F. McKinney to S. M. Williams, January 5, 1842, Williams Papers.

moros as many urged. The Galvestonians feared an invasion from
the sea. The once-fine navy was useless: the one seaworthy ship in
port was not prepared for duty, and the remainder were either in-
capacitated or away. The islanders' panic subsided, however, when
George W. Hockley, formerly in Houston's cabinet, arrived to direct
defense efforts. But commerce continued to stagnate because New
Orleans shippers hesitated to send vessels and goods to Texas. Then,
in September, the coast experienced the most severe hurricane since
1837. The cotton crop, already damaged by worms, was destroyed,
and residents estimated the total damage as high as eighty thousand
dollars. These events helped to ruin Henry Howell Williams's investments and led him into bankruptcy.[4]

The Mexican attacks on Texas rekindled public sympathy in the
United States, and the annexation issue surfaced again in spite of
the continued opposition from abolitionists, who feared any exten-
sion or expansion of slavery. Houston sent James Reily as minister to
Washington with instructions to explore the possibility of annexation, but the time was unfavorable. The British preferred an independent Texas for economic and political reasons, and one of three
treaties between England and the Republic (commerce, suppression
of the African trade, and mediation with Mexico) provided that
pressure would be exerted on Mexico for the recognition of Texan
independence. Though many Texas residents desired annexation to
the United States, Sam Williams and several other businessmen in
Galveston did not. Whether or not President Houston favored annexation at this time remains unclear, but he began a series of canny
diplomatic maneuvers that ultimately resulted in union.[5]

In the spring of 1843, Houston summoned Williams and George
W. Hockley back into public service as commissioners for the osten-
sible purpose of negotiating a permanent armistice between Texas
and Mexico. Until this time, Williams usually had backed the hero

---

[4] Joseph Milton Nance, *Attack and Counter-Attack: The Texas-
Mexican Frontier, 1842*, pp. 27, 47–48, 194, 257, 261–268, 297–299,
316–323, 424–426; W. Eugene Hollon and Ruth Lapham Butler (eds.),
William Bollaert's Texas, pp. 136–143, 155–157; Galveston *Civilian*, Sep-
tember 24, 1842; H. H. Williams to S. M. Williams, December 24, 1842,
Williams Papers.

[5] Llerena B. Friend, *Sam Houston: The Great Designer*, pp. 115–161.

of San Jacinto in politics, and in return Houston had favored Williams's financial schemes. At one time, the president had presented his supporter with an engraved silver spectacles case.[6] This diplomatic mission, however, would lead to a complete rupture of their friendship.

While Texas agents in Washington suggested that the door might be open for an offer to join the United States, Houston was actively cultivating the friendship of Captain Charles Elliot, the British chargé d'affaires in Texas, and urging him to secure Mexican recognition of the Republic's independence. Early in 1843, Houston received a message from President Santa Anna that unexpectedly provided time for the Texas executive's stratagems to mature. Santa Anna released James W. Robinson, provisional lieutenant governor in 1836, who had been captured during the raid on San Antonio in 1842 and incarcerated at Castle Perote. In return for his freedom Robinson carried an offer of amnesty from the Mexican president if Texas would return to the Mexican republic. The constitution adopted in 1836 provided that the states were departments of the federal government and totally subservient. To make this centralized arrangement more palatable to Texas, Santa Anna personally guaranteed that no troops would be stationed within its borders and that the Anglo-Americans might initiate local laws and elect representatives to the national congress, favors not enjoyed by the other departments. This offer, of course, was unacceptable to most Texans, but, in order to gain time, Houston proceeded as if he were willing to consider the plan. In June the president announced a one-year armistice with Mexico, during which time commissioners would meet to draw up a permanent proposal.[7]

Why the president selected Williams and George W. Hockley to be commissioners to Mexico is not explained in extant correspondence. Both men had long supported Houston, though Hockley had resigned as secretary of war and marine during the past year when he disagreed with certain aspects of executive policy. He had served as artillery officer at San Jacinto and had accompanied Santa Anna from Texas to Washington in 1836; on his new mission he

[6] The spectacles case (n.d.) is on display at the Rosenberg Library in Galveston.

[7] Friend, *Sam Houston*, pp. 85–86.

would act as the military representative, while Williams would be a general commissioner. The latter, of course, understood Latin American culture in addition to speaking Spanish fluently, an important consideration in view of Houston's plan for lengthy negotiations in order to gain time for the achievement of his ulterior diplomatic objectives. In addition to these qualifications, the pair were personally loyal to Houston. Moreover, they were quite acceptable to the Mexican officials, for neither favored annexation to the United States. In fact, Williams and Hockley were both willing to accept some sort of dignified relationship with Mexico.[8]

The president needed representatives who could convince Mexico of the sincerity of their deliberations, because, while they were so employed, he intended to use the mission as a diversionary tactic. In later years he described his diplomatic moves preceding annexation as "more coy than forward" in regard to his dealings with Great Britain.[9] The same phrase might well apply to the dalliance with Mexico, which Houston intended to whet the appetite of the United States. The older republic would then become the pursuer, determined to add Texas to the union.

Williams probably conferred with the president in April, soon after reading the published letter from Santa Anna's envoy, James W. Robinson, explaining the Mexican offer. The Galvestonian took the steamer to Houston on April 4 and could have connected with the stagecoach to Washington-on-the-Brazos.[10] Obviously, tentative oral arrangements preceded the instructions sent by Secretary of State Anson Jones in August indicating that the pair had agreed to go to Mexico. In order to persuade Hockley and Williams to undertake what was, because of the degrading terms initially offered by Mexico, a delicate mission, Houston must have assured his commis-

    [8] William Kennedy to Lord Aberdeen, June 18, 1844, in Ephraim Douglass Adams (ed.), British Diplomatic Correspondence Concerning the Republic of Texas, 1838–1846, pp. 338–342; G. W. Hockley to Anson Jones, February 28, 1844, in Anson Jones, Memoranda and Official Correspondence Relating to the Republic of Texas, pp. 324–325.

    [9] Friend, Sam Houston, p. 115.

    [10] Telegraph and Texas Register, April 5, 1843. This issue also reprinted Robinson's March 27 letter to the Galveston Civilian outlining the terms offered by Mexico.

sioners that he would support them against charges of entertaining unpatriotic motives. He had privately promised to stand by Robinson, although he warned him that his role as bearer of Santa Anna's proposition would be misunderstood by the public. Most Texans believed that Robinson had acted only in self-interest and was willing to go through with the charade in order to gain his freedom. Williams's and Hockley's motives were more difficult to fathom; many contemporaries supposed that the pair accepted the inglorious mission to Mexico as a means of striking a blow against annexation.[11]

As the mission was first envisioned, the commissioners were to meet with their Mexican counterparts in late September somewhere on the Rio Grande, possibly at Matamoros or Laredo. There they were to discuss the terms of the truce with General Adrián Woll. It was anticipated that they would then continue on to Mexico City to negotiate the release of the Texas prisoners taken in the raids on San Antonio and those who had surrendered to the Mexican army after the abortive attack on Mier in December, 1842.[12] The latter was an unauthorized invasion of Mexico executed by a band of three hundred volunteers seeking revenge—and booty—for the incursions at San Antonio. Those taken at Mier aroused popular sympathy after Santa Anna ordered a decimation following their escape and recapture during the march south to prison. Seventeen of the 170 men drew black beans and were shot, thus making martyrs out of the participants.

During the preliminary exchanges by letter, the Mexican authorities insisted that Texas must submit to the absolute sovereignty of Mexico. Elliot, the British chargé and a close friend of both President Houston and Williams, suggested that in order to secure peace, Texas should appear to acquiesce. A veteran army officer in the Queen's service, Elliot believed that by a judicious choice of words, Texas might "reunite" with Mexico, if Texas secured the Rio Grande

---

[11] Joseph William Schmitz, *Texan Statecraft, 1836–1845*, pp. 199–200; Justin H. Smith, *The Annexation of Texas*, p. 172.

[12] Charles Elliot to Percy W. Doyle, July 30, August 2, 1843; G. W. Hill to Adrián Woll, July 29, 1843, in Adams, *British Diplomatic Correspondence*, pp. 239, 243.

as its boundary in return.[13] Although Texas had claimed the Rio Grande as its boundary in 1836, the land between it and the Nueces historically belonged to the states of Tamaulipas and Nuevo León. A legal right to this area between the rivers would add land reputed to be rich in minerals and would also give Texas navigational rights on the Rio Grande, an important consideration for the future development of commerce.

In August Secretary of State Anson Jones sent Hockley and Williams explanations of the administration's intentions. These letters, no longer extant, probably encouraged the pair to proceed carefully and slowly. The president advised Jones not to set a specific time for the meeting with General Woll until later and to "hint" to the commissioners what was expected of them. The major concern at this time seemed to be the return of the Texas prisoners.[14]

Having accepted the presidential commission and awaiting their final instructions in Galveston, Hockley and Williams found themselves in an awkward position on July 14 when Commodore Edwin W. Moore triumphantly returned to the island from an unauthorized cruise to Yucatan. In order to reduce expenses and avoid a confrontation with Mexico, Houston had appointed Williams one of three commissioners to de-activate the Texas Navy the preceding January.[15] Williams had declined because, like Hockley and most Galvestonians, he favored the sagacious use of the vessels for which he had contracted in 1838. President Houston had misjudged his man in this instance. Moore convinced James Morgan and William Bryan, the two remaining commissioners, that he should sail from New Orleans to attack the Mexican fleet, and Morgan even joined the cruise in defiance of Houston's orders. Morgan explained later that he was surprised to find the ships and crews in "such apple pie order" and believed that an attack on the Mexican fleet would end

---

[13] Charles Elliot to Percy W. Doyle, July 30, 1843, *ibid.*, p. 239; Charles Elliot to Anson Jones, August 28, 1843, in Jones, *Memoranda*, p. 248.

[14] Sam Houston to Anson Jones, July 30, August 3, 1843; Charles Elliot to Anson Jones, August 28, 1843, in Jones, *Memoranda*, pp. 233, 241–242.

[15] G. W. Hill to S. M. Williams, January 23, 1843, Williams Papers.

the plan to invade Texas. Responding to this insubordination, "Old Sam" declared Moore a pirate and ordered his arrest. On board his six-hundred-ton flagship, *Austin*, and accompanied by the four-hundred-ton brig, *Wharton*, Moore broke through the Mexican blockade of rebel Yucatan on May 1, 1843. By the end of June, the Texas ship assisted by the small Yucatan navy forced the withdrawal of the Mexican fleet including two large British-built steamers, one of which was the first iron vessel constructed at the Laird shipyard at Birkenhead, England, in 1842. Arriving in Galveston on July 14, Moore received a hero's welcome, and the sheriff refused to follow the executive order to arrest the commodore. While rowdies hanged Houston in effigy, a committee organized a testimonial dinner in honor of the victorious navy. Williams and Hockley diplomatically sent their regrets, stating that their health prevented their attending such functions.[16]

The Old Hero won in the end. His order that Moore be dishonorably discharged prompted the other officers to resign in protest, thus saving him the trouble of abolishing their commissions. He tried to sell the vessels, but the Galvestonians prevented the disposal of the ships by raising a fund toward their purchase. For the time being, the ships remained in storage and ultimately were transferred to the United States. When annexation negotiations resumed, Houston requested a United States patrol in the Gulf to prevent attack from irate Mexico.[17]

Williams also had an embarrassing personal quarrel with Moore. The thirty-three-year-old commodore, a veteran of fifteen years in the United States Navy, was an opportunist in advancing both his career and his fortune. In 1842 he gave Samuel St. John, Williams's brother-in-law, $20,000 in unsigned exchequer notes given to him by Houston to offer in payment for naval repairs in New Orleans. In return, St. John surrendered shares of stock belonging to his wife and her two sisters. Later each participant accused the other of dishonest dealing; the commodore said that St. John had

---

[16] James Morgan to J. Reed, May 11, 1843, Morgan Papers, Rosenberg Library; Tom Henderson Wells, *Commodore Moore and the Texas Navy*, pp. 128–162; Galveston *Independent Chronicle*, August 1, 1843.

[17] Wells, *Commodore Moore*, pp. 163–165.

secreted the notes that he had offered only as security, causing Moore great embarrassment. The Williams brothers believed that Moore had appropriated the stock for himself, shares that St. John had offered only as a loan to be used as security.[18] While cruising that same year, Moore heard of "unfavorable remarks" purportedly made by Sam Williams; he angrily addressed a letter to the Galvestonian demanding an explanation of the affront to his honor. He never received a reply. When the commodore landed in July, he saw Williams in the crowd and pointedly ignored him. A week later Moore sent the banker a note demanding redress of past grievances; if not satisfied, he threatened to "resort to another course." Drafting his reply on the reverse of the note that he had just received, Williams acknowledged having received the 1842 letter from Moore. He had not replied to it, however, because he thought that the commodore had only been venting his hostility rather than seeking an explanation. If Moore sincerely wanted the alleged remark explained, he had only to ask. The next day Williams received a polite request which he immediately answered. Three days later Moore apologized for the "disagreeable" occurrence at the dock, thus ending the immediate affair.[19]

Williams and Hockley reported to Washington-on-the-Brazos in September, 1843, to receive their official commissions. The conference with the Mexican representatives had been delayed, and they now hoped to hold the meetings in November and return by Christmas. George W. Hill, secretary of war and marine, gave them written orders for the establishment of a one-year armistice during which time two other commissioners would journey to the Mexican capital with full powers to settle all differences. In the meantime, the Houston administration postponed naming the plenipotentiaries, pleading lack of funds; the excuse was partially true, but the intent was to gain time. Part of the delay stemmed from diplomatic procedures. Mexico refused to acknowledge that she was dealing with an independent power and continued to address correspondence to

[18] *Ibid.*, pp. 6–7, 100–101; David Reed to William H. Williams, July 26, 1857, Williams Papers.

[19] E. W. Moore to S. M. Williams, July 21, 24, 1843; S. M. Williams to E. W. Moore, July 21, 1843, Williams Papers.

"Mr." Houston, an insult to the Republic. Santa Anna intended to recognize the Texas agents only as supplicants for amnesty.[20]

The secretary of state instructed the commissioners to prolong the meetings and may also have issued a memorandum that has since disappeared. Houston intended to capitalize on both the leisurely discussions and the delay in communication caused by the remoteness of the conference. Neither Williams nor Hockley was privy to the annexation maneuvers being carried out; Williams understood that the delays would permit the British minister more time to work in the Mexican capital for the recognition of Texan independence.[21]

One article in the instructions from the war department demanded that no troops woud be stationed in a neutral ground between the Rio Grande and the Nueces River, a request so blatantly hostile to Mexican interest that it was possibly designed to upset the negotiations. The Texas Republic unilaterally claimed the Rio Grande as its southwestern boundary and in the 1836 treaty with Santa Anna had forced his acquiescence. General Martín Perfecto de Cós had withdrawn his force "across the Rio Grande" in 1835, and so had General José Urrea, acting under orders from Santa Anna in 1836. Mexico, of course, continued to recognize the Sabine River as its northeastern boundary with the United States, a view that remained in force until 1848 at the end of the war between Mexico and the United States. Besides a more readily identifiable boundary than the Nueces and the potential of navigation, the Rio Grande would give Texas the rich trading center at Santa Fe. Crucial to the immediate problem were the Mexican garrisons at Laredo and Brazos Santiago, the pass north of the ill-defined mouth of the

[20] Republic of Texas to S. M. Williams, September 25, 1843, Williams Papers; G. W. Hill to G. W. Hockley and S. M. Williams, September 26, 1843, in Charles Adams Gulick et al. (eds.), *The Papers of Mirabeau Buonaparte Lamar,* IV, pt. 1, 23–24; Charles Elliot to Aberdeen, October 10, 1843, in Adams, *British Diplomatic Correspondence,* pp. 267–268; *Telegraph and Texas Register,* July 26, 1843.

[21] Herbert P. Gambrell, *Anson Jones: The Last President of Texas,* p. 290; G. W. Hockley to Anson Jones, February 28, 1844, in Jones, *Memoranda,* pp. 324–325; S. M. Williams to the Voters of the Second Congressional District, March 13, 1846, *Lamar Papers,* VI, 17–19.

Rio Grande, both within the Texas "neutral ground" as defined in the instructions. Either through ignorance or by intent, Anson Jones led the commissioners to believe that Santa Anna would agree to the withdrawal of such troops.[22]

Williams and Hockley sailed for Matamoros on the sloop *Cutter* the second week in October, 1843, although some unknown person who apparently opposed the mission tried unsuccessfully to scuttle the ship. The people of Matamoros welcomed the Texans, but rainy weather prevented them from starting up the river for Woll's headquarters. Williams warned his wife that she might not hear from him for some time because of the poor communications once they ascended the river. He and Hockley hoped "to do something beneficial to our country," he wrote, but if unsuccessful in this endeavor, they would at least try to do no harm.[23]

Early in November they finally started upriver and several days' travel brought them to Mier, the scene of the Texan attack only eleven months before. Here the townspeople prepared a banquet in their honor, surprising the commissioners, who had expected hostility. Before leaving the village, the pair received a communiqué from Woll changing the place of meeting from Laredo to Sabinas, a small remote village west of Mier on the road between Laredo and Monterrey. Although Woll provided them with every courtesy upon their arrival in Sabinas, they could not begin the discussions, because one of the Mexican commissioners appointed by Woll was ill. The enforced inactivity depressed Williams, since he knew it would delay the return to his family.[24]

The agents finally met with Colonels Alexander Ybara and Cayetano Montero in December and reported only slow progress

[22] G. W. Hockley to Anson Jones, January 7, 1844, in Jones, *Memoranda*, pp. 299–300.

[23] *Ibid.*; Charles Elliot to Aberdeen, October 10, 1843, in Adams, *British Diplomatic Correspondence*, pp. 267–268; J. D. Marks to A. P. Upshur, October 19, 1843, Dispatches Received by the Department of State from U.S. Consuls in Matamoros, 1826–1906, microfilm copy in Latin American Collection, University of Texas at Austin; S. M. Williams to wife, October 24, 29, 1843, Williams Papers.

[24] Galveston *Civilian*, December 9, 1843; S. M. Williams to wife, November 24, 1843, Samuel May and Austin May Williams Papers, Barker History Center, University of Texas at Austin.

during the first week of conferences. Ybara and Montero politely studied the Texan proposals, but they refused to accept any limitation on stationing troops east of the Rio Grande until they could consult with their superiors in the capital. Three weeks passed in this manner, but on Christmas Day Williams wrote to his brother that they momentarily expected a favorable reply satisfactory to all parties.[25] Because of their isolation and poor communication, rumors persisted in Texas that one of the commissioners had died from fever and that the conferences had broken down completely.[26]

The four negotiators met again on January 1, 1844, but to Williams's dismay the supreme government delivered an ultimatum directing the consultation to close eight days after signing the protocol just received from the capital. That document included all the proposals submitted by Hockley and Williams except the one providing for the neutral ground, which the Mexican authorities labeled "inadmissable." Unsure of the proper course to pursue in response to the abrupt and puzzling order to close the discussions by January 9, Williams and Hockley labored to draft a reply. After expressing a sincere desire for peace and harmony, Williams asked Woll to grant them more time, twenty to twenty-five days, so that they might consult with the Texas government. The commander in chief, however, refused to deviate from the clear and final instructions received from Santa Anna. The official memorandum stated that no concession would be made to the controversial article or in granting additional time to agents who appeared with insufficient power to negotiate. Colonel Ybara tried to soften the haughty reply by adding that the Texans could remain at Sabinas to await a response from Mexico City.[27]

Disappointed that they had to wait for replies from Mexico City and Washington-on-the-Brazos and thus delay their return home, Hockley and Williams settled down to wait at Sabinas. They

---

[25] Charles Elliot to Aberdeen, January 15, 1844, in Adams, *British Diplomatic Correspondence*, pp. 295–297; New Orleans *Bee*, quoted in the Galveston *Civilian*, January 31, 1844. For a copy of the Texan terms, see *Lamar Papers*, IV, pt. 1, 24–25.

[26] Houston *Morning Star*, December 7, 1843, January 4, 1844.

[27] Adrián Woll to the Texas commissioners, [January, 1844]; draft by Williams, [January 2, 1844]; Alexander Ybara and Cayetano Montero to Texas commissioners, January 3, 1844, Williams Papers.

sent reports to the president and secretary of state on January 7 explaining the temporary breakdown in negotiations; although they could not fathom the peremptory orders from the capital, Williams optimistically believed that the talks would resume.[28]

Williams and Hockley, of course, remained ignorant of the events taking place in the United States and Texas during their absence. President John Tyler's secretary of state, Abel P. Upshur, had offered to reopen annexation negotiations about the time that the pair had left Galveston. "Old Sam" cautiously declined the invitation, which made Upshur even more determined. In January, he sent assurances to Texas that the administration controlled sufficient votes for passage of the annexation treaty. Houston received this message at about the same time that he heard from his weary representatives at Sabinas. Santa Anna learned about the pending annexation talks and instructed Juan N. Almonte, the Mexican minister in Washington, D.C., to warn President Tyler that such a step would mean war between Mexico and the United States. Williams and Hockley probably speculated that loose talk of union with the United States had prompted the curt order they had received from the dictator, but they apparently believed that such reports were false. Hockley, for one, preferred war with Mexico to annexation to the United States.[29]

The commissioners' message reached Sam Houston the first week in February, and by return courier he expressed his sympathy that matters had not been "consummated" but added that one cannot always have the things one desired. He directed them to capitulate, saying, "But if nothing else can be done, and it should be necessary so to do, you will admit the article in question as presented by the Mexican Commissioners, and as communicated by you to his government."[30] The letter from Anson Jones instructed the negotia-

[28] S. M. Williams to wife, January 7, 1844, *ibid.*; G. W. Hockley to Anson Jones, January 7, 1844, in Jones, *Memoranda*, pp. 299–300; Charles Elliot to Aberdeen, March 15, 1844, in Adams, *British Diplomatic Correspondence*, pp. 301–302.

[29] G. W. Hockley to Anson Jones, February 28, 1844, in Jones, *Memoranda*, pp. 324–325.

[30] Sam Houston to Hockley and Williams, February 3, 1844, in George P. Garrison (ed.), *Diplomatic Correspondence of the Republic of*

tors to end their talks by March 1, a phrase that General Woll interpreted to mean that Texas would indeed be soon annexed.[31]

Even before this reply was returned from Texas, Santa Anna sent his own commissioners to Sabinas with new, more rigid, instructions. Brigadier General Antonio María Jaurequi and Colonel Manuel María Landeras replaced Woll's two representatives, and the new commissioners offered no concessions at all to the Texas agents. Humiliated by their limited power and possibly feeling that they might be imprisoned as mere agents of a rebellious department, Williams and Hockley apprehensively awaited the express rider from Texas. Upon receipt of their new instructions, the pair felt justified in signing the protocol offered by Santa Anna's agents: Texas would return to the Mexican republic on the same footing as the other states—as a mere department subservient to the central government. Although the document offered no advantage to Texas, Williams and Hockley affixed their signatures on February 15. Because of their lack of power, the convention in no way bound the Houston administration to adopt the provisions, nor would the agreement have any meaning until formally approved by both governments. According to a contemporary historian friendly toward Houston, Hockley and Williams could not refuse to sign the document, because they feared for their safety. Yet Anson Jones maintained that the commissioners had made a "great mistake" and exceeded their powers by endorsing the compact.[32]

Williams and Hockley immediately left Sabinas for the coast, where they wrote dispatches to be carried by courier to San Antonio while they waited for a ship to take them to Galveston. Learning that no vessel was expected soon, the men set out on horseback along the coast to Corpus Christi, where a regular packet called

Texas, II, 786–789. The Galveston *Civilian*, January 31, 1844, reported the arrival of the dispatch and understood it was "favorable."

[31] G. W. Hockley to Anson Jones, February 28, 1844, in Jones, *Memoranda*, pp. 324–325.

[32] Galveston *Civilian*, April 17, 1844; S. M. Williams to the Voters of the Second Congressional District, March 13, 1846, *Lamar Papers*, VI, 17–19; Henderson Yoakum, *History of Texas from Its First Settlement in 1685 to Its Annexation to the United States in 1846*, II, 422; M. P. Norton to Anson Jones, April 24, 1844, in Jones, *Memoranda*, p. 342.

each week. High water and a cold norther plagued the travelers, but they had ample opportunity to see the formidable sand dunes that formed tiers along Padre Island. They made connections with the boat at Corpus and landed at Galveston on March 26, where they paused with their families and friends before reporting in person to the president. They refused to comment on their mission, and their acquaintances speculated that they were very disappointed in their accomplishments.[33]

When Houston and Jones received the copies of the Mexican proposals in March, the tentative plans for annexation to the United States were underway. During the first part of February, 1844, just after he had sent the consoling letter and new instructions to Williams and Hockley at Sabinas, Houston had dispatched James Pinckney Henderson to aid the Texas chargé, Isaac Van Zandt, in negotiating a treaty to join Texas to the union. Unfortunately, Secretary of State Upshur died the last day in February after an explosion aboard a naval vessel, and for almost a month the negotiations were at a standstill until John C. Calhoun assumed the portfolio. Some doubt existed that the South Carolinian could shepherd the proposed treaty through the United States Senate, but on April 12 the Texas agents signed the document and the Texans waited impatiently for that body to take action.[34]

Williams and Hockley met with the president on April 5 in Houston. Although Anson Jones had accurately described the protocol as "different" from what had been agreed upon, there seemed to be no reproach from "Old Sam." Silently rejecting the Mexican document, Houston filed it in the archives as a curiosity. In a letter to Jones the following day, Houston blamed the failure of the Sabinas mission on the furor over annexation.[35] Later that same day, the

[33] Andrew Neill to Anson Jones, March 10, 1844, in Jones, *Memoranda*, pp. 325–326; W. Eugene Hollon and Ruth Lapham Butler (eds.), *William Bollaert's Texas*, pp. 329, 334; Houston *Morning Star*, March 30, 1844.

[34] Friend, *Sam Houston*, pp. 130–136.

[35] Anson Jones to Charles Elliot, March 18, 1844, in Jones, *Memoranda*, pp. 327–328; Sam Houston to Isaac Van Zandt and James Pinckney Henderson, May 10, 1844; Sam Houston to Anson Jones, April 6, 1844, in Amelia W. Williams and Eugene C. Barker (eds.), *The Writings of Sam Houston*, IV, 317–319, 295–296.

president and his two disappointed agents took the steamer to Galveston, where Houston held an informal private interview with the British consul. Elliot surmised that Houston had little faith in the success of the plan for annexation and that instead he relied on the British and French to force Mexico into recognizing Texan independence.[36] The Old Hero remained on the island impatiently waiting for word about the treaty, but he soon discovered that the United States senators intended to use the matter for political advantage during the early maneuvering in a presidential election year.[37]

The unacceptable terms offered by Santa Anna did not remain secret for long. In April the New Orleans *Bee* printed the details, copied from the official journal in Mexico City.[38] Within three weeks the Texas papers were publishing the armistice agreement, and, with the exception of the anti-Houston *Telegraph*, none censured Hockley and Williams, who had been "deceived" throughout. Even the *Telegraph* absolved the commissioners when their instructions appeared in May, and instead blamed the president for issuing secret instructions that caused such "patriotic" men to "flounder badly." The request to publish the original instructions came from those supporting Anson Jones for the presidency in the autumn elections. While Houston approved the request, he added a note to send "only" the orders from the war department, a word that suggests other, possibly more politically damaging instructions did exist.[39] If such a memorandum existed, it has since been lost or destroyed, possibly in the fire at the capitol in 1881.

President Houston's disavowal of their mission alienated Hockley and Williams from the Old Hero, and they blamed his activities for ruining any chances of success at Sabinas. The Houston news-

[36] *Telegraph and Texas Register*, April 10, 1844; Charles Elliot to Aberdeen, April 7, 1844, in Adams, *British Diplomatic Correspondence*, pp. 304–308.

[37] Friend, *Sam Houston*, pp. 137–138.

[38] DuBois de Saligny to Guizot, April 2, 1844, in Nancy Nichols Barker (trans. and ed.), *The French Legation in Texas*, II, 513.

[39] *Telegraph and Texas Register*, April 24, 1844; Houston *Morning Star*, May 4, 1844; *Telegraph and Texas Register*, May 15, 1844; M. P. Norton to Anson Jones, April 24, 1844, in Jones, *Memoranda*, p. 342; instructions are printed in *Lamar Papers*, IV, pt. 1, 23–25.

papers capitalized on this estrangement, and the commissioners complained about their rough treatment in the press. Close friends said that they had been "used" by Houston and Jones to facilitate annexation, not "duped" by the Mexicans. In the future, Williams would cooperate with Houston for political expediency, but his regard for the president diminished and by the late 1850's disappeared entirely.[40]

While the unhappy commissioners defended their honor in Texas, the United States Senate rejected the treaty of annexation. At about the same time, Santa Anna notified Houston that hostilities would resume because Texas had failed to send qualified agents to the capital as provided by the preliminary agreement signed at Sabinas. Jones, quite correctly, replied that neither side was bound by the treaty until both had signed, and therefore the terms remained inoperative.[41]

Disillusioned by the political chicanery, Williams returned to devote himself to business and remained aloof from political activities. He probably relished the disappointment of the pro-annexation party and wasted little sympathy on the president when the Galveston anti-Houston element heckled and jeered the Old Hero during a speech on the island.[42] The Mexican invasion failed to materialize because of political upheavals that ultimately removed Santa Anna from the presidency. Thus Texans could devote themselves to political squabbling prior to the September presidential election, a noisy contest between Secretary of State Jones and Vice-president Edward Burleson.

[40] William Kennedy to Aberdeen, June 18, 1844, in Adams, *British Diplomatic Correspondence*, p. 338; *The Galveston Weekly News*, May 11, 1844. Tura Compton Cressey (great-granddaughter of Williams) in "Col. Williams, Texas Pioneer" (typescript, 1932, Barker History Center), mentions Williams's hatred of the "general" but fails to explain the reason for it. Descendants continue to dislike Houston, explaining that Houston ordered the burning of Williams's house in San Felipe in 1836, which is untrue (Virginia Harshman to author, January 20, 1971).

[41] Anson Jones to Van Zandt, July 13, 1844, in Garrison, *Diplomatic Correspondence*, II, 289–290.

[42] Friend, *Sam Houston*, pp. 140–142.

CHAPTER 9

Enlightened Self-Interest
1844-1852

OVER twelve thousand men voted to select the fourth Texas president in September, 1844, but it is doubtful that Samuel May Williams cast a ballot for either candidate. Had Williams known that Anson Jones, the victor, had favored the British plan to encourage Mexico to recognize Texas's independence, he might have overcome his sense of betrayal and voted his interest. The secretary of state, however, had failed to forward President Houston's instructions to accept the Diplomatic Act to Ashbel Smith, the Texas chargé at London in June, 1844. Instead, he recalled the agent and planned to save the glory of negotiating such a solution for his own administration, after the fall election.[1]

Shortly after Jones's success at the polls, James K. Polk scored a narrow victory over his Whig opponent, Henry Clay, in the presidential race in the United States. Since Polk and the Democratic party had campaigned on an expansionist platform, his triumph revived hopes for the immediate annexation of Texas. After several months of debate, the United States Congress passed a joint resolution that would allow Texas to enter as a state as soon as the Texas voters agreed and approved a suitable constitution. A unique feature in this proposal permitted Texas to retain its public lands so that subsequent sales would raise sufficient revenue to pay the indebtedness incurred during the Republic.

While Congress was debating the terms of the joint resolution, British and French agents intensified their efforts to secure recog-

[1] Ashbel Smith, *Reminiscences of the Texas Republic*, pp. 61–63.

nition of the Republic from Mexico in order to prevent the proposed merger with the United States. Though successful in obtaining such terms from the Mexican government, they misjudged popular feeling in Texas. The Lone Star congress endorsed annexation in June, 1845, and a convention met in July to confirm the action and to write a state constitution. At the convention the only dissenting vote on annexation came from the Galveston delegate, Richard Bache, known for his antipathy toward Polk. Bache's vote reflected the opinion of Sam Williams and many other islanders. A popular referendum on annexation was scheduled for October.

Williams composed arguments against annexation for public consumption. In particular, he objected to the transfer of the Republic's customs house receipts to the United States and Polk's dispatch of federal troops to Corpus Christi even before the Texans voted on the merger. How, he asked, would the proposed state pay the bondholders and other legitimate creditors when its only assets, the public lands, brought in such little revenue?[2] Some islanders feared that their port might become a mere appendage to New Orleans; one observer estimated that a majority of Galvestonians preferred not to join the United States.[3] But in spite of this opposition, 4,500 Texans—about one-third the number who had participated in the presidential canvass thirteen months earlier—turned out and overwhelmingly endorsed annexation. Reporting the widespread voter apathy, the Houston *Telegraph* noted that Galveston recorded 121 negative votes, more than any other county, while 270 there approved union. In contrast, only 41 out of 285 persons in Harris County failed to affirm annexation.[4]

In spite of his recent disagreeable experience in public service, Sam Williams coveted a seat in the United States Congress as representative from the Second District, which encompassed the area west of the Trinity River. He consequently announced his candidacy

[2] "Memorandum of the present situation in Texas," [1845], in Williams's hand, Samuel May Williams Papers, Rosenberg Library, Galveston.

[3] *Telegraph and Texas Register*, April 23, 1845; James Morgan to Samuel Swartwout, January 22, 1845, quoted in Herbert P. Gambrell, *Anson Jones: The Last President of Texas*, p. 382; Smith, *Reminiscences*, pp. 72–73, 81.

[4] *Telegraph and Texas Register*, October 15, 22, 1845.

prior to the special election called for March 30, 1846, to choose the new state's congressmen to serve the remainder of the Twenty-ninth Congress. A number of candidates entered the lists in addition to Williams: Timothy Pillsbury and Thomas Jefferson Chambers of Brazoria, John M. Lewis and Joseph C. Megginson of Montgomery, and William C. Cooke of Bexar. Williams may have sought the congressional seat to restore his tarnished reputation, damaged by the unfavorable press treatment after his mission to Sabinas in 1844, but his primary reason for entering the race was undoubtedly self-interest. The firm of McKinney and Williams had not yet been reimbursed for the supplies it had furnished the revolutionary authorities in 1835 and 1836, and, in addition, the entire Williams clan held certificates of the funded debt.[5] As congressman, he intended to introduce legislation to shift the burden of paying the indebtedness from Texas to the United States.

He ordered circulars from the Galveston *News* explaining his position.[6] Capitalizing on the current popularity of the Democrats, Williams endeavored to associate himself with the party of annexation, although the Williams family had had previous connections with the Whig party in Baltimore.[7] He was, he said, a "Jeffersonian democrat" and in agreement with the Democratic party's Texas policies. The eight-million-dollar debt ought to be settled immediately, even if it meant transferring the public domain to the federal government. Under other circumstances, Williams preferred that Texas retain control over her land, but that was a luxury she could now ill afford. Once the creditors had been paid, proceeds from the sale of land should be spent on education and the expenses of state government in order to keep taxes low. On national issues, the Galvestonian assured the voters that he stood with the administra-

[5] Galveston *News*, March 3, 1846; T. F. McKinney to S. M. Williams, May 21, 1848; Sophia St. John to H. H. Williams, August 25, 1845; David Reed to W. H. Williams, July 26, 1857, Williams Papers; Hans P. N. Gammel (comp.), *The Laws of Texas, 1822–1897*, III, 996, IV, 126, 244–245.

[6] Statement to Williams from Bangs and Fletcher, March 25, 1846, Williams Papers. No issues of the Galveston *News* for this period survive except February 24, 27, and March 3, 1846.

[7] H. H. Williams to S. M. Williams, September 17, 1838, Williams Papers.

tion—in favor of a low tariff for revenue only and limited expenditures on internal improvements, though Texas admittedly stood in the need of improved river navigation.[8] Williams's statement, which offered little to the ordinary voter, was aimed to attract support from others of his own class. Merchants, large landholders, and investors who had speculated in Texas bonds would benefit by the measures he advocated.

The staunchly Democratic Houston *Telegraph* immediately labeled Colonel Williams a "pewter Democrat," a former Whig opponent of annexation who now tried to join the victorious party for mere expediency. Editor Francis Moore chided the Galveston *News* for altering its stand against the exclusion of Whigs from the party in order to support Williams, but Willard Richardson defended his course, saying that anti-annexation Democrats should be allowed to join. The Galveston editor ignored the jibe about Whigs, a delicate subject on the island, where several prominent men admitted belonging to that party. The *Telegraph*, insisting that apostates should first prove themselves before seeking high office, supported Pillsbury.[9] This newspaper war reflected the developing rivalry between merchants in Houston and Galveston over the domination of the Brazos cotton trade.

Five days before the election, Moore, to whom paper money was an anathema, warned voters that Williams had said nothing about banking in his circular. He also rebuked the colonel for his "lame apology" concerning the concessions he had made at Sabinas. Moore explained that Williams had really intended to return Texas to Mexico in order to activate his bank charter and "flood the country with rag money."[10] Such insinuations injured Williams's chances among the numerous antibanking voters, and his plan to alienate the public domain aroused even more opposition.

On March 30, 1846, a cold rainy day, Galvestonians went to the polls to vote for Williams, who received 466 of the 558 votes cast

---

[8] S. M. Williams to the Voters of the Second Congressional District, March 13, 1846, in Charles Adams Gulick *et al.* (eds.), *The Papers of Mirabeau Buonaparte Lamar*, VI, 32.

[9] *Telegraph and Texas Register*, January 7, February 11, March 4, 1846.

[10] *Ibid.*, March 25, 1846.

Enlightened Self-Interest, 1844–1852 135

in the county. Unlike elections during the Republic, when folded secret ballots had been used, a system of *viva voce* voting was employed. The clerk recorded the name of each voter in a large, ruled election book as each citizen approached his desk, and then, on the same line, he marked the publicly announced preference in the appropriate column for all to see.[11] Obviously, few Galvestonians wished to be recorded in opposition to one of their community's most prominent and influential citizens.

Elsewhere in the Second District, the voters were decidedly less enthusiastic about Colonel Williams. Many remembered his aristocratic manner and undemocratic practices while colonial secretary, behavior sufficiently remarkable that Stephen F. Austin, in his last letter to Williams, urged him to change his attitude. Other Texans disliked the Galveston commercial interests and preferred a representative from the planter class. The unusually wet spring delayed the final tally for two months, and as late as May 2, one islander predicted that Williams would be the victor. When Secretary of State David G. Burnet, Williams's old adversary, finally published the results, it was revealed that Pillsbury was the winner by forty-three votes over Williams, the runner-up.[12]

Even as the tally was being made, tension mounted along the Rio Grande. Encounters between small units of Mexican and American forces led President Polk to request a declaration of war, which Congress granted on May 13. Williams's eldest son, Joseph, joined the volunteer rifle company in Galveston and sailed to Point Isabel in May, where he trained for combat under Colonel Albert Sidney Johnston, a fellow Galvestonian. At the end of August, he transferred to Ben McCulloch's Texas Ranger company, attached to Colonel Jack Hays's First Texas Mounted Regiment, which served General Zachary Taylor as scouts. Joseph shared in the action at San Jeronimo near Monterrey on September 21, and several days

[11] *Ibid.*, April 1, 8, 29, 1846; John Henry Brown, *History of Texas from 1685 to 1892*, II, 347; Gammel, *Laws of Texas*, II, 1517.

[12] S. F. Austin to S. M. Williams, November 3, 1836, Williams Papers; *Telegraph and Texas Register*, April 29, 1846; Asa P. Ufford to Edward C. Hanrick, May 2, 1846, Edward C. Hanrick Papers, Barker History Center, University of Texas at Austin; *Telegraph and Texas Register*, May 20, 27, 1846.

later, he received a wound that resulted in the amputation of his left arm. As soon as he was able, Joe received a discharge and returned to Galveston.[13]

Most of the Texas volunteers were home before the regular congressional election the first week in November, 1846. Williams endeavored to unseat Pillsbury, and he again ordered political broadsides, including some printed in German to aid in winning support among the immigrants.[14] The Houston newspapers rallied to the incumbent, a man "free from censure," while the challenger was described as a "self important" man who had fled to Texas using an *"assumed name"* and had a "sullied" reputation. The *Telegraph* added that Williams was unworthy to serve as congressman because he entered the race solely to hypothecate land to make good the Texas bonds owned by his friends in Baltimore and Philadelphia. When the Galveston *Civilian* objected to this personal attack, the vitriolic Moore retorted that the people should be warned against a man who urged legislation favoring "Shylocks and avaricious speculators." Moreover, the colonel's supporters had induced two others to enter the race in order to split the vote, but that plan was working against him instead of for him. The Houston *Morning Star* maintained that one of these hopefuls, Judge R. E. B. Baylor, not only campaigned from the stump but also from his pulpit and the bench. Colonel Williams, the *Star* wryly noted, lacked such an advantage, and moreover, he got "stumped whenever he attempts to make *stump* speeches."[15] Just before the election, the *Telegraph*, republishing the armistice agreement negotiated by Williams in 1844, editorialized against electing a man whose idea of statesmanship included returning Texas to Mexico. "Was it for this," asked Moore, "that Milam, Travis, Bowie, Fannin . . . fell?" According to the *Telegraph*, Williams should be elected only to the Mexican

[13] Thomas H. Kreneck, "The Lone Star Volunteers: A History of Texas Participation in the Mexican War" (M.A. thesis, University of Houston, 1973), pp. 79–93; disability certificate, October 13, 1846, Williams Papers.

[14] Statement to Williams, October 13, 1848, Williams Papers. There are no extant copies of the Galveston *News* or *Civilian* during the summer and fall of 1846.

[15] *Telegraph and Texas Register*, September 23, October 7, 14, 28, 1846; Houston *Morning Star*, quoted in *Telegraph*, October 21, 1846.

congress. The same issue displayed a touching testimonial from the messmates of Wingate Pillsbury, son of the congressman, who had recently died in the service of his country at Veracruz.[16] In the face of such developments, Williams had little chance of winning. On election day, Williams, in keeping with the custom of the day, treated his supporters at the Tremont Hotel bar. He carried Galveston, winning 249 more votes than Pillsbury, but his local margin of victory was smaller than at the previous balloting. The other counties in the Second District favored the incumbent by a plurality of almost 1,100 votes. Williams's rout on his second bid for a congressional seat signalled the end of his political aspirations.[17]

Yet one of Williams's objectives in seeking election to Congress, the assumption of the defunct Republic's debts by the United States, was partially realized in the Compromise of 1850. One of its provisions called for the United States to pay Texas for the land awarded to New Mexico west of the 103rd meridian, the money earmarked to erase the long-standing debt of the Republic. The following year, Thomas F. McKinney again petitioned the Texas legislature for reimbursement of the firm of McKinney and Williams in the amount of $150,000, representing the principal and interest on the original investment. Politics and the continuing lack of funds delayed payment until 1856, when McKinney secured $40,729 from the state treasury. But he and Williams realized only $8,000 each, because McKinney had made "loans" of over $9,000, contingent on the successful collection of the sum, to those who could help pass the bill, and the remainder was allocated to cover an earlier indebtedness.[18] McKinney continued to press the legislature for the

[16] *Telegraph and Texas Register*, October 21, 1846.

[17] Statement to Williams from Seymour and Tichenor, December 26, 1846, Williams Papers (for a description of electioneering practices, see Francis Richard Lubbock, *Six Decades in Texas; Or Memories of Francis Richard Lubbock, Governor of Texas in War Time, 1861–63: A Personal Experience in Business, War, and Politics*, ed. C. W. Raines, pp. 99–100); *Telegraph and Texas Register*, November 9, 1846.

[18] Petition no. 37, T. F. McKinney to Senate, November 15, 1851, Secretary of State File Box 2-9/125, Archives of the State Department, State of Texas, Texas State Library Archives, Austin; T. F. McKinney to S. M. Williams, November 15, 1851, Williams Papers; Gammel, *Laws of*

rest of their money, and in 1871 and 1873, the year McKinney died, the state recognized a scaled indebtedness of $16,942.80 but was unable to pay the sum. McKinney's heirs, the grandchildren of his oldest sister, successfully petitioned the legislature in 1929, but Governor Dan Moody vetoed all such claims because of insufficient funds in the state treasury. Payment was finally authorized in 1935, but none of Williams's heirs appeared as claimants.[19]

Fortunately for Williams, his primary interest was in banking, and after his resounding defeat in 1846 he submerged himself in work. The modest "little bank," which had been authorized in 1841 as a relief measure for the firm, became increasingly useful to commerce. But until 1848, banking remained an appendage of the commission house because of the continued political opposition to banks of issue. Contemporaries did not understand how it was ethical to "create" money with a printing press, and they blamed the paper money for the economic ills that persisted in both the United States and Texas. Some of the repugnance toward Williams's bank was personal, stemming from enmities that had arisen because of his land-speculating ventures and his involvement in politics. While he was on his diplomatic mission to Mexico, the antibanking faction in the Texas congress had secured the enactment of a law to suppress all private banking.[20] The colonel, however, continued to operate in spite of such hostility, assuming that his charter was inviolable.

This suspicion of corporations and banking was evident in the deliberations of the state constitutional convention of 1845, in which attempts were made to restrict and eliminate banks of issue. In its final form, the constitution, as approved by the Texas voters, forbade the legislature to create, renew, or extend charters that in-

---

Texas, IV, 244–245; T. F. McKinney to S. M. Williams, January 26, February, 1856; [1856 b], Williams Papers. The exact figures are obscure because the firm received small sums from time to time and cancelled some of the debt by accepting credits at the Galveston Custom House, plus other such exchanges, including 58,538 acres of land below Corpus Christi.

[19] *Journal of the Senate of Texas at the First Called Session,* pp. 177, 202.

[20] Bray Hammond, *Banking and Politics in America from the Revolution to the Civil War,* p. 146; Gammel, *Laws of Texas,* II, 1031.

cluded banking or discounting privileges; it provided that two-thirds of both houses might revoke existing incorporations; and it specifically prohibited the issuance of paper designed to circulate as money. In spite of the efforts of McKinney, a member of the senate, the First Legislature implemented the organic law by enacting a bill providing a maximum fine of fifty dollars for each promissory note, check, or bank note issued in Texas.[21]

For the next two years Williams experienced no difficulty in continuing his banking activities in spite of the adverse law. He assumed that the 1841 relief act remained in force and made his operation an exception; like others who held charters from legislative bodies, he relied on the doctrine of vested rights and the sanctity of contracts that had been upheld time and again by the federal courts. In a brief written in 1835 regarding the upper colony controversy, Williams had cited *Fletcher* v. *Peck* (1810) and the Dartmouth College case (1819) as precedents for the validation of his contract. Entrepreneurs like Williams preferred not to acknowledge the decision handed down in the Charles River Bridge case in 1837, which allowed the public interest to intrude into the sanctity of contract. His more democratic neighbors, however, attacked "that sometime-fiction in law called vested rights."[22]

Feeling confident of his position, Williams, with the aid of his brother, Henry Howell, decided to expand the bank in 1847 by opening the Commercial and Agricultural Bank as provided in the 1835 charter obtained at Monclova. The charter had been approved by the Texas congress in 1836, but the following year the antibanking faction had passed the law prohibiting banks of issue. Williams had quietly waited for a more propitious time. The Mexican document was particularly generous, requiring a minimum of capital and allowing the almost unrestricted issuance of paper.[23] He could rely on support from local merchants, because Galveston, more than

[21] *Debates of the Convention of 1845*, pp. 452–453, 458, 460–461; Gammel, *Laws of Texas*, II, 1294–1295, 1359.
[22] Briefs written by S. M. Williams and Spencer H. Jack, undated, "Upper Colony Controversy," Rosenberg Library; Brown, *History of Texas*, I, 342.
[23] Charter, April 30, 1835, Williams Papers; also Gammel, *Laws of Texas*, I, 406.

other Texas cities, required banking facilities in order to develop its potentialities as a port to rival New Orleans. Improved economic conditions and the consummation of annexation made raising the $300,000 necessary to open the bank an easier task than during the previous decade.

After being approached by Henry Howell Williams, Joseph S. Lake of New York City, in conjunction with his New Orleans colleague, Warrick Martin, agreed to advance the major portion of the sum by becoming stockholders in the Galveston enterprise. Lake & Martin, plus their associates, J. and R. Milbank and Company of New York and R. W. Milbank of New Orleans, formed a consortium that already owned a bank in Akron, Ohio, and held stock in banks in several other commercial cities. Lake ordered the engraved plates for the notes and also furnished the cashier, J. M. McMillen, formerly of Akron. After surveying the scene, McMillen and another knowledgeable employee of the Lake enterprises, O. Klemm, correctly predicted that the Texas political climate was unfavorable toward banking. Although they feared that either an unfriendly legislature or court might negate the Mexican charter, Williams proceeded with the plans.[24]

The Commercial and Agricultural Bank opened on New Year's Day, 1848, when the directors employed a somewhat disingenuous scheme to certify that the vault contained $100,000 in specie and that an additional $200,000 was on deposit in New York and New Orleans. The inspector, Niles F. Smith, had been appointed by President Sam Houston in 1837 under the terms of the joint resolution that permitted Williams to activate his Mexican charter as a relief measure for the firm. When the bank did not open in 1837, Smith put aside his commission for over ten years, until called upon to make the necessary certification permitting the C & A Bank to begin operation.[25] Not unexpectedly, the board of directors selected Sam Williams as president and approved McMillen for cashier. The first board included Michel B. Menard, George H. Ball, Jacob L. Briggs, Henry Hubbell, and B. A. Shepherd. During the next decade, these

[24] J. S. Lake to H. H. Williams, November 3, 1847, Williams Papers.
[25] Gammel, *Laws of Texas*, I, 1135; *Attorney General v. S. M. Williams*, Galveston *Weekly News*, February 2, 1849.

men resigned and were replaced by James N. Reynolds of New York, and Jesse J. Davis, Allen Lewis, John L. Sleight, Andrew Moore, Lent M. Hitchcock, and George Delesdernier, all of Galveston. To house his new bank, Williams bought the two-story brick building on the southwest corner of Tremont and Market streets, plus the adjoining lots on the west.[26]

Even as the C & A Bank opened, the Second Legislature debated a bill intended to kill Williams's institution. As passed on March 20, 1848, the act made the emission of paper money without authority a misdemeanor, punishable by a maximum fine of five thousand dollars for each offense within every thirty days. The attorney general was instructed to institute suits against the offenders in the district courts. Politics had inspired the measure. Besides the popular antipathy toward paper money, the representatives from the inland counties, already jealous of Galveston's position as the state's leading port, did not wish the island city to obtain the added advantage of superior financial facilities. The restriction against banking was introduced by Jacob de Cordova, an Austin commission merchant and land broker, and Elisha M. Pease, a representative from Brazoria, shepherded the bill to its final passage. Just who, or even how many, voted for the act is not recorded in the official journal. Williams had antagonized many influential legislators by his inability or unwillingness to produce the large loans necessary for the advancement of their special interests.[27]

A certain amount of personal revenge also entered the picture. Guy M. Bryan, the nephew of Stephen F. Austin, formed a strong dislike for both Williams and McKinney. He represented Brazoria County in the state house of representatives from 1847 to 1853, when he moved up to the senate. During this period he blocked

[26] *State of Texas* v. *S. M. Williams*, 8 *Texas* 255 (1852): Ben C. Stuart, "Some More Trite Tales of Tremont Street," Galveston *News*, January 16, 1910; Galveston County Deed Records, F, 586, 642; J. W. McMillan to S. M. Williams, February 22, 1849, Williams Papers.

[27] Gammel, *Laws of Texas*, III, 234–235; Texas Legislature, *Journal of the House of Representatives*, 2 Leg., 1 sess., 1848, pp. 944–945, 166, 1100, 1102, 1135; Earl Wesley Fornell, *The Galveston Era: The Texas Crescent on the Eve of Secession*, p. 50; T. F. McKinney to S. M. Williams, August 13, 1850, Williams Papers.

measures favored by McKinney and Williams, assisted by his close friend, Elisha M. Pease, who became governor in 1853.[28]

Shortly after the prohibitive law took effect on May 1, 1848, a rumor that Lake and Company had failed in New York caused a brief panic in Houston. Cautious men feared that such news might blow the C & A Bank "sky-high" and refused to accept Williams's paper for several days. A friend of the bank assured his fellows that the directors would not allow the people to suffer and would pay specie; this unauthorized pledge served to restore faith in the Galveston currency.[29]

The bank had done well since its opening, and possibly as much as $30,000 in C & A bills had gone to New Orleans during the first six months. Williams redeemed these notes in specie in a ploy to bolster his reputation for stability. Overly cautious, he retained $36,000 in specie to cover the estimated $18,000 circulating in Texas. If necessary, Williams could liquidate his affairs within two or three months by redeeming all the outstanding notes with coin, thereby preserving his credit with the community. In this fashion, he hoped to retain his charter for future use, even though he might temporarily be forced to suspend operations.[30]

Such prudent procedures were necessary because the newly appointed attorney general (and former law partner of E. M. Pease), John W. Harris, had filed a suit against Williams in June as required by the March 20 law. Harris contended that for issuing and passing paper notes during the month of May, Williams and the other officers might each be assessed at least the two-thousand-dollar minimum penalty for each note circulating. The case would be heard in the Galveston district court during the fall term, but in the meantime the C & A Bank continued to function in the absence of an injunction. Williams's friends considered that the law was unconsti-

[28] T. F. McKinney to S. M. Williams, December 4, 1850, February 5, 1856, Williams Papers; Texas House Journal, 2 Leg., 1 sess., 1848, pp. 480–481, 492, 542, 576–577.

[29] Telegraph and Texas Register, June 1, 1848, quoting the Houston Morning Star; H. C. Stowell to [J. V. Williams], June 10, 1848, Williams Papers.

[30] J. S. Lake to S. M. Williams, May 12, June 1, 1848; R. W. Milbank to S. M. Williams, July 17, 1848; S. M. Williams to Warrick Martin (draft), July 28, 1848, Williams Papers.

tutional because it was specific, not general, and they maintained that individuals could not be held accountable.[31]

Legal problems were not the only crises Williams faced during his first year of operation. Joseph S. Lake discovered that Warrick Martin was trying to gain control of the C & A Bank, and the matter became critical when Lake and Company was forced to close during a brief recession in 1848.[32] Williams hurriedly dispatched J. W. McMillen to New Orleans to forestall Martin's acquisition of Lake's Commercial and Agricultural Bank stock, and by July, he had possession of the certificates in the Galveston vault. He tried to make peace between Lake and Martin by calling them both "the fathers" of his "little" operation, but they continued to make wild accusations against each other.[33] Finally, Martin threatened a suit unless Lake and Williams bought his interest at his price, but after a trip to Galveston, Martin was persuaded to drop his demands. Both he and Lake concluded that their differences had largely been due to their lawyers, who had exaggerated matters out of proportion.[34]

The bank case came before District Judge Joseph C. Meggison late in 1848 and continued into January, 1849. Williams retained the Galveston firm of Ebenezer Allen and William G. Hale, and their arguments proved more convincing than the case prepared and presented by the special assistant to the attorney general, Andrew Jackson Hamilton. The state endeavored to prove that Williams's charter was invalid, but Meggison's opinion reaffirmed the 1841 relief law that permitted banking privileges, and he denied that subse-

[31] *State of Texas* v. *S. M. Williams*, 8 *Texas* 255 (1852); *Attorney General* v. *S. M. Williams*, Galveston *Weekly News*, February 2, 1849; J. S. Lake to S. M. Williams, November 4, 1848; T. F. McKinney to S. M. Williams, December 13, 1849, Williams Papers.

[32] J. S. Lake to S. M. Williams, January 10, April 15, July 1, 1848, Williams Papers.

[33] J. S. Lake to S. M. Williams, July 1, 7, September 20, 1848; S. M. Williams to Warrick Martin (draft), July 28, 1848; W. Martin to S. M. Williams, November 3, 1848, *ibid.*

[34] J. S. Lake to S. M. Williams, October 11, 16, 1848, March 13, 1849; W. Martin to S. M. Williams, September 19, 1848, May 5, 1849, *ibid.* There are over seventy letters detailing the role played by these men from November 3, 1847, to June 18, 1849, when the correspondence abruptly ends. This suggests that another file of letters once existed.

quent acts of the legislature abrogated the vested interest of the grantees. Williams termed the decision "creditable," and Galveston merchants asked permission of the judge to publish his argument. A few days later, the editor of the *News* devoted four front-page columns to record the full proceedings of the case.[35] Because either party might appeal, Williams's attorneys expected that the state would carry the matter to the higher court, but they felt confident of winning there, too.

The Galveston banker hoped to have the distasteful 1848 law repealed by the next legislature. McKinney had been elected to the lower house, and, from Austin, he assured his former partner that he was working for a reversal of the banking act. A procedural question had forced a delay in the state's plan to appeal: could the governor employ counsel in suits in which the state was a party? The legislators finally agreed that outside assistance, such as the previous employment of Hamilton in the bank case, was unnecessary, and that the governor could employ legal aid only when the office of the attorney general was vacant.[36] Retiring Attorney General Harris had filed four suits against the C & A Bank with penalties amounting to $75,000 for the fifteen months that it had violated the law. Though the district court had ruled unfavorably for the state, the first case had been appealed and the other suits had received continuances.[37]

A man of quick temper and vengeful spirit, McKinney held a grudge against "Colossal Jack" Hamilton, and, while searching the archives for material relative to his land claims, he discovered evidence harmful to the ambitious young lawyer, who had been appointed to fill the vacant attorney general's office. Various state revenue officers had failed to remit complete returns, and the attorney general had been negligent in assessing penalties against the de-

[35] J. W. McMillan to S. M. Williams, February 22, 1849; Niles F. Smith to S. M. Williams, December 7, 1848, *ibid.*; Galveston *Weekly News*, February 2, 1849.

[36] T. F. McKinney to S. M. Williams, November 23, December 1, 13, 1849, January 2, 1850, Williams Papers; Texas *House Journal*, 3 Leg., 1 sess., 1849, p. 14; Gammel, *Laws of Texas*, III, 471.

[37] Texas *House Journal*, 3 Leg., 1 sess., 1849, pp. 39–40.

faulters. McKinney became chairman of a special investigating committee appointed by the legislature to determine culpability, and he told Williams that he would "show off our friend Jack in his true colors. . . ."[38] The inquiry revealed that neither the auditor nor the comptroller had reported the omissions found in the accounts of the taxing and licensing agents, and that the attorney general had taken no steps to remedy the widespread corruption. Reacting to the scandal, the legislature removed the position of attorney general from the patronage powers of the executive and made it an elective office. McKinney immediately commenced a successful campaign to elect Galveston attorney, Ebenezer Allen, to that position.[39] Allen, who was Williams's legal advisor, had served as attorney general and secretary of state during Anson Jones's presidency in 1844 and 1845. Friendly toward banking, the new attorney general managed to forestall new suits for awhile.

The success of the bank prompted offers to open agencies in various cities, but the directors seriously considered only New York and New Orleans and a branch bank for the growing city of Brownsville near the mouth of the Rio Grande.[40] Lake directed the New York agency, and after the trouble with Martin, J. W. McMillen and later O. Klemm, a young protégé of Lake's, assumed the responsibility in New Orleans.[41] Although the Brownsville branch was scheduled to open in the autumn of 1848 after President Polk had announced ratification of the treaty ending the war with Mexico, the court cases and the bickering among the partners delayed the plans until early 1850. James N. Reynolds, a New York speculator in

[38] T. F. McKinney to S. M. Williams, November 5, December 1, 13, 1849, January 2, 15, 1850, Williams Papers.

[39] Report of the Joint Committee to Investigate the Office of Comptroller and Treasurer, February 7, 1850, appendix, *Journal of the Senate of the State of Texas*, 3 Leg., 1 sess., 1850, pp. 274–276, 286; Gammel, *Laws of Texas*, III, 599; T. F. McKinney to S. M. Williams, August 29, 1850, Williams Papers; *Telegraph and Texas Register*, September 11, 1850.

[40] M. C. Rogers to S. M. Williams, January 17, 1848; H. H. Williams to S. M. Williams, June 8, September 8, 1848, Williams Papers.

[41] J. S. Lake to S. M. Williams, May 12, July 7, October 11, 1848; O. Klemm to H. H. Williams, February 14, 1850, *ibid.*

land and mining, was persuaded to head the branch, and though he declined the title of president, that was his position.[42] Warren Jenkins, formerly associated with the Canal Bank of Cincinnati and a friend of the Lake associates, became cashier at Brownsville, while his son, Henry, assumed that position in Galveston when McMillen retired.[43]

As the decade drew to a close, the discovery of gold in California brought a small flurry of business through the port of Galveston, advertised locally as the most accessible route to the west. From Galveston, travelers took a steamer to Houston and then traveled overland to Fredericksburg on the fringe of Indian country, from there to El Paso, and on to San Diego, only two months after landing in Galveston if all went well. Among those Texans who succumbed to the gold fever were George W. Scott, Sarah Williams's brother, and Ephraim W. McLean, McKinney's nephew. One returning adventurer brought Sam Williams a twenty-ounce nugget of "pure gold," which he proudly displayed at the bank.[44]

By the end of the 1840's, Williams no longer possessed a monopoly of banking in Galveston. As early as 1849 Robert Mills, formerly of Brazoria, had transferred his commission house to the Strand in Galveston and begun circulating his own paper notes in apparent violation of the 1848 law. His operation differed from Williams's in two ways: first, he did not officially call his institution a bank; and, second, he did not print his own paper. Mills had bought up the notes of a wildcat bank in Mississippi, and, after endorsing each bill, he put them into circulation in Texas. But in spite of the rantings of the antibanking party, "Williams paper" and "Mills money" served a useful purpose and circulated at par along the Gulf coast. Even his opponents admitted that Williams never suspended specie payments and attributed the success of the C & A Bank to the "judicious manner in which it is managed." The only valid criticism

[42] J. S. Lake to S. M. Williams, May 23, August 1, 1848, May 25, 1849; J. N. Reynolds to S. M. Williams, August 19, 1848; S. M. Williams to Joseph P. Conthony, March 6, 1852, *ibid.*

[43] *Commercial and Agricultural Bank* v. *Simon L. Jones,* 18 *Texas* 811 (1857); Warren Jenkins to S. M. Williams, September 28, 1848; J. W. McMillen to S. M. Williams, August 15, September 20, 1848, March 21, 26, 1859, Williams Papers.

[44] *Telegraph and Texas Register,* January 18, 1849, July 4, 1850.

leveled against the Galveston bankers was the high rate of interest charged in contrast with New Orleans.[45]

The Houston financial community continued to be jealous of the Galveston paper money. Editor Francis Moore, while declaring that "we regard all banks as evil," noted that "private institutions" on the island continued to circulate paper, supported by the courts and public opinion. Perhaps, Moore suggested, Houston merchants should also seek banking privileges so they too might profit in substituting paper for specie. He feared that the Galveston money might finance a canal or railroad to connect the island with the Brazos, thus seriously injuring Houston commerce. Ever alert to the dangers of counterfeits in using paper money, Moore also warned his readers to beware of the influx of bills from Mississippi that resembled Mills money but were not being honored at his bank.[46]

Moore's suspicions were correct. The bankers were involved with a scheme to dredge a channel through the shallow bays west of Galveston island to join the Brazos at Velasco. Williams, McKinney, Michel B. Menard, and others in Galveston met at the close of 1848 and drew up plans for a survey and financing, but the charter for the Galveston and Brazos Navigation Company was not granted by the legislature until February, 1850. The state allowed the company ninety-four sections of land in uninhabited South Texas, and dredging began in 1851 on the fourteen-mile canal, one hundred feet wide and four feet deep. It was completed in 1854, but high tides caused the banks near the mouth of Oyster Bayou to collapse, so that the company had to have that section reworked in 1857.[47] Plans for a railroad were more complicated. Williams, Robert Mills,

[45] Jacob de Cordova, *Texas: Her Resources and Her Public Men*, p. 7; Fornell, *Galveston Era*, p. 42.

[46] *Telegraph and Texas Register*, January 10, 1848, April 11, 1850, January 17, 1851.

[47] Copy of petition of the Galveston and Brazos Navigation Company, December 20, 1848, and bond from Galveston City Company to Joseph Osterman, July 1, 1850, Rosenberg Library; Gammel, *Laws of Texas*, III, 571–576, IV, 1095; Galveston *Weekly News*, December 22, 1848, April 20, 1849, February 18, 1851, October 27, 1857; *Telegraph and Texas Register*, January 28, July 22, September 30, November 4, 1853; Willard Richardson *et al.* (eds.), *Galveston Directory, 1866–1867*, p. 101.

and the editor of the *News*, Willard Richardson, preferred that such a project be financed privately by traditional stock companies, but a plan to build a railway to the island using public money gained popularity in the early 1850's. Williams viewed state ownership with apprehension, regarding the idea as a dangerous precedent that might threaten his bank. On July 7, 1856, Williams presided at a meeting of conservative residents to denounce the proposal. Private enterprise, aided by land grants and government loans, triumphed, and by 1859 Galvestonians had train service connecting with Houston three times a week. They remained dependent on a ferry from the island until the following year, when the bridge was completed and leased to the Galveston, Houston, and Henderson Railroad.[48]

Between 1849 and 1852, when the court finally heard the appeal in the bank case, Wiliams devoted himself to his role as prosperous banker. Portraits of the colonel and his wife hung in the recently redecorated parlor. In addition to groceries and liquors, tradesmen delivered oil and coal for cooking and heating, and in summer, brought ice for the comfort of the family.[49] Moreover, Williams kept two horses, a carriage, and a barouche in the stable behind the house, and sixteen head of cattle grazed on the salt grass surrounding his twenty-acre homesite west of the city. Four slaves served the family and lived in the outbuildings near the kitchen. Meticulous in dress, the colonel affected white linen clothing in summer, and during the colder weather, enhanced his somber suits with black silk or velvet waistcoats. A gold watch and diamond stickpin added the final touch of opulence.[50]

At midcentury the Williams household in Galveston abounded with young people. Though Joe no longer lived at home, Austin

[48] Kenneth W. Wheeler, *To Wear A City's Crown: The Beginnings of Urban Growth in Texas, 1836–1865*, pp. 94–101; Fornell, *Galveston Era*, pp. 159–179, 183–184; Galveston *News*, July 9, 11, 1856.

[49] The portraits, undated and unsigned, belong to the Rosenberg Library and hang in the Williams house; statements from various merchants, 1848–1849; silver from Hyde and Merrit, February 24, 1848; furniture from J. A. Sauter, Williams Papers.

[50] Galveston County Tax Assessor to Williams, November 20, 1850; statements for clothes from Briggs and Yard, George and Albert Ball, *ibid.;* jewelry itemized in the inventory of Williams's estate, Galveston County Probate Records, File Box 397.

and William Howell, known as "Beaver," were there quite often, while Molly, aged twelve, and Caddy, eight, attended the recently opened Ursuline school as day students. Williams bought an elegant German piano for his daughters, who studied music with the nuns.[51] Samuel May Williams, Jr., born in 1845, completed the immediate family, but nieces, nephews, and children of friends often joined the menage in order to attend school or work on the island. In 1850 the older boys attended Western Military Institute at Blue Lick Springs near Louisville, Kentucky. Founded in 1847, the academy was popular with southern planters as a preparatory school. Beaver went from there to Harvard in 1852; Austin returned to Texas.[52]

The colonel remained a major landholder; according to the 1850 tax roll, he owned 49,000 acres scattered around the state valued at $44,000, in addition to island property worth $10,000.[53] He gradually sold portions of his acreage, or leased it to tenants, except for an 1,100-acre sugar plantation near the mouth of the San Bernard River. He had purchased this valuable tract in 1844 when sugar-growing promised to be profitable, but in 1850, he sold his interest to Joseph J. Bates of Galveston.[54] During the last year that Williams operated the plantation, Joe and Austin had served as overseers for the sixteen Negro slaves who planted and harvested the cane and made the syrup. Besides the 120 head of cattle, there were 14 horses, 11 mules, and 3 yoke of oxen used to plow and haul cane.[55]

[51] Statements to Williams, January 29, 1849, November 5, 1852, Williams Papers. The piano is on display at the house.

[52] W. H. Williams to mother, September 24, 1850, Samuel May and Austin May Williams Papers, Barker History Center, University of Texas at Austin; checks for tuition, June 2, 4, 12, September 11, 1850, February 19, 1852; brochure for W.M.I., 1856; W. H. Williams to father, July 25, 1852, Williams Papers.

[53] Statement from Assessor and Collector at Galveston, November 20, 1850, Williams Papers.

[54] Brazoria County Deed Records, F, 502 (this is the northern quarter of the T. and W. Alley league); agreement between J. Bates and S. M. Williams, March 20, 1852, Williams Papers. See the General Land Office's map of Brazoria County.

[55] J. V. Williams to S. M. Williams, February 13, 20, March 28, April 6, 16, June 14, 1849; inventory, June 28, 1849, by J. V. Williams, Williams Papers.

Williams quit sugar-growing at a propitious time, because the same year a severe drought stunted the cane and deformed the ratoons; two years later, a bumper crop caused a price decline and the industry failed to return to its former prosperity. His brothers, Nathaniel and Matthew, continued to produce cane at Oakland Plantation in Fort Bend County on Williams's former league on Oyster Creek. Though Nat had left Texas and had moved first to New Orleans and then to Baltimore in 1845, he had retained interest in the plantation. Matthew and his wife, Mary Ann Dunlavy, lived on Oyster Creek with their six children, overseeing the production of cane and the processing of the sugar. Matt died from a stomach hemorrhage October 10, 1852, and the widow and children moved to Houston when Nat sold Oakland later that year. The fine brick sugar house and other buildings became the property of Benjamin Franklin Terry and William F. Kyle.[56] Terry became well known during the Civil War as the commander of Terry's Texas Rangers. After the deaths of Terry and Kyle during the war, the plantation passed to Colonel Edward H. Cunningham. Renamed Sugarland, the property was rescued in the early twentieth century by I. H. Kempner and W. T. Eldridge, who formed the Imperial Sugar Company.

The prosperity enjoyed by Williams and his family was short-lived, however. By the end of 1852, the enemies of banking had gained control of state politics, thus foreshadowing the end of the colonel's wealth and happiness.

[56] William R. Johnson, *A Short History of the Sugar Industry in Texas*, pp. 26, 28, 30, 32; N. F. Williams to H. H. Williams, March 3, 1848; M. R. Williams to S. M. Williams, August 1, 1848, Williams Papers; Fort Bend County Deed Records, C, 112, 113, 115, E, 551.

CHAPTER 10

The Defeat of Texas'
First Banker
1852-1858

THE confidence that Samuel May Williams felt in 1849 about the ultimate favorable disposition of the bank case gradually eroded. The Texas Supreme Court was to rule on the matter at Galveston in March, 1852, and Williams became fretful as the time neared. The year had opened inauspiciously when Robert Mills's New Orleans associate failed, and Texans rushed to exchange their paper money. Only the prompt action of Galveston merchants who continued to redeem the notes at par prevented a run on the island banks. When some residents questioned the solvency of the Commercial and Agricultural Bank, the Galveston *News* loyally, although erroneously, assured the public that the colonel always maintained sufficient specie in his vault to redeem all his paper *"ten times over."* Williams, who was less sanguine, complained to a colleague that his activities were labeled criminal while others operating in a similar manner received no such condemnation. He believed that he and his family had been marked for persecution by the antibanking faction.[1]

In late March the court finally reached a decision favorable to the bank by unanimously confirming the 1849 ruling of the district court. Three experienced men composed the high bench: Chief Justice John Hemphill, a cautious and conservative scholar who had served in the same capacity during the Republic, Associate Justice

[1] Galveston *News*, quoted in *Telegraph and Texas Register*, January 30, February 20, 1852; S. M. Williams to Joseph P. Conathy, March 6, 1852, Samuel May Williams Papers, Rosenberg Library, Galveston.

Abner S. Lipscomb, who had sat as Alabama chief justice before emigrating to Texas, and Associate Justice Royall T. Wheeler, a former district judge.[2] Andrew Jackson Hamilton argued the case for the state, maintaining that the lower court had erred in its decision, but Williams's attorneys, Ebenezer Allen, the present Texas attorney general, his partner, William G. Hale, and John B. Jones, a former district judge, made a competent denial. The opinion, written by Lipscomb, who was considered an expert on adjudicating statutory and common law, stated that the 1835 charter and the special relief law of 1841 were valid and permitted banking activities.[3] Williams no doubt felt vindicated and relieved after the decision. The action taken by the state supreme court also reassured merchants at Palestine, Texas, who requested that a branch bank be established there. Francis Moore, however, warned the readers of the Houston *Telegraph* that northern capitalists intended to increase the bank stock and then double the amount of circulating paper.[4]

The antibanking clique, led by Guy M. Bryan and Andrew J. Hamilton, soon reorganized and decided on a new plan of attack. Having failed to kill the C & A Bank by declaring the charter illegal, Williams's enemies now intended to end his operation by levying huge fines on the board of directors for passing illegal paper. Toward the end of 1852, the new attorney general, Thomas J. Jennings, who assumed office on August 2, 1852, filed suit in the Galveston district court, alleging that the bank officials continued to operate an illegal institution. The petition asked that the court levy a $35,000 fine against the board for issuing paper notes during the past seven months from April through October. (Five thousand dollars per month was the maximum fine permitted by the 1848 statute.) Allen and Hale filed a general demurrer that District Judge Peter W. Gray sustained, and, in the absence of a further petition

[2] Oran M. Roberts, "The Political, Legislative, and Judicial History of Texas, 1845–1895," in Dudley G. Wooten (ed.), *A Comprehensive History of Texas, 1845–1897*, II, 17.

[3] *State v. Williams*, 8 *Texas* 255 (1852). It was not considered a conflict of interest for a public official to continue private practice, and until 1853 the United States attorney general also was permitted this dual role. Allen held office until August 2, 1852.

[4] Scott and Holmes to S. M. Williams, May 17, 1852, Williams Papers; *Telegraph and Texas Register*, June 25, 1852.

from the state, Gray dismissed the suit. Subsequently the attorney general instituted another suit in March, 1853, requesting a penalty of $20,000 for the offenses from November, 1852, to March, 1853, but Gray treated it in a similar manner. At the same time, the state began action against Robert Mills for circulating paper notes from April, 1852, through February, 1853, and asked for a fine of $55,000. Again, Judge Gray dismissed the case, ruling that the state failed to have grounds for a suit because the charges against the Galveston bankers were general, not specific.[5]

Williams's attorneys interpreted the new harassment by the attorney general to mean that the banker's opponents were more interested in collecting the excessive penalties permitted than in eliminating banking. If they really wanted to do away with the bank, the legislature could accomplish that goal at any time. Aware that the popularly elected high court was sensitive to public opinion regarding the bank, Allen advised his client to adopt delaying tactics so that the justices would have ample time to weigh the will of the electorate. The former attorney general believed that the populace now favored banking. Besides slow and careful preparation, the canny lawyer suggested that Williams lobby for a bill to exempt his institution from the penalties assessed illegal banks by stressing his financial conservatism. Finally, Allen suggested that Williams appeal any cases brought against him to the United States Supreme Court —or at least imply that he so intended.[6]

The bank question intruded into political alignments in Texas. The state Democratic convention meeting in Austin in February, 1848, just after opening of the C & A Bank, had specifically endorsed the use of hard money and denounced as dangerous the fluctuating paper issue of private banks. Subsequent platforms continued to be antibanking in tone, but they used more general language. In 1852, the Texas Whigs named the brother of a C & A Bank director as a delegate to the national convention, and, even more significantly, the party platform recommended that the legislature alter the state constitution to permit banking, "which we deem to be of

---

[5] *State of Texas* v. *S. M. Williams and others; State of Texas* v. *Robert Mills and others*, 14 *Texas* 98 (1855).

[6] Ebenezer Allen to S. M. Williams, confidential brief for *State* v. *S. M. Williams et al.*, [1853], Williams Papers.

such vital importance to the future growth and prosperity of our State."[7] Although the national presidential campaign of 1852 generated little interest in Texas, the gubernatorial race the following year stimulated a heated contest between the Democrats and the Whigs. Elisha M. Pease, long an active worker in the Democratic party, triumphed over the Whig candidate, William B. Ochiltree. On December 23, Pease delivered an "able" inaugural message outlining many progressive reforms, but he said nothing at all about paper money or the bank question.[8]

Williams, who preferred the Whig platform, was disappointed by the Democratic victory. Nevertheless, following the advice of his attorney, he attended the entire session of the Fifth Legislature from November 7, 1853, to February 13, 1854.[9] The banker found Austin changed since 1839, when he had served in the Fourth Congress; the old wooden capitol had just been abandoned, and the legislators gathered in the new limestone statehouse at the head of Congress Avenue.

The friends of paper money introduced a bill to amend the constitution to sanction the creation of banks, but it failed to pass in spite of intensive lobbying. Many members personally opposed banking and ignored the growing sentiment in favor of such institutions. Even the Houston *Telegraph* finally discovered advantages in well-regulated paper money and chided the timid "democrats" for believing that all banks represented privileged monopoly; only "Federalists" would hesitate to allow the people to express their wishes at the polls. The *Telegraph* noted with irony that judges, attorneys, and legislators all used the paper notes in spite of laws to the contrary. But the Democrats continued to avoid reform legislation, preferring to stick with their traditional antibanking views.[10]

---

[7] Ernest W. Winkler (ed.), *Platforms of Political Parties in Texas*, pp. 47, 50, 52, 53.

[8] *Telegraph and Texas Register*, January 6, 1854.

[9] A. M. Williams to S. M. Williams, December 20, 1853, Samuel May and Austin May Williams Papers, Barker History Center, University of Texas at Austin; A. M. Williams to mother, February 1, 1854, Williams Papers.

[10] *Telegraph and Texas Register*, December 30, 1853; Francis Richard Lubbock, *Six Decades in Texas; Or Memoirs of Francis Richard Lub-*

In the meantime, Attorney General Jennings, frustrated by the Galveston district court in his efforts to prosecute the bank cases as required by statute, asked Justice Lipscomb for permission to re-argue "the question of the mode of pleading" that had been used in the previous cases involving Williams and Mills. Lipscomb, the author of the 1852 opinion, assented, and the plea came before the Texas Supreme Court in Galveston in early 1855. Allen and Hale, on behalf of Williams, rejected the state's petition on the previously maintained grounds that the indictments were in general, not specific, terms. They also explored the various interpretations given to the words, *offense, banking, discounting,* and *privilege,* presumably to gain time and delay a decision, in accordance with the strategy previously outlined by Allen. Mills's attorneys questioned the intent of the 1848 law and argued that because the situation had changed, the law was obsolete. Moreover, why should Mills be fined, they asked, for passing Mississippi paper that was readily accepted at par in New Orleans?[11] One of Mills's counselors was former Attorney General John W. Harris, who had supervised the 1848 suit against Williams and was considered by many to be the finest lawyer in the state.[12] Lipscomb again wrote the majority opinion in which Chief Justice Hemphill concurred. They upheld the ruling of the lower court that the state's petition was defective in its omission of specific allegations against the banks. Justice Wheeler, however, dissented, and, though he admitted that the law was vague, he denied that the court should inquire into the meaning of the statute. In his opinion, the law had been violated and punishment should be meted out to the Galveston banks.[13]

Twice in seven years Williams had survived the efforts of his enemies to destroy his bank in the courts. Although the high court had again sustained the favorable decision rendered in the district court, the dissent by one of the three justices suggested that the victory perhaps was only transitory.

The colonel suffered a personal tragedy during the court session

---

bock, *Governor of Texas in War Time, 1861–63: A Personal Experience in Business, War, and Politics,* ed. C. W. Raines, p. 210.

[11] *State* v. *Williams; State* v. *Mills,* 14 *Texas* 98 (1855).

[12] James Daniel Lynch, *The Bench and Bar of Texas,* p. 369.

[13] *State* v. *Williams; State* v. *Mills,* 14 *Texas* 98 (1855).

that lessened any happiness he felt over the outcome of the legal maneuvering. Nine-year-old Sam, Jr., died on February 11, 1855, after a brief illness, and the bereaved family followed the small coffin from the house to the Episcopal cemetery on Broadway, where he was buried in the family plot.[14] Sarah, who mourned the passing of her youngest child, increasingly complained of her own infirmities. At forty-seven she was an old woman. She suffered a congenital eye problem, possibly cataracts, as did both her brothers and her youngest daughter. Twice she visited a surgeon in Lexington, Kentucky, in the early 1840's, with only moderate improvement, but in 1854 she journeyed to Boston for a successful operation, after which she could again read and sew with the aid of strong eyeglasses.[15]

After their second defeat in 1855, the opponents of paper money resumed pressure on state officials to prosecute illegal banking, and, by a series of technical moves, the attorney general submitted specific charges against Williams and Mills. The officers of the Commercial and Agricultural Bank were to be fined for issuing fifty one-dollar notes dated January 1, 1848, but actually circulated on February 18, 1853. Williams's attorneys countered with demurrers and amended petitions, and the case finally came before Judge Gray in the district court in January, 1857.[16] Previous rulings by Gray had been in favor of the banks, but the political scene had abruptly changed. Abner S. Lipscomb had died the previous November, and Gray was an eager contender for the vacant seat on the state supreme court in the election to be held in February, 1857.

The judge heard the Mills case first, and on January 19 he gave very explicit instructions to the jury to find Mills guilty, which they

[14] Statements to Williams from the doctor, sexton, and coffinmaker, February 11, 21, 23, 1855, Williams Papers; marker in the Episcopal Cemetery, Galveston.

[15] A. M. Williams to Mary Anna, November 22, 1855; S. M. Williams to Sarah, May 24, June 1, July 5, 1842; May 19, 31, June 10, 19, July 8, 1844; June 23, 29, July 9, August 27, 1854, Williams Papers, Barker History Center. There is a high incidence of cataracts among the descendants of Austin M. Williams.

[16] Brief for S. M. Williams et al., Appellants v. the State of Texas, [1853], Williams Papers.

did. Gray set the fine at $100,000, an exorbitant penalty applauded by those who believed that men of wealth had regarded themselves as "beyond the law" for too long. Two days later, the jury in the Williams trial failed to reach a verdict, and the judge discharged them. Allen and Hale, acting on advice from the bench and the attorney general, agreed to accept a $2,000 judgment against the bank for passing a single dollar bill in order to carry the appeal against the excessive fine to the state supreme court.[17]

While awaiting the appeal, Williams and Mills continued to conduct business as usual in spite of the adverse ruling. The Galveston *News*, sympathetic toward the bankers, reported that many accused Judge Gray of making a "political" decision less than a month before the election. Previously his conduct had been friendly toward the commercial interests, but his recent ruling had put banking in jeopardy.[18]

Newspapers around the state argued the merits of banking for the next four months. Sentiment in Austin followed the traditional Jefferson-Jackson view that monopolies endangered the common man and that bankers charged usurious interest. Former New Englander Edward H. Cushing assumed control of the Houston *Telegraph* in 1856 and reversed its antibanking policy. He feared that the recent decision would restrict business and also might make the Texans dependent upon questionable Louisiana bank notes. The editor of the Galveston *News* admired Cushing's style and reprinted the probanking editorials. Richardson attacked the antibanking faction for its concentration on the Galveston institutions while Swenson and Swisher of Austin, a commission house with banking functions, used Union Bank of Louisiana notes and went unscathed.[19]

The *News* supported Gray for the seat on the court. Richardson commended his dignity and wisdom, although he personally disagreed with the recent banking decisions. But the state's voters

[17] Galveston *News*, January 20, 31, February 3, 5, 1857.

[18] *Ibid.*, January 31, February 3, 1857.

[19] Austin *Gazette* and Austin *Intelligencer*, quoted in the Galveston *News*, February 10, March 24, 1857; *Telegraph and Texas Register*, February 11, May 6, 1857; Galveston *News*, February 3, 5, 7, 17, March 3, 1857.

passed over the Houstonian in favor of Oran Milo Roberts, district judge of Shelby County, who won by a small plurality. The East Texas judge was noted for his devotion to Jeffersonian principles, including agrarianism, states' rights, and strict construction of the constitution.[20] His lack of sympathy for the commercial interests along the coast forecast trouble for the bankers' pending appeals.

Under this mounting tension, Williams suggested that his board of directors resign. Each man might be fined as much as two hundred thousand dollars, and to avoid such penalties, Lent M. Hitchcock, G. H. Delesdernier, Andrew Moore, John L. Sleight, Allen Lewis, and Jacob L. Briggs announced their withdrawal in a letter to the News. Williams's sons urged their father to sell the bank, even at a loss, just for his "peace of mind," but the colonel refused to bow under pressure.[21]

In addition to the concern about bank paper during the first half of 1857, Texans heard that specie might disappear. The bank question intruded into the summer gubernatorial campaign between Senator Sam Houston, running as an independent, and Hardin R. Runnels, the regular Democratic candidate. The Galveston News "understood" that Runnels favored banking whereas Houston opposed altering the state constitution to permit such activity.[22] Unpopular in Texas since his negative vote on the Kansas-Nebraska Act three years before, Old Sam suffered his only political defeat on August 3, 1857. Williams doubtless cast his ballot for Runnels, the winner by almost fifteen thousand votes.

Almost before the results of the race were known, news of widespread financial failures in the northeast arrived in Galveston. The Panic of 1857 began August 24, when the New York City branch of the Ohio Life Insurance and Trust Company closed, and other commercial and financial institutions soon followed. On October 16 the steamer from New Orleans confirmed a rumor that three banks there had suspended specie payments. Islanders immediately began a run on Williams and Mills that continued through the next

[20] Galveston News, February 3, 1857; Roberts, "Political, Legislative, and Judicial History," p. 40; Lynch, Bench and Bar, pp. 273–277.
[21] Galveston News, May 19, 1857; A. M. Williams to W. H. Williams, April 20, May 3, 1857, Williams Papers.
[22] Galveston News, August 18, 1857.

day. The Commercial and Agricultural Bank generally paid specie on demand, although during the crisis Williams refused to honor depositor checks even in paper, giving preference instead to redeeming the small notes presented by women and laborers. Both institutions curtailed their bills, and merchants had to rely on New Orleans paper, accepting it at par in order to lessen hysteria. On the following day, when Williams's bank closed early, a panic caused local paper to be discounted that evening at a rate of 25 percent; however, when he resumed paying gold on demand, confidence was quickly restored.[23] However Williams and Mills managed the affair, the Panic of 1857 insofar as Galveston was concerned soon subsided. The new year brought hope for economic improvement, but the bankers uneasily awaited the Galveston session of the supreme court, which was delayed by inclement weather in January. In the interim, Mills had to suspend specie payments for a brief time, while Williams discovered a large amount of counterfeit paper circulating as Commercial and Agricultural bank notes.[24]

Another personal tragedy occurred in December, 1857, when the colonel learned that his eldest son was dying at the home of a friend in Trinity County. After his return from the war, Joe had failed to adjust to the loss of an arm, and in spite of a series of positions obtained for him by his father, the embittered young man became "dissipated." Late in 1855, Joe "reformed" and engaged in commerce in Polk and Trinity counties until his death.[25]

The Texas Supreme Court heard arguments by the bankers' lawyers in March, 1858, but Justice Wheeler fell ill, and at the end

[23] Ibid., September 1, 15, 22, October 6, 14, 20, 1857; Telegraph and Texas Register, October 19, 21, 1857, quoted in Earl Wesley Fornell, The Galveston Era: The Texas Crescent on the Eve of Secession, p. 49.

[24] Galveston News, January 12, 1858.

[25] C. W. Mervin to S. M. Williams, December 11, 1857; Warneken and Kirchoff to S. M. Williams, May 26, June 9, 1849, Williams Papers; bond, August 1, 1851, Galveston County Deed Records, J, 487 (J. V. Williams served as deputy clerk; see pp. 488–505); A. M. Williams to S. M. Williams, December 20, 1853; T. F. McKinney to S. M. Williams, [1856], J. V. Williams and Company to S. M. Williams, February 4, March 17, 1856, April 15, October 23, 1857, Williams Papers.

of the month, the court suspended action on the two cases.[26] Although Williams had successfully defended his bank in the courts for almost a decade, his future prospects as a banker did not appear auspicious. Both Roberts and Wheeler were hostile toward private banking. Chief Justice Hemphill had recently been elected to fill Sam Houston's senatorial seat, and in January, 1858, the Democratic convention endorsed Wheeler for chief justice. This was the first time that judicial candidates had been nominated by a political convention, an innovation that was expected to force the judges to "adhere to the truths of Democratic equality and justice."[27] The chances that the bank cases would be considered during the Tyler session later in 1858 were slim because Hemphill was deeply involved in political maneuvering to force Houston's resignation before the end of his term in the Senate.[28] The court's docket, therefore, was already crowded, and it appeared that the decision on the banks would be delayed until 1859, when a new member would be elected to fill Wheeler's place.

Richardson continued to support Williams's interests in the *News*. While the court was in session, he printed excerpts from Mary Austin Holley's 1836 history of Texas, in which she applauded the efforts to establish the bank. She compared Williams's goals to those of Robert Morris in the 1780's and indicated that both men desired to stabilize the fluctuating currencies of their respective republics. Invoking the hallowed name of Stephen F. Austin, Richardson credited Mrs. Holley with insight into the empresario's views on banking; he further explained that the only way to develop the potential of the state was by supporting private enterprise, such as banks and railroads.[29]

For more than a decade, Williams had struggled to provide conservative banking facilities for Texas, but his enemies refused to allow him to succeed and he was exhausted—mentally, physically, and financially. His sons grew to hate the bank and urged him to retire from business, suggesting that he join them on the Colo-

[26] Galveston *News*, March 16, 23, April 13, 1858.

[27] Winkler, *Platforms*, p. 75.

[28] Galveston *News*, March 16, 1858.

[29] Mary Austin Holley, *Texas*, pp. 183–187; Galveston *News*, March 9, 1858.

rado River above Bastrop where they operated a sawmill on his cedar tract.[30] The colonel, however, refused to consider the attractive proposal to spend his remaining years in rural isolation.

The summer passed quietly, interrupted only by a request from Williams's nephew, William Henry St. John, to settle the old court-adjudicated debts owed by the firm of McKinney and Williams to his father.[31] The heat was the most oppressive that Galvestonians could remember. In August, the editor of the *News* visited the C & A Bank, where Williams kept a thermometer and recorded weather data, a practice the colonel had developed in 1828 when General Terán had inaugurated scientific weather observations at San Felipe. Williams confirmed that the temperatures had remained above ninety degrees for several weeks, a most unusual occurrence on the island.[32] The city physician assured residents that Galveston was the healthiest that it had been in the past eight years, but within two weeks yellow fever struck suddenly, with three deaths and twenty quarantined during one weekend. The following Tuesday, September 7, the *News* sorrowfully reported that Colonel Williams was "fatally" ill, though "of course his is no case of yellow fever."[33]

Williams died late Monday afternoon, September 13, having been confined to his bed for nearly two weeks. Just three weeks short of his sixty-third birthday, he succumbed to old age and "general debility," according to his doctor, who had advised Beaver and Austin to hurry home from Bastrop three days before his passing. Austin remained at the mill, but Beaver arrived early Wednesday morning, the day of the funeral, to find the coffin, packed in ice, in the front parlor awaiting the service. Black-plumed Knights Templar conducted the brief ceremony at the house and acted as pall-bearers to escort the founder of their chapter to his grave. Williams had also organized the local Royal Arch chapter in 1840, and, in the early 1850's, he had served as the highest state officer of each order. Members of these groups led the impressive cortege of other Free-

[30] A. M. Williams to S. M. Williams, July 7, 1855, Williams Papers.
[31] W. H. St. John to S. M. Williams, May 9, 1858; subpoena to U.S. District Court, July 6, 1849, *ibid.*
[32] Galveston *News*, August 10, 17, 1858.
[33] *Ibid.*, August 24, September 7, 14, 1858.

masons, ship captains, city and state dignitaries, and friends down the sandy road between the rows of townspeople lining the route to the Episcopal cemetery. Business houses had closed the previous day, and the public buildings and ships in the harbor lowered their flags to half mast until after the funeral. The largest crowd in many years assembled to pay its respects to one of the last old settlers.[34]

Six months later the Commercial and Agricultural Bank died at the hands of the Texas Supreme Court. When the Galveston session opened early in 1859, Wheeler presided as chief justice and the voters had chosen James H. Bell to fill the vacant seat. Son of Josiah H. Bell, one of Stephen F. Austin's earliest colonists, the new justice had received his legal training at Harvard and had previously served as a district judge. On February 28, 1859, in one of his first opinions, Bell dismissed the Mills case and absolved the banker of the $100,000 fine imposed by the lower court. Few politicians, including supreme court justices, wanted to antagonize Robert Mills, whose influence was increasing daily. Williams, on the other hand, was dead and powerless. Associate Justice Oran M. Roberts delivered the ruling in the C & A Bank case in March. He denied that Williams had a vested interest derived from the 1835 charter because the bank had not opened until 1848, three years after the state constitution clearly prohibited such activity. Thus banking was a crime against the state, and Roberts affirmed the minimum fine set by the lower court.[35]

Williams died intestate, leaving property valued at $95,000, not including parcels of land still in litigation. When Beaver returned from the Harvard Law School in 1845, he had assumed responsibility for unraveling the overlapping surveys, improperly recorded deeds, and squatter's claims that affected his father's land. The court appointed Beaver and Philip C. Tucker, a family friend, as

[34] C. W. Trueheart to W. H. Williams, September 10, 1858; W. H. Williams to A. M. Williams, September 16, 1858, Williams Papers; Galveston *News*, September 14, 21, 1858. Williams's Masonic activities are detailed in the *Texas Grand Lodge Magazine*, January, 1936, and the Rosenberg Library possesses a daguerreotype of Williams in his regalia, circa 1854.

[35] Lynch, *Bench and Bar*, p. 293; *R. and D. G. Mills and others v. The State of Texas; S. M. Williams and others v. The State of Texas*, 23 *Texas* 295 (1859).

administrators of the estate in 1858, but before the matter was settled, Sarah also died while on a visit to Bastrop in 1860. The heirs
sold the Galveston homesite to Tucker and divided the remaining
clear property among the four surviving children, but when the
debts were finally settled in 1872, the actual cash value of their pat-
rimony was very modest.[36]

The court assigned Jacob L. Briggs and B. A. Shepherd to liq-
uidate the assets of the C & A Bank and to redeem and destroy all
Williams paper. The goodwill of the organization passed informal-
ly to Ball, Hutchings and Company, a commission house owned by
former C & A director George Ball. Neither company papers nor
court house records reveal any legal connection between the two institutions, but former patrons of Williams's bank transferred their
business to Ball, Hutchings. Although Ball continued to exchange
and discount paper money, he never issued his own notes. A series
of mergers eventually joined Ball, Hutchings with its tenuous association with the C & A Bank to the present First Hutchings-Sealy
National Bank of Galveston. Thus Williams may be claimed as the
father of Texas banking.[37]

Williams did not have to witness the destruction and dismantling of his life's work. The ten-year court battle with its political
overtones had eroded his once robust health, and, despairing of vin-
dication, he relinquished the struggle and allowed despondency to
triumph. His entire life had been spent in commerce, a familiar
place where he understood the values and practices, but his sophis-
ticated manner and overweening self-confidence were ill suited to
frontier politics. After his arrival in Texas in 1822, Williams had
used his talents to develop the potential of his adopted home while
furthering his own interests. His brusque practicality complemented the ability and skill of Stephen F. Austin, though his friend er-

[36] Inventory, April 30, 1855; A. M. Williams to S. M. Williams, July
7, 1855, Williams Papers; Galveston County Probate Records, Box 397;
T. J. League to W. H. Williams, September 10, 1860, Williams Papers;
Galveston County Deed Records, P, 150–151, U, 73–74, 266, and W, 308.

[37] Avery L. Carlson, *A Monetary and Banking History of Texas from
the Mexican Regime to the Present Day, 1821–1929*, p. 9; Ruth G. Nichols, "Samuel May Williams," *Southwestern Historical Quarterly* 56 (October 1952): 209; Galveston *News*, June 16, 1926, September 21, 1955,
September 25, 1965.

roneously labeled Williams a dreamer and misinterpreted his ambition and vision for idle reverie.[38] Although little understood by his contemporaries, Sam Williams made a major contribution toward the successful development of Texas and her economy in the nineteenth century.

[38] S. F. Austin to T. F. McKinney, January 16, 1836, in Eugene C. Barker (ed.), *The Austin Papers*, III, 304–305.

Genealogy of the Williams Family

SAMUEL MAY WILLIAMS's ancestors included many notables, beginning with Robert Williams of Roxbury (1608–1693), a cordwainer
from Norwich, England, who arrived in Massachusetts in 1637 with
his wife and four children. Among Roberts's numerous grandchil-
dren were the mother of Mrs. Paul Revere, the mother of Dr. Joseph
Warren (who fell at Bunker Hill in 1775), and the Reverend John
Williams (1664–1729), a Harvard graduate who married Eunice
Mather. Eunice perished in the 1704 Deerfield massacre. Samuel
Williams (1656–1735), grandson of Robert, married Sarah May, and
subsequent generations repeated the combination of their names for
the first son. A number of militia officers and Congregational minis-
ters are found in all branches of the family, but it is unclear when
seafaring became a family tradition.

The father of Samuel May Williams (1795–1858), the subject of
this biography, was Howell Williams (1769–1819), a ship captain.
His father, William Williams of Mortlake Manor (1723–1785), married a distant cousin, Martha Williams (1734–1815), whose great-
grandfather was Stephen Williams (1640– ?), a son of Robert of
Roxbury, born in Massachusetts. Howell Williams was named for
his maternal grandmother, Martha Howell (1712–1766), the wife of
Colonel Joseph Williams of Roxbury (1708–1798), grandson of
Stephen. Howell Williams married Dorothy Wheat (1768–1823)
and settled in Providence, Rhode Island, where their eight children
were born.

Samuel May Williams was the first born. The next child was

SAMUEL MAY WILLIAMS
1795–1858

m

SARAH PATTERSON SCOTT
1807–1860

| Joseph Guadalupe Victoria 1825–1857 | Sophie Caroline 1829?–1831? | Austin May 1830–1869 | Eliza Ann 1831?–1831 | William Howell (Beaver) 1833–1924 | Sarah McKinney 1837–1838 | Mary Dorothea (Molly) 1838–1922 | Caroline Lucy (Caddy) 1842–1876 | Samuel May, Jr. 1845–1855 |

Austin May
m
Mary Anna Adams 1837–1916

| Sarah Matura 1856–1934 | Annie Eliza 1857–1940 | Samuel May 1860– | Henry Howell 1863– |

William Howell
m
Edwina Eliza Campbell 1834–

| Ann Clarke 1861– | Wm. H. 1863? | Campbell 1865– | Sarah 1867– | Ethel 1870– | League 1872– | Kathryn 1873– | St. John 1876– | Caroline Louise 1878– |

Mary Dorothea
m
Thomas Jefferson League 1834–1874

| Esther W. 1863–1907 | Thomas Jefferson 1865–1923 | Clinton Wells | Sam'l Williams | Charles Henry –1916 |

Caroline Lucy
m
Dr. Marcus L. Campbell –1883

| Samuel May W. 1864–1941 | John Wesley 1866–1940 | Marcus Lafayette 1868– | St. John 1869? | Sarah P. 1870– | Mary Caroline 1872–1955 | Ann W. (Nancy) 1875– |

Henry Howell Williams (1796–1873), who went to sea, finally settling in the 1830's in Baltimore, where he married Rebecca Wilkins. The third child of Howell and Dorothy Williams was Sophia Jenkins (1798–1854?), who married Samuel P. St. John, Jr., of New York. Next in line, Nathaniel Felton Williams (1800–1884) was named for his father's youngest brother, a Baltimore merchant who apprenticed his nephews. Nat married Elizabeth Dobson, the sister of his partner in the Mobile commission house of Dobson and Williams. After her death in 1838, Nat married Martha E. Williams, the daughter of Uncle Nathaniel of Baltimore. The fifth child was Eliza Yeisor Williams (1802– ?), who married Otis Sweet but apparently was widowed before 1830 when she appeared in Texas. Eliza spent much of her life visiting her brothers and sister, and about 1848 she married John B. Toulmin, a business associate of Samuel P. St. John, Jr.; in 1856, the Toulmins lived abroad. William Joseph Williams (1803–1822) went to sea and died at Santiago, Cuba. The last two children were twins born in 1805. Mary Ann Williams married the Reverend David Reed of Boston, who published the *Christian Register* in the 1850's; she died at an early age, leaving young children. Matthew Reed Williams joined Sam in Texas and married Mary Ann Delany, formerly of New York, in 1835. He died in 1852, leaving two daughters and two sons. One of the sons was known as Samuel May Williams "of Houston" to differentiate him from his deceased uncle and from his nephew, the son of Austin May Williams also named Samuel May.

Critical Essay on
Selected Sources

THE major source of material about Samuel May Williams is the large collection of papers deposited with the Rosenberg Library in Galveston. In 1922, Mary Dorothea Williams League gave the library a trunk filled with family correspondence, statements, ledgers, receipts, and checks—almost five thousand separate items. The collection is indexed and the library published a calendar for the period from 1819 to 1864, omitting only documents that pertained primarily to Austin M. and William H. Williams. In addition to this valuable archive, the University of Texas photostated a small number of family papers still in the possession of a descendant of Austin M. Williams. The Barker History Center of the University of Texas also received a brief essay by Williams's great-granddaughter, Tura Compton Cressy, "Col. Williams, Texas Pioneer," which was based on family sources. Besides these gifts from members of the Williams family, a biographical sketch of the Galvestonian appears in Charles W. Hayes, *Galveston: History of the Island and the City* (1974), compiled by the editor of the Galveston *News* in 1879, who interviewed still-living contemporaries and used local sources then available. Hayes also corresponded with Williams's brother, Nathaniel Felton, for additional information. The two M.A. theses, Siddie R. Armstrong, "Chapters in the Early Life of Samuel May Williams, 1795–1836" (University of Texas, 1929) and Duane Howard, "Historical Studies in the Life of Samuel May Williams: A Builder of Texas, 1795–1858" (Texas Christian University, 1947) used the Galveston collection to write adequate but somewhat superficial monographs about Williams. Armstrong had intended to continue her history beyond 1836, at a later date.

Once Williams arrived in Texas, his private life and official duties are better documented. Gossip such as that of Angelina Bell Peyton Eberly in the notes made by Mary Austin Holley in 1844, "Interviews with Prominent Texans of Early Days," Mary Austin Holley Papers, Barker History Center, and that found in J. H. Kuykendall (ed.), "Reminiscences of Early Texans," published in 1903 in *The Quarterly of the Texas State Historical Association,* gives color and substance to Williams's liaison with Mrs. Eccleston. A careful reading of *The Austin Papers,* vols. I and II, edited by Eugene C. Barker in the *Annual Reports, 1919, 1922* of the American Historical Association, and *The Austin Papers,* vol. III (Austin, 1927), indicates Williams's activities and whereabouts from 1823 to 1836 when used in conjunction with the Williams Papers. Checking certain originals in the Barker History Center's collection of Austin Papers confirmed Williams's handwriting as Eccleston and shed additional details in some cases. Barker's excellent biography of Austin, *The Life of Stephen F. Austin: Founder of Texas, 1793–1836* (originally published in Dallas, 1925, republished in 1949 and 1969), provides a useful framework of the events during that period, although Williams's role and contributions are neglected.

Williams's official duties as revenue collector and postmaster are revealed in the many communications from his superiors that appear in the Williams Papers, and his association with the *ayuntamiento* is chronicled in Barker (ed.), "Minutes of the Ayuntamiento of San Felipe de Austin, 1828–1832," published quarterly between 1918 and 1920 in the *Southwestern Historical Quarterly.* Again, a check of the original minute books in the Spanish Archives of the General Land Office indicated which documents were written by Williams. The Registro of the deeds for Austin's first colony, also in the Spanish Archives, illustrates the amount of time Williams spent recording titles.

The secretary's land speculation activities have never been closely documented. The Edward C. Hanrick Papers in the Barker History Center reveal the extent of the "Alabama" speculation when used with certain letters in the Williams Papers and the *Austin Papers.* The Robertson Colony controversy deserves a separate book.

Extant papers belonging to Sterling C. Robertson relating to his claim and his accusations against Williams are in the possession of Malcolm D. McLean at Texas Christian University. Other documents, unfavorable to Austin and Williams, are published in John Henry Brown's *History of Texas from 1685–1892* (1892). Williams's letters to Thomas McQueen in February, 1834, refuting Robertson's testimony, and the two briefs outlining his case, one written by Williams and the other by Spencer H. Jack, entitled "Upper Colony Controversy," are available at Rosenberg Library.

Williams's activities at Monclova and his sympathy with the federalist party in 1835 need more study. Unfortunately no journal for the 1835 session of the Monclova legislature exists, and historians have discovered few of the documents that should be in the Saltillo Archive. In 1869 Brown found material that he subsequently published in his book, and in the 1940's, the University of Texas made photocopies of all material relating to Texas then at Saltillo. The best account of the activities in Monclova is Frank W. Johnson's reminiscences as a participant in his *History of Texas and Texans*, edited by Barker and Ernest William Winkler (1914). Several unpublished monographs written at the University of Texas offer insight into the federalist party and what individuals believed they were fighting for between 1834 and 1839. All are excellent studies and deserve wider reading: Raymond Estep, "The Life of Lorenzo de Zavala" (Ph.D. dissertation, 1942); Cecil Alan Hutchinson, "Valentín Gómez Farías: A Biographical Study" (Ph.D. dissertation, 1948); Bessie Lucille Letts, "George Fisher" (M.A. thesis, 1929); and David Martell Vigness, "The Republic of the Rio Grande: An Example of Separatism in Northern Mexico" (Ph.D. dissertation, 1951). The Gómez Farías Papers, Latin American Collection, University of Texas at Austin, are calendared but not indexed; they offered nothing on Williams, although there are letters from Thomas F. McKinney. The Fisher Papers and Zavala Papers available at the Texas State Library and the Barker Center yielded nothing about Williams. Alessio Robles, *Coahuila y Texas* (1945–1946), considered the authority on northeastern Mexico, is somewhat disappointing in that he cites Barker's *Life of Austin* for the details of the land speculation. Robles does use heretofore unexplored Mexican sources, but he has a pronounced antagonism toward Gómez Farías that distorts objective accounting of the events of 1835.

The struggle for independence and Williams's subsequent activities on behalf of the new Republic from 1835 through 1838 may be traced through receipts and letters in the Williams collection at the Rosenberg Library. The McKinney and Williams Company papers in the Texas State Library archives indicate the firm's contributions but are incomplete and must be augmented by other sources, such as William C. Binkley (ed.), *Official Correspondence of the Texan Revolution, 1835–1836* (1936). George P. Garrison (ed.), *Diplomatic Correspondence of the Republic of Texas* (1907, 1908), Seymour V. Conner (ed.), *Texas Treasury Papers . . . 1836–1846* (1955), and Charles Adams Gulick and others (eds.), *The Papers of Mirabeau Buonaparte Lamar* (1921–1927) also offer pertinent documents concerning negotiations for the loan and the acquisition of the Second Texas Navy. Three diaries of this period add interesting details of Williams's wanderings: *From Virginia to Texas, 1835: Diary of Col. Wm. F. Gray* (1965); J. P. Bryan (ed.), *Mary Austin Holley: The Texas Diary, 1835–1838* (1965); and that of James Ogilvy, attorney for Hugh Grant, brother of the deceased Monclova speculator, which forms parts one through three of Harriet Smither's "Diary of Adolphus Sterne," published in 1926 and 1927 in the *Southwestern Historical Quarterly*.

The part played by Williams in developing the Galveston City Company is explained in Hayes, *Galveston,* and in measures and charters approved by the congresses and legislatures of Texas in Hans P. N. Gammel (comp.), *The Laws of Texas, 1822–1897* (1898). The latter plus the *Journals of the Fourth Congress of the Republic of Texas, 1839–1840,* edited by Harriet Smither, provide documentation of Williams's efforts to represent his constituents in Congress. The abortive mission to Sabinas depends on the Williams Papers, newspapers, and Anson Jones, *Memoranda and Official Correspondence relating to the Republic of Texas* (1859). Charles Elliot's correspondence with his superiors in the British Foreign Office also gives interesting details of the border diplomacy and annexation in Ephraim D. Adams (ed.), *British Diplomatic Correspondence Concerning the Republic of Texas, 1838–1846* (1917). Neither Llerena B.

Friend, *Sam Houston: The Great Designer* (1954), nor *The Writing of Sam Houston* (1938–1943), edited by Amelia W. Williams and Eugene C. Barker, offers insight into the relationship between Houston and his commissioners to Mexico.

Williams's banking efforts must be followed in his correspondence, contemporary newspapers, and the decisions of the Supreme Court of Texas. No satisfactory political history of the Lone Star State during the 1850's has been written, in part because of the destruction of archival material by the fire in the capitol in the 1880's. This deficiency compels the historian to depend on monographs, biographies, or highly personal histories by participants, such as Francis Richard Lubbock, *Six Decades in Texas,* edited by C. W. Raines (1900), or Oran M. Roberts, "A Political, Legislative, and Judicial History of Texas, 1845–1895," in Dudley G. Wooten (ed.), *A Comprehensive History of Texas, 1685–1897* (1898).

Bibliography

PRIMARY SOURCES

Manuscript Collections: Private Papers

Moses and Stephen F. Austin Papers. Barker History Center, University of Texas at Austin.

Nicholas Biddle Papers. Library of Congress, microfilm in the University of Houston Library.

Guy Morrison and Moses Austin Bryan Papers. Barker History Center, University of Texas at Austin.

David G. Burnet Papers. Rosenberg Library, Galveston.

Valentín Gómez Farías Papers. Latin American Collection, University of Texas at Austin.

Galveston City Company Papers. Rosenberg Library, Galveston.

Edward C. Hanrick Papers. Barker History Center, University of Texas at Austin.

Mary Austin Holley Papers. Barker History Center, University of Texas at Austin.

Thomas F. and James P. McKinney Papers. Barker History Center, University of Texas at Austin.

McKinney and Williams Papers. Texas State Library Archives, Austin.

Oran M. Roberts Papers. Barker History Center, University of Texas at Austin.

Sterling C. Robertson Papers. Harllee Collection and Sutherland Collection in the possession of Malcolm D. McLean, Fort Worth.

John G. Tod Papers. Rosenberg Library, Galveston.

Samuel May Williams. Two documents in private collection of Frell Albright, Houston.

Samuel May and Austin May Williams Papers. Barker History Center, University of Texas at Austin.

Samuel May Williams Papers. Rosenberg Library, Galveston.
Lorenzo de Zavala Papers. Barker History Center, University of Texas at Austin.

Manuscript Collections: Public Documents

Bexar Archives. Barker History Center, University of Texas at Austin.
Dispatches Received by the Department of State from United States Consuls in Matamoros, 1826–1906. Microfilm, Latin American Collection, University of Texas at Austin.
Legislative Memorials and Petitions. Archives of the State Department, State of Texas, Texas State Library Archives, Austin.
Saltillo Archives. Selected photostats from the state of Coahuila, 1824–1834, Barker History Center, University of Texas at Austin.
Spanish Archives of the General Land Office. Austin.
Texas County Archives. Deed Records, Marriage Records, Probate Records in Austin, Brazoria, Fort Bend, Galveston, Harris, Matagorda, and Travis counties.

Published Correspondence and Diaries

Adams, Ephraim Douglass, ed. *British Diplomatic Correspondence Concerning the Republic of Texas, 1838–1846.* Austin: Texas State Historical Association, 1917.
Barker, Eugene C., ed. *The Austin Papers.* Vols. I, II, American Historical Association, *Annual Report, 1919, 1922.* 3 vols. Washington, D.C.: Government Printing Office, 1924, 1928. Vol. III, Austin: University of Texas Press, 1927.
Barker, Nancy Nichols, trans. and ed. *The French Legation in Texas.* 2 vols. Austin: Texas State Historical Association, 1971–1973.
Binkley, William C., ed. *Official Correspondence of the Texan Revolution, 1835–1836.* 2 vols. New York: D. Appleton-Century Company, 1936.
Bryan, James Perry, ed. *Mary Austin Holley: The Texas Diary, 1835–1838.* Austin: University of Texas Press, 1965.
Conner, Seymour V., ed. *Texas Treasury Papers: Letters Received in the Treasury Department of the Republic of Texas, 1836–1846.* 4 vols. Austin: Texas State Library, 1955.
Davis, Robert E., ed. *The Diary of William Barret Travis, August 30, 1833–June 26, 1834.* Waco: Texian Press, 1966.
Garrison, George P., ed. *Diplomatic Correspondence of the Republic of Texas.* American Historical Association, *Annual Report, 1907, 1908.* 3 vols. Washington, D.C.: Government Printing Office, 1908, 1911.
Gray, William Fairfax. *From Virginia to Texas, 1835: Diary of Col. Wm. F. Gray.* Houston: Fletcher Young Publishing Co., 1965.
Greer, James K., ed. "Journal of Ammon Underwood, 1834–1838." *Southwestern Historical Quarterly* 32 (October 1928): 124–150.

Gulick, Charles Adams, et al., eds. The Papers of Mirabeau Buonaparte Lamar. 6 vols. Austin: Von Boeckmann-Jones Co., 1921–1927.

[Harris, Lewis Birdsall]. "Journal of Lewis Birdsall Harris, 1836–1842." Southwestern Historical Quarterly 25 (1921–1922): 63–71, 131–146, 185–197.

Hollon, W. Eugene, and Ruth Lapham Butler, eds. William Boellaert's Texas. Norman: University of Oklahoma Press, 1956.

Jones, Anson, Memoranda and Official Correspondence Relating to the Republic of Texas. New York: D. Appleton, 1859.

[Langworthy, Ashael]. A Visit to Texas: Being the Journal of a Traveller through Those Parts Most Interesting to American Settlers. . . . New York: Goodrich & Wiley, 1834.

Pratt, Willis W., ed. Galveston Island: Or a Few Months Off the Coast of Texas: The Journal of Francis C. Sheridan, 1839–1840. Austin: University of Texas Press, 1954.

Sanchez, José María. "A Trip to Texas in 1828." Translated by Carlos E. Casteñeda. Southwestern Historical Quarterly 29 (April 1926): 258–288.

Smither, Harriet, ed. "Diary of Adolphus Sterne." Southwestern Historical Quarterly 30 (1926–1927): 139–156, 219–232, 305–324.

Williams, Amelia W., and Eugene C. Barker, eds. The Writings of Sam Houston. 8 vols. Austin: University of Texas Press, 1938–1943.

Published Documents and Reports

Almonte, Juan Nepomuceno. "Statistical Report on Texas." Translated by Carlos E. Casteñeda. Southwestern Historical Quarterly 28 (January 1925): 177–222.

An Abstract of the Original Title of Record in the General Land Office. Houston: Niles and Company, 1838.

Austin, Stephen F. Translation of the Laws, Orders, and Contracts on Colonization, from January 1821, up to 1829. Houston: Borden and Moore, 1837.

Barker, Eugene C., ed. "Minutes of the Ayuntamiento of San Felipe de Austin, 1828–1832." Southwestern Historical Quarterly 21 (1918): 299–326, 395–423; 22 (1918–1919): 78–95, 180–196, 272–278, 353–359; 23 (1919–1920): 69–77, 141–151, 214, 223, 302–307; 24 (1920): 81–83, 154–166.

Congressional Globe. 35th Congress. 1st and 2nd sessions. Washington, D.C., 1858.

Debates of the Convention of 1845. Houston: J. W. Cruger, 1846.

Gammel, Hans P. N., comp. The Laws of Texas, 1822–1897. 10 vols. Austin: Gammel Book Company, 1898.

Henry Sampson volume of briefs and Obituary Addresses in Honor of J. C. Calhoun. Washington: U.S. Senate, 1850. In Rosenberg Library, Galveston.

Sandusky, William H. Map of the City of Galveston, Texas, 1845. Philadelphia: Wagner and McGuigan, n.d.

Smither, Harriet, ed. *Journals of the Fourth Congress of the Republic of Texas, 1839–1840.* 3 vols. Austin: Von Boeckmann-Jones Co., n.d.

———, ed. *Journals of the Sixth Congress of the Republic of Texas, 1841–1842.* 3 vols. Austin: Von Boeckmann-Jones Co., 1940–1945.

Texas Congress. *Journals of the House of Representatives.* Austin, 1840–1841.

Texas Legislature. *Journals of the House of Representatives.* Austin, 1847–1848.

———. *Journals of the Senate.* Austin, 1847–1851, 1935.

Winkler, Ernest W., ed. *Platforms of Political Parties in Texas.* Austin: University of Texas Press, 1916.

———, ed. *Secret Journals of the Senate, Republic of Texas, 1836–1845.* Austin: Austin Printing Company, 1911.

Legal Decisions

Commercial and Agricultural Bank v. *Simon L. Jones.* 18 *Texas* 811 (1857).

R. and D. G. Mills and others v. *The State of Texas.* 23 *Texas* 295 (1859).

Samuel May Williams v. *F. W. Chandler and others.* In P. C Tucker volume of briefs, Rosenberg Library, Galveston.

Samuel May Williams and others v. *the State of Texas.* 23 *Texas* 264 (1859).

Spencer v. *Lapsley.* 20 *Howard* 264 (1858).

State of Texas v. *Samuel May Williams.* 8 *Texas* 255 (1852).

State of Texas v. *S. M. Williams and others, Robert Mills and others.* 14 *Texas* 98 (1855).

Newspapers and Periodicals

Austin *Texas Sentinel,* 1840–1841.

Baltimore *American and Commercial Advertiser,* 1808, 1811, 1818.

Brazoria *Advocate of the Peoples' Rights,* 1834.

Brazoria *Texas Republican,* 1834–1835.

Galveston *Civilian,* 1838–1845.

Galveston *Independent Chronicle,* 1843.

Galveston *News,* 1842–1858, 1910, 1926.

Houston *Morning Star,* 1843–1848.

San Felipe *Texas Gazette,* 1829–1830.

Telegraph and Texas Register (San Felipe, Harrisburg, Columbia, Houston), 1835–1858.

Texas Grand Lodge Magazine, January, 1936.

The Galvestonian, 1839, 1841.

SECONDARY SOURCES

Books

Armstrong, James. *Some Facts on the Eleven League Controversy.* Austin: Southern Intelligencer Book Establishment, 1859.

Baker, J. W. *A History of Robertson County, Texas.* Waco: Texian Press, 1970.

Barker, Eugene C. *The Life of Stephen F. Austin: Founder of Texas, 1793–1836.* Austin: Texas State Historical Association, 1949.

Brown, John Henry. *History of Texas from 1685 to 1892.* 2 vols. St. Louis: I. E. Daniell, 1892.

Callcott, Willfrid Hardy. *Santa Anna: The Story of an Enigma Who Was Once Mexico.* Norman: University of Oklahoma Press, 1936.

Carlson, Avery L. *A Monetary and Banking History of Texas from the Mexican Regime to the Present Day, 1821–1929.* Fort Worth: Fort Worth National Bank, 1930.

Carter, James David. *Masonry in Texas: Background, History, and Influence to 1846.* Waco: Committee on Masonic Education and Service, 1955.

Courtney, Jovita. *After the Alamo: San Jacinto from the Notes of Doctor Nicholas Decomps Labadie.* New York: Vantage Press, 1964.

Davidson, Marshall B. *History of Notable American Houses.* New York: American Heritage Publishing Co., Inc., 1971.

DeCordova, Jacob. *Texas: Her Resources and Her Public Men.* Austin: DeCordova and Frazier, 1856.

DeGrummond, Jane Lucas. *The Baratarians and the Battle of New Orleans.* Baton Rouge: Louisiana State University Press, 1961.

Dixon, Sam Houston, and Louis Wiltz Kemp. *The Heroes of San Jacinto.* Houston: Anson Jones Press, 1932.

Dobie, J. Frank, ed. *Foller de Drinkin' Gou'd.* Austin: Texas Folklore Society, 1928.

Edward, David B. *The History of Texas: Or, The Emigrant's, Farmer's, and Politician's Guide to the Character, Climate, Soil, and Productions of That Country.* Cincinnati: J. A. James and Co., 1836.

Foote, Henry Stuart. *Texas and the Texans: Or Advance of the Anglo-Americans to the Southwest.* 2 vols. Philadelphia: Thomas, Cowperthwait and Co., 1841.

Fornell, Earl Wesley. *The Galveston Era: The Texas Crescent on the Eve of Secession.* Austin: University of Texas Press, 1961.

Frantz, Joe B. *Gail Borden: Dairyman to a Nation.* Norman: University of Oklahoma Press, 1951.

Friend, Llerena B. *Sam Houston: The Great Designer.* Austin: University of Texas Press, 1954.

Gambrell, Herbert P. *Anson Jones: The Last President of Texas.* Austin: University of Texas Press, 1964.

Hammond, Bray. *Banks and Politics in America from the Revolution to the Civil War*. Princeton: Princeton University Press, 1957.

Hayes, Charles W. *Galveston: History of the Island and the City*. 2 vols. Austin: Jenkins Garrett Press, 1974.

Helm, Mary (Sherwood) W. *Scraps of Early Texas History*. Austin: B. R. Warner and Co., 1884.

Hogan, William Ransom. *The Texas Republic: A Social and Economic History*. Norman: University of Oklahoma Press, 1946.

Holley, Mary Austin. *Texas: Observations, Historical, Geographical, and Descriptive*. . . . Baltimore: Armstrong & Plaskitt, 1833.

————. *Texas*. Lexington, Ky., J. Clarke & Co., 1836.

Ikin, Arthur. *Texas: Its History, Topography, Agriculture, Commerce, and General Statistics*. London: Sherwood, Gilbert, and Piper, 1841.

Johnson, Frank W. *A History of Texas and Texans*. 5 vols. Edited by Eugene C. Barker and Ernest William Winkler. Chicago: American Historical Society, 1914.

Johnson, William R. *A Short History of the Sugar Industry in Texas*. Houston: Texas Gulf Coast Historical Association, 1961.

Lindley, E. R., comp. *Biographical Directory of the Texan Conventions and Congresses, 1832–1845*. [Austin]: Texas Legislature, [1941].

Long, Walter Ewing. *Stephen F. Austin's Legacies*. Austin: Steck-Vaughn Co., 1970.

Lubbock, Francis Richard. *Six Decades in Texas: Or Memoirs of Francis Richard Lubbock, Governor of Texas in War Time, 1861–63: A Personal Experience in Business, War, and Politics*. Edited by C. W. Raines. Austin: Ben C. Jones and Co., 1900.

Lynch, James Daniel. *The Bench and Bar of Texas*. St. Louis: Nixon-Jones, 1885.

Magrath, C. Peter. *Yazoo: Law and Politics in the New Republic*. Providence: Brown University Press, 1966.

Miller, Thomas Lloyd. *Bounty and Donation Land Grants of Texas, 1835–1888*. Austin: University of Texas Press, 1961.

Morton, Ohland. *Teran and Texas: A Chapter in Texas-Mexican Relations*. Austin: Texas State Historical Association, 1948.

Muir, Andrew Forest, ed. *Texas in 1837: An Anonymous, Contemporary Narrative*. Austin: University of Texas Press, 1958.

Nance, Joseph Milton. *Attack and Counter-Attack: The Texas-Mexican Frontier, 1842*. Austin: University of Texas Press, 1964.

Rabasa, Emilio. *La constitución y la dictadura: Estudio sobre la organización política de México*. Mexico City: Tip. de "Revista de Revistas," 1912.

Richardson, Willard, *et al.*, eds. *Galveston Directory, 1859–1860*. Galveston: Galveston News Book and Job Office, 1859.

————. *Galveston Directory, 1866–1867.* Galveston: Galveston News Office, 1866.

Rieder, Milton P., Jr., and Norma Gaudet Rieder, eds. *New Orleans Ship Lists.* 2 vols. Metaire, Louisiana: privately printed, 1966, 1968.

Robles, Vito Alessio. *Coahuila y Texas desde la consumación de la independencia . . . hasta el tratado de paz de Guadalupe Hidalgo.* 2 vols. Mexico City: Imprenta Univertaria Talleres Gráficos de la Nación, 1945–1946.

Rutter, Frank R. *South American Trade of Baltimore.* Baltimore: Johns Hopkins University Press, 1897.

Schmitz, Joseph William. *Texan Statecraft, 1836–1845.* San Antonio: Naylor Company, 1941.

Ship Registers and Enrollments of New Orleans, Louisiana. 4 vols. Baton Rouge: Louisiana State University Press, 1941.

Siegel, Stanley. *A Political History of the Texas Republic, 1836–1845.* Austin: University of Texas Press, 1956.

Smith, Ashbel. *Reminiscences of the Texas Republic.* Galveston: Historical Society of Galveston, 1876.

Smith, Justin H. *The Annexation of Texas.* New York: The Baker and Taylor Co., 1919.

Smithwick, Noah. *The Evolution of a State: Or Recollections of Old Texas Days.* Austin: Gammel Book Co., 1900.

Stiff, Edward. *The Texan Emigrant: Being a Narration of the Adventures of the Author in Texas . . . down to the Year 1840.* Cincinnati: George Conclin, 1840.

Taylor, Virginia H. *The Spanish Archives of the General Land Office of Texas.* Austin: The Lone Star Press, 1955.

Ward, Henry George. *Mexico.* 2 vols. London: Henry Colburn, 1829.

Webb, Walter Prescott, ed. *The Handbook of Texas.* 2 vols. Austin: The Texas State Historical Association, 1952.

Wells, Tom Henderson. *Commodore Moore and the Texas Navy.* Austin: University of Texas Press, 1960.

Wheeler, Kenneth W. *To Wear a City's Crown: The Beginnings of Urban Growth in Texas, 1836–1865.* Cambridge: Harvard University Press, 1968.

Williams, Elgin. *The Animating Pursuits of Speculation: Land Traffic in the Annexation of Texas.* New York: Columbia University Press, 1949.

Williams, Stephen W. *History of the Williams Family.* Greenfield, Massachusetts: Merriam & Mirick, 1847.

Wooten, Dudley G., ed. *A Comprehensive History of Texas, 1685–1897.* 2 vols. Dallas: William G. Scarff, 1898.

Wortham, Louis J. *A History of Texas from Wilderness to Commonwealth.* 5 vols. Fort Worth: Wortham-Molyneaux Company, 1924.

Yoakum, Henderson. *History of Texas, from Its First Settlement in 1685 to Its Annexation to the United States in 1846.* 2 vols. New York: J. S. Redfield, 1855.

Ziegler, Jesse A. *Wave of the Gulf.* San Antonio: Naylor Company, 1938.

Articles

Amsler, Robert. "General Arthur G. Wavell: A Soldier of Fortune in Texas." *Southwestern Historical Quarterly* 69 (1965): 12–21, 186–209.

Bacarisse, Charles A. "The Texas Gazette, 1829–1831." *Southwestern Historical Quarterly* 56 (October 1952): 239–253.

Barker, Eugene C. "Land Speculation as a Cause of the Texas Revolution." *The Quarterly of the Texas State Historical Association* 10 (July 1906): 76–95.

———. "The Finances of the Texas Revolution." *Political Science Quarterly* 19 (December 1904): 612–635.

———. "The Government of Austin's Colony, 1821–1831." *Southwestern Historical Quarterly* 21 (January 1918): 223–252.

Bugbee, Lester G. "The Old Three Hundred." *The Quarterly of the Texas State Historical Association* 1 (October 1897): 108–117.

Dienst, Alex. "The Navy of the Republic of Texas." *The Quarterly of the Texas State Historical Association* 12 (1909): 165–203, 249–275; 13 (1909): 1–43, 85–127.

Elliott, Claude. "Alabama and the Texas Revolution." *Southwestern Historical Quarterly* 50 (January 1947): 315–328.

Franklin, Ethel May. "Joseph Baker." *Southwestern Historical Quarterly* 36 (July 1932): 130–143.

Greene, A. A., trans. and ed. "The Battle of Zacatecas." *Texana* 7 (Fall 1969): 189–200.

Griffin, Charles C. "Privateering from Baltimore during the Spanish American Wars of Independence." *Maryland Historical Magazine* 35 (March 1940): 1–25.

Heusinger, Edward W. "The Monetary History of the Republic of Texas." *Southwestern Historical Quarterly* 57 (July 1953): 82–90.

Holbrook, Abigail Curlee. "Cotton Marketing in Antebellum Texas." *Southwestern Historical Quarterly* 73 (April 1970): 431–447.

Hord, Arnold Harris. "Genealogy of the Triplett Family." *William and Mary Quarterly*, 1st ser., 21 (July 1912): 115–134.

Howren, Alleine. "Causes and Origin of the Decree of April 6, 1830." *The Quarterly of the Texas State Historical Association* 16 (April 1913): 378–422.

Kuykendall, J. H., ed. "Reminiscences of Early Texans." *The Quarterly of the Texas State Historical Association* 6 (January 1903): 236–253; 7 (July 1903): 29–64.

Lewis, Carroll A., Jr. "Fort Anahuac: The Birthplace of the Texas Revolution." *Texana* 1 (Spring 1969): 1–11.

Nichols, Ruth G. "Samuel May Williams." *Southwestern Historical Quarterly* 56 (October 1952): 189–210.

Nielson, George R., ed. "Lydia Ann McHenry and Revolutionary Texas." *Southwestern Historical Quarterly* 74 (January 1971): 323–408.

Pearson, P. E. "Reminiscences of Judge Edwin Waller." *The Quarterly of the Texas State Historical Association* 4 (July 1900): 33–53.

Rowe, Edna. "The Disturbance at Anahuac in 1832." *The Quarterly of the Texas State Historical Association* 6 (April 1903): 265–299.

Schoen, Harold. "The Free Negro in the Republic of Texas." *Southwestern Historical Quarterly* 40 (October 1936): 85–113; 41 (July 1937): 83–108.

Winkler, Ernest William. "The Seat of Government of Texas." *The Quarterly of the Texas State Historical Association* 10 (January 1907): 185–245.

Winterbotham, J. M. "Some Texas Correspondence." *Mississippi Valley Historical Review* 11 (June 1924): 109–119.

Unpublished Monographs

Armstrong, Siddie Robson. "Chapters in the Early Life of Samuel May Williams, 1795–1836." M.A. thesis, University of Texas, 1929.

Bacarisse, Charles A. "The Baron de Bastrop: The Life and Times of Philip Hendrick Nering Bogel, 1759–1827." Ph.D. dissertation, University of Texas, 1955.

Bradfield, Ganey W. "A List of Property Owners within the Limits of the Model of San Felipe de Austin, ca. 1830." Manuscript. Josey Store Museum, San Felipe, Texas, 1967.

Cressy, Tura Compton. "Col. Williams, Texas Pioneer." Typescript. Barker History Center, University of Texas at Austin, 1932.

Estep, Raymond. "The Life of Lorenzo de Zavala." Ph.D. dissertation, University of Texas, 1942.

Harris, Helen Willits. "The Public Life of Juan Nepomuceno Almonte." Ph.D. dissertation, University of Texas, 1935.

Howard, Duane. "Historical Studies in the Life of Samuel May Williams: A Builder of Texas, 1795–1858." M.A. thesis, Texas Christian University, 1947.

Hutchinson, Cecil Alan. "Valentín Gómez Farías: A Biographical Study." Ph.D. dissertation, University of Texas, 1948.

Kreneck, Thomas H. "The Lone Star Volunteers: A History of Texas Participation in the Mexican War." M.A. thesis, University of Houston, 1973.

Letts, Bessie Lucille. "George Fisher." M.A. thesis, University of Texas, 1929.

Vigness, David Martell. "The Republic of the Rio Grande: An Example of Separatism in Northern Mexico." Ph.D. dissertation, University of Texas, 1951.

Index

184